Charles Jewett

A forty Years' fight with the drink Demon

Charles Jewett

A forty Years' fight with the drink Demon

ISBN/EAN: 9783337135898

Printed in Europe, USA, Canada, Australia, Japan

Cover: Foto ©ninafisch / pixelio.de

More available books at **www.hansebooks.com**

A FORTY YEARS' FIGHT

WITH THE

DRINK DEMON,

OR

A HISTORY OF THE TEMPERANCE REFORM AS
I HAVE SEEN IT,

AND OF

MY LABOR IN CONNECTION THEREWITH.

BY

CHARLES JEWETT, M. D.

NEW YORK:
NATIONAL TEMPERANCE SOCIETY AND PUBLISHING HOUSE,
58 READE STREET.
1882.

PREFACE.

HAD the temperance enterprise, commenced substantially in 1826, received from the American people a support, financial and otherwise, commensurate with its importance, and been prosecuted on the plan adopted by its originators, the promise which its early and wonderful successes gave of a speedy triumph would have been realized, and this volume would not have been given to the public, but in place thereof, its author, or some fellow-laborer, would have published, ere this, a more ample and worthy history of one of the grandest achievements of this nineteenth century.

The consummation of this great and needful work has been prevented by a concurrence of causes not generally understood, because not carefully studied; the study, unlike most others, bringing no present and promising no future pecuniary reward.

First among the causes referred to, I must place the strange and deplorable mistakes of our American churches, in the aggregate, which, with a few notable exceptions, have busied themselves with matters having generally a far less direct bearing on their own or the world's welfare, rather than in worthy and *direct* efforts to crush their own worst enemy, whose wounded and reeling victims meet us in our streets as we walk to our houses of worship—and, worse still, whose marked and doomed ones often look up from the cushioned pews of magnificent churches, into the faces of our Christian teachers while they are eloquently urging us to put forth efforts for the salvation of men in Burmah or Hindostan. But something worse than mistakes have hindered the progress of the cause.

The too general and criminal indifference of our best educated and influential classes to the just claims of the temperance enterprise, in years that have past, has permitted it to form unnatural associations, to take questionable forms, and its honest and earnest friends sometimes to mistake and adopt harmful expedients; and now, when we appeal for aid to those classes, they point us to our past mistakes and the imperfection of our present arrangements, as a justification of their continued neglect. As *one* of the *many* deplorable results of such a course, thousands and tens of thousands of the classes complained of, will pay the penalty of their folly in the ruin of their sons.

When and how have occurred the mistakes I deplore, the reader will learn by the perusal of the following chapters. It is not too late to correct the errors of the past. Ten years, perhaps less, of wisely directed, properly sustained, and persistent effort, on the part of the aggregate Christianity of this country, would be ample to complete the grandest work ever committed to any generation since the commencement of the Christian era.

The general and thorough education of all our teachable people in relation to the nature and use of intoxicating elements—the entire abolition of the drinking usages of society and what would inevitably and directly follow, the suppression by law of the traffic in those substances, as thoroughly as other crimes against society are suppressed, would be fraught with more blessings to our country than any or all those products of inventive genius and mechanical skill which have distinguished the present century, splendid and beneficent as they are.

We have some reasons to fear that a stern and general grapple with the great scourge of modern civilization calls for a larger measure of courage, self-denial, and consecration to God and the best interests of man, than the present generation seems likely to furnish. If so, the work of demoralization and ruin wrought always by the general use of intoxicants, will go on for the present, and the triumph of the temperance enterprise will be reserved for a wiser, more self-denying, and courageous generation.

It was no part of my purpose in the production of this work, to give a general history of the temperance reform in this country, or to assign to all who have distinguished themselves in connection with it their just meed of praise for the good work they have done.

The time has not arrived when such a work could be written with justice to all parties concerned or profit to the great interests involved. Various expedients are now employed to secure increased attention to our views and measures, and to hasten the downfall of the liquor system, the value of which time alone can determine; and many of the present and active promoters of the temperance reform will never be rightly estimated, until the work in which they are engaged be completed, or their mission on earth shall be ended.

The undersigned is fully sensible that the facts of his personal history would be scarcely worth recording but for his intimate and almost life-long connection with one of the great reform movements of the age. The expressed belief of many friends that such a history might interest and perhaps instruct my fellow-laborers, has led to the production of this volume. If its publication shall justify the expectations of my co-laborers and contribute, in any measure, to the advancement of the cause, I shall never regret its publication, however it shall be regarded by those who look on our efforts only to criticise them.

Let me not be misunderstood. I do not deprecate criticism, but the personal indolence and selfishness of those who make fault-finding their *only* contribution to a struggling enterprise. Reformatory movements are aggressive always, and those who labor in and for them are constantly attacking the opinions, customs, and habits of others which they seek to change. They have therefore no right to complain of sharp criticism in return. For one, I ask no *personal* favors, as I never grant any where loyalty to the truth and the interests of **humanity** forbid.

THE AUTHOR.

CONTENTS.

CHAPTER I.

Incentives to the Battle—A sad state of things—A little Light—Set on—Considering the matter—The Whipping Post—The first Blow—Signing the pledge—Rev. Dr. Hewitt—The Fathers—Missionary work with Pills—William Goodell—A blow from Elder Meech—My first Speech—What came of it—Pure Gold.   13

CHAPTER II.

Organization—A Commissary Department wanting—Little Money, but Rich—Ben Johnson cures the Doctor—Cider Experience—Out of the Scrape—Rhymes and Retailers—Still Rhyming—Argumentum ad Hominem—The Winding Sheet—They Dislike but Patronize him.   29

CHAPTER III.

A Visitor—Thomas P. Hunt—His Speech at Aponaug—"An excellent sentiment, madam"—Facing the question—Yes or No?—He loves but votes against it—A victory for Rum—An "Open House"—A song furnished gratis.   41

CHAPTER IV.

A CONTROVERSY.

A "Plucky" Wholesaler—Retreating, he gets "a shell"—A Retailer hit—Rinsing the glasses—Providence Votes down the Traffic—A laughable incident—The way to do it—A shot that hit—Enlisting a Sharp Shooter—He hits the "bull's eye"—"Crack up"—Shoot, but don't hurt folks—"Father Bonney's Prayer—First extemporaneous Speech.   48

CHAPTER V.

A COWARDLY ATTACK.

"Smith's hat"—Giving up the lancet—My co-workers—A sick wife—Trouble—A visit to Boston—Dreaming in Rhyme—Laugh and be fat—Encouraging progress—Doubt and uncertainty—A Wife's Counsel—A timely suggestion—Seventy Dollars! . . 65

CHAPTER VI.

INVITED TO A WIDER FIELD.

Packing up—"Cast down but not destroyed"—A dialogue—Was it brotherly or wise?—A Christian hero—A Clergyman and three Churches—The poor-house preacher—"If I had let rum alone"—Rum and horrors—We "went for" the buckwheat cakes—Crane's store—What'll you have?—"Didn't I call for 't, ha?"—"You can't cheat me"—Doubted! 76

CHAPTER VII.

REVIEW OF THE PAST.

The Convention of 1838—The great petition—A committee worth remembering—Looking ahead—Hats off, gentlemen!—The Law of 1838—Wholesale Dealers to the front!—They meet—A Paixhan shell—The lesson of past events—Study and reorganization. 93

CHAPTER VIII.

TREASON.

Robert Rantoul and Massachusetts Democracy—"Up Guards, and at them"—A practical illustration—A shallow Trickster—A laugh out of place—Hard at work, but happy—Judge Crosby—Wise counsel. 113

CHAPTER IX.

Money, how will you get it?—Financial Plan—Duties of Agents—The way our plan worked—Illustrative Reports—The Washingtonian movement—The Temperance Union breaking down, why? An explanation—Local organizations essential—Washingtonianism, its errors—Washingtonianism, its power—Summing up. 122

CONTENTS. ix

CHAPTER X.

The Clergy and their general faithfulness—Mistakes and their results—" Experiences," their potency—More blunders—The Clergy disaffected—Close organizations, their origin—Practical results—Different organizations compared—What is needed. . . 140

CHAPTER XI.

Open societies, their advantages—Discussion before the masses wonderfully effective—Comparisons—Our progress too slow—Why I thus speak—Our younger brethren—Progress before the year 1840—Some change essential to a triumph—Three classes will not join the Orders—Why?—Regalia—They love the drink—Out of date? No—How they work in California—A glorious success—A supposition—Policy our ground of choice. . 154

CHAPTER XII.

OPERATIONS OF THE MASSACHUSETTS TEMPERANCE UNION.

Sad results of wrong measures—Our temperance Poets—Fourteen o'clock—A Cotton Speculation—Jimmy's Mill—The Distiller's Disaster—A grist from Jimmy's Mill. 172

CHAPTER XIII.

BOUND, AND HOW.

The Widow's Son—In the " Slough of Despond "—A fight for Life—Victorious—The Moral—A Speculation—Still moralizing—The Longevity of Reformers. 188

CHAPTER XIV.

OUR LEADERS AND CHAMPIONS.

Rev. Dr. Justin Edwards—The First New England Regiments—Personal Peculiarities—Rev. John Pierpont—The freedom of the Pulpit assailed—A Masterly Defence—Logic—Logic Versified—The License System—Sarcasm—Legitimate employment of it—Awful Exposures—Shall we give it wings? Yes—"Lament in Rhyme, Lament in Prose"—Square hits—Summing up. . 196

CHAPTER XV.

"THERE WERE GIANTS IN THOSE DAYS."

L. M. Sargent—Personal peculiarities—The Temperance Tales—A Damascus blade well employed—"Deacon Giles' Distillery"—Providential and grand results—Father Taylor—Word painting—Eloquence. 214

CHAPTER XVI.

Joseph Breck—A glass of Gin—Compare them, Sir—Frightened—A laugh all round—A cup of tea—A home question—What do *you* say?—A new patron—Our best hold—Gough, Gough!—Discussion, its value—The tipsy Son—Afflicted—The old story—Converted at a blow—Temperance Conversions, how effected—Ruminating—Only to travelers—Travelers on short routes—Pretty much burned out—The poor old Doctor—Expelled—Why is it? The Major—" Take him off"—Threatened—Satisfaction—Recovered—Trying it again—"Ten cents"—The whole cost. . 231

CHAPTER XVII.

Incompetent Advocates—Their influence—Our early Advocates—District Societies—On time—The Christian way—The Lunch—A Good Time—The lesson of it—Visit the Brethren—Rhymes—A new Field—How shall we fix it?—Plan of operations—Trouble in the Camp. 265

CHAPTER XVIII.

Moving—Guerrilla Warfare—Almost discouraged—Retreating—Arrested and sent to the front—One thousand dollars—Getting into type—Front to Front—We rout them—Comfortable—Visiting the Prisoners—Sham Democracy—Republicans unsound and timid—A glorious opportunity—Political action—They beg off—A venal Press. 288

CHAPTER XIX.

The Maine Law—Reaction, how created—False Witnesses—Working up a "reaction"—A Prophesy—Its fulfillment—How it goes—

Search and Seizure—Cleaned out—A Viper without fangs—Trying it on—Terrible threats—Nobody hurt—We roll them out—Legs—Three cheers for the Law—Cargoes or Pint Bottles? Either!—Property—Pour it out. 305

CHAPTER XX.

Will you come? Yes—A Challenge—A four days Debate—The Whisky Champion—A Bill of Indictment—Plausible but baseless—Still Debating—Parallel Cases—Shad in Connecticut River! Ha, ha—A good time—A capital arrangement—A Colloquy—A Distiller at the front—Political Economy—Still-fed Pork—" Tender"—Hard Work but poor Pay. 325

CHAPTER XXI.

Westward ho!—On the Prairies—A Thanksgiving extemporized—Whisky and the Indians—Life on the Farm. . . . 342

CHAPTER XXII.

Return to New England—Organization and Finance—Instruction the Great Want—Sensation versus Education—What might have been—Poverty and its results—Mistakes of Good Men—Why is it permitted?—A "New Departure" suggested—Will you attend to it, Sir.? 348

CHAPTER XXIII.

The Million Fund—Massachusetts Alliance—Old Dr. Beecher—To the West again—Thurlow W. Brown. 360

CHAPTER XXIV.

Charles Dickens—The Logic of Facts—What we must Teach—Foundations and Connections—Starvation and Consequent Feebleness—Slightly Intoxicated—Temperance and the Doctors—The Longevity of our Temperance Fathers—Form of Organization for Local Temperance Societies—Conclusion. . 378

A FORTY YEARS FIGHT

WITH THE

DRINK DEMON.

CHAPTER I.

Incentive to the Battle—A sad state of things—A little light—Set on—Considering the matter—The Whipping Post—The first blow—Signing the pledge—Rev. Dr. Hewett—The Fathers—Missionary work with Pills—William Goodell—A blow from Elder Meech—My first Speech—What came of it—Pure Gold.

In the year 1826, while at the home of my father in Lisbon, Conn., engaged in certain studies supposed to be necessary as preliminary to the study of medicine, in which it had been settled that I should subsequently engage, rumors reached our family circle that movements in opposition to the sale and use of intoxicating liquors had originated, not only in our own state, but in other New England states as well. These rumors, aided by local circumstances which I cannot here detail, directed our thoughts to the pernicious results of the drinking customs which at that time universally prevailed, and of the liquor traffic which was then carried on in every town and village under the sanction of law and apparently without awakening a suspicion on the part of the masses of the people that there was anything wrong about either. Our attention having thus been called to the subject, it was frequently discussed around our hearth, in the field, and by the way. Facts to classify and compare and from which to draw conclusions, were all around us and were of the most startling character. More than one-tenth of our male population who had passed the age of thirty were occasional, if not habitual, drunkards. With that statement the results otherwise need not here be described. And yet, on all public occasions, intoxicating liquors, the cause of all this mischief, were present. At auctions, military trainings and elections, at the raising of houses, barns, or bridges, at public celebrations, on New Years days and the annual Thanksgivings, at funerals and even at the ordination of ministers, the presence of intoxicating liquors was deemed indispensable. They were relied upon to sustain the farmer during the severe labors of the haying and harvest; and the best men then living drank them freely, and many such were engaged in the traffic. That great changes have been wrought in the customs and habits of the people in relation to these matters since that date is obvious, and will not be denied by any honest man. Notwithstanding the general and deplorable blindness of the people at the period named, in reference to truths which millions even of our children and youth *now* understand, certain facts existed even then quite sufficient to enable awakened and inquiring minds seeking for truth and light, to find them, at least to a sufficient extent for practical guidance. To be sure we could not *then*, even with the help of the facts to which I am about to call attention, see the whole truth. It was not necessary that we should; but we could see enough to guide us in the right direction, to make the path of duty plain for some distance before us, and that is all we have ever a right to demand; because a resolute walking in that path so far as we can see it, will always secure additional light by the time it is needed.

Here and there an individual was found, who, from the possession of some personal peculiarities would not follow the general custom, and refused, utterly, to drink spirituous liquors under any circumstances, and it was perfectly plain to all observers, when attention was directed to the matter, that by their persistent abstinence they lost nothing on the score of health or the power of endurance. A brother of mine was of that number. It was in vain that, in the field or elsewhere, the bottle or its contents were pressed upon Joseph. He would not drink. He did not like the taste of it. The fiery stuff burned his mouth and he would not swallow it. "But Joseph, you cannot stand it on water alone, through these long, hot days, and in the midst of such severe labor, without a little stimulus. You will be faint and give out before night." "Well, when I do, you will know it," was Joe's uniform reply. We soon discovered that he endured the fatigue of the hay and harvest field as well as the rest of us. In fact, if anybody failed, it was never Joe.

Here, and in other similar cases, was a practical refutation of prevailing opinions; and some of us saw it and were instructed. My first earnest effort in opposition to the existing state of things occurred in this wise:

Events had occurred in the immediate neighborhood, growing out of the use of liquor, which greatly interested our family; and the subject had been discussed around our hearth during a certain evening with a good deal of earnestness. At the conclusion of this discussion, my father said to me, in a very earnest way, (I seem almost to hear his words ringing in my ears now, after the lapse of forty-five years,) "Charles, you are always scribbling about something, and for the most part, I think, on matters of very little importance; and now, if you have any gifts in connection with the use of the quill, try your hand for once on a subject of some consequence." "What would you have me do?" I asked. "Go into your chamber to-morrow morning and write an address to the authorities of this town and endeavor to show them the folly and wickedness of granting men license to destroy the peace and happiness of the neighborhood by selling liquors; for that is the result of the sale any way, and men with but half an eye ought to see it."

The reader will perceive that my venerated father, though he was not at the time a personal abstainer, had begun to get his eyes open to see things as they were. As I had been educated from my childhood to find pleasure in always gratifying, as far as possible, the wishes of my parents, (that was an ancient fashion which has become almost obsolete,) and as I had become considerably interested in the matter myself, I went to my chamber the following morning to undertake the task assigned me.

The first thing to be done, of course, was to consider the subject earnestly and in all its aspects, so far as my boy-brain and limited observation would enable me. I planted myself, in imagination, over at the store, not eighty rods from my father's door, and in my thought followed the jugs of liquor from thence to the homes of the people. From the center of the town, or parish, (Lisbon Green, we called it,) five roads diverged in as many directions, and I knew, personally, every inhabitant for miles. On every road within a mile and a half of the "meeting-house" was the home of one or more men ruined by drink; on one of the roads there were three, and a barn is now standing on that road, within a mile of the meeting-house, in which two intemperate men have, in fits of desperation, hanged themselves since 1828. I saw distinctly that the mission of the liquor which was daily carried out of that store was a different one from that of the sugar, the coffee, and the cotton warps which the farmer's wives in those days filled in their own looms with home-spun woolen and wrought into blankets and garments for the boys. The liquor supplied no natural want, but, on the contrary, created an artificial one, which clamored increasingly for gratification, until the ruin of its subject was often effected, involving in most cases the ruin of domestic happiness, and sometimes of different members of the family.

While I mused upon these things I became excited over them, and set about the task before me, and I wrote an address to the Selectmen in rhyme. Youth, and very limited knowledge, is the only apology I can offer for having done so. Although the work of a boy, and very imperfect, yet it was an honest, earnest, and truthful, though clumsy, expression of thought and feeling, and it wrought good results. My father had a hundred copies of the address printed, privately, at his own expense, and on a certain Saturday night, while the people generally slept, these were distributed about the town, or parish, rather. Here a copy was stuck on the front gate with a tack, (my father made tacks,) there, one carefully folded, was slipped under the door-knocker, or thrust under the front door. One copy was tacked on the whipping-post, or rather, on the wooden box surmounting it; for, although scourging as a penalty for crime had ceased to be practiced, (old Betty Green was the last whipped for stealing from the church the table cloths used at the communion service,) that old relic of barbarism still stood on the "Green" in front of the "meeting-house." One copy had been tacked pretty securely on the aforesaid box, and was not observed until the people came to "meeting," and it was then too late for any party who might be aggrieved to tear it down; for to do so would be to proclaim that he was among the wounded pigeons. There it remained, therefore, through the day; and during the interval of public worship was read probably by every man and boy who had come to the meeting, and who was tall enough to read it from the ground. The post was about six feet high.

Here was "moral suasion" applied in a very direct way; and it was interesting to note the amount of rum wrath which this anonymous production awakened in certain of the readers. I noted it with interest, for I was present; and, to prevent any suspicion attaching to me as its author, I elbowed my way through the staring crowd and read the article with apparently as much interest as any of the group. That the curious reader may be enabled to form some idea of the character of the document, I will give him here a brief extract; but I must once more earnestly beg him while reading it to remember that its author was but a country boy, whose reading had been pretty much confined to the Bible and Psalm Book, the old Westminster Catechism, The American Preceptor, Columbian Orator, Robinson Crusoe, Weam's Life of Washington, and a weekly, and most excellent newspaper, The Norwich Courier. Referring to the liquor shop and the drinking customs of the people as a source of mischief this was written:—

> "Most other evils to this fount we trace,
> Which blast our pleasures and destroy our race.
> For *this*, the widow mourns—her husband dead;
> For *this*, the starving children cry for bread;
> For this, the wife sits waiting for her spouse,
> At midnight hour, and ponders o'er her woes,
> While he, poor wretch, all power of moving fled,
> Sleeps by the fence, or in yon crazy shed.
> In vain she goes and listens at the door;
> The sighing breeze, the torrent's distant roar
> Are all she hears. Now, where her children sleep,
> She casts one look, and then lies down to weep.
> Now, tell me, what on earth can comfort bring,
> Or from what source shall smiling pleasure spring?
> Pleasure! 'tis what on earth she ne'er can know,
> Where every passing hour augments her woe."

In the conclusion of the article, which was of considerable length, though thrown off at one sitting, the boy made the following appeal to the Fathers of the town, its civil authorities, who, as far as licensing men to sell liquors was concerned, had all power in the premises:—

"Oh, banish grog shops, and *thus* check this ill,
Delay no longer, but your part fulfill,
Rescue the fallen, sinking age regard,
And Heaven's best blessings will be your reward."

A temperance society was formed in my native town, I think, in 1827, the pledge of which I, with most of my father's family, signed. It pledged its subscribers only against the sale and use of spirituous liquors. Among many others, some very aged men of the town, at the earnest solicitation of our venerable clergyman, Rev. Levi Nelson, joined the society and signed its pledge, fully expecting to suffer in their health from the change it involved; but were afterwards surprised to find that what they had done for the sake of benefiting others through their example, had really been blessed to the improvement of their own health.

From the time when these events occurred in that usually quiet, rural community, to the year 1840, the store at the "Green" was successively occupied by four individuals. I knew them all, and can testify that they were kind-hearted, social, and agreeable gentlemen, good neighbors, and, excepting their ruinous traffic, were useful, well-disposed, and public-spirited men. Alas! three out of the four went down to their graves the lamented victims of their own traffic, and the fourth suffered severely in his own family from the same cause. But one, of all the intemperate men of that community, ever reformed, and he was so far broken down physically, by long and free drinking, that he never regained his health, remaining to his death but the feeble wreck of his former self.

No event occurred worthy of special notice, as connected with temperance, during the three years which I devoted to the study of medicine, except a visit to Pittsfield, Mass., where I attended medical lectures, by the Rev. Dr. Hewett, then in the employment of "The American Temperance Society" as a lecturing agent. That learned, able, and eloquent man delivered two public lectures on the subject in that town, which were largely attended, and which so moved the influential portion of its citizens, that a committee was *at once* appointed to take measures to stop the destructive traffic in liquors; but the influence of his appeals soon died away to such an extent that the traffic was continued and still curses the town, one of the most beautiful of Western Massachusetts.

The startling view of the liquor system, presented by Dr. Hewett in those lectures, was not, however, without permanent results. Undoubtedly they left impressions on many minds as lasting as life. Certainly they deepened in the mind of one young doctor, who heard them, a hatred, already pretty strong, of the liquor traffic and the drinking usages of society, and fixed, more firmly than ever before, his determination to wage upon both, while life should last, perpetual and uncompromising war.

More than forty years after listening, at Pittsfield, to that excellent man and intellectual giant, I had the happiness to meet him at a temperance gathering in Bridgeport, Conn. It was during the last year of his life. He had learned that I was to address the people there on the good old theme, and, though in feeble health, he attended the meeting, opened it by prayer, at the request of the chairman, P. T. Barnum, Esq., and listened with attention while I addressed a crowded congregation. At its close he arose and gave a hearty endorsement to the doctrines advanced, and to the counsel given, and, grasping my hand in his earnest way, thanked me in the presence of the congregation for my earnest advocacy of a cause he loved. When such earnest advocates of this noble cause pass away, as Hewett, Edwards, Beecher, Pierpont, Marsh, Sargent, and Nott, I am ready to exclaim in the language of one of old, " My father, my father, the chariot of Israel, and the horsemen thereof!" God give to those of us who follow them a double portion of the Spirit by which those noble men were actuated.

In the year 1829, I commenced the practice of medicine at East Greenwich, Rhode Island. In the western part of the town where I located not a single individual practised abstinence from intoxicating liquors from any conviction that it was wrong to drink, if in moderation. Here, therefore, the work was to be commenced *de novo*. I had to convert my first man, and I set to work on a favorite theory of mine, in reference to missionary operations in general, viz: aim at the conversion of those nearest to you *first*, and extend operations as opportunities offer. I am apt to distrust a missionary zeal that burns to do good to somebody a thousand miles away, but neglects opportunities of doing good just at hand. I secured the conversion to my temperance faith of the excellent family with whom I boarded, that of Andrew Pitcher, and their hearty coöperation in every movement I afterward made for the advancement of the cause in their neighborhood. That family has been passed by by the destroying angel of the still. God grant that they may continue to be thus favored, they and their children's children to the latest generation.

For the first year of my professional life I labored for the advancement of the temperance cause only in the private circle, in the intervals of professional labor. Often, while waiting to watch the operation of medicines on the sick, there would be opportunities to talk about something, and somehow it would frequently happen that the conversation would turn on the fearful prevalence of intemperance, and on the serious injury therefrom to all the best interests of the community. Careful not to give needless offense, I sought thus to interest and influence those with whom I daily came in contact. With a little medicine I mixed a little temperance, and despite all my skill and caution in compounding the latter I found it more difficult to render it agreeable to certain parties than even my pills and powders.

The only source of instruction on the subject then within my reach, except my daily observation of the practical working of the drinking system, was a most excellent paper, "The Genius of Temperance," edited by Wm. Goodell. Its weekly visits were most welcome to me, and greatly aided me in my warfare on the wicked and destructive system I was fighting with all the weapons I could command—a work which I had come to regard as a part of my daily duties. I believe it to be a part of the daily duties of every man, especially of every Christian, to wage a constant and uncompromising war on every demoralizing and destructive habit, custom, or institution of the community in which he resides. We share, in my opinion, in some degree the guilt of every wicked system existing within the sphere of our influence against which we do not utter our earnest and continued protest, and which we do not study and perseveringly labor to annihilate. If I am wrong in holding such opinions Wm. Goodell is in part responsible, for his editorials taught me such doctrines in my early manhood.

During the spring of 1832 the Rev. Levi Meech, (Elder Meech they called him,) a Baptist preacher, a man of decided ability, and a genuine reformer, preached in the neighboring town of Exeter a discourse in relation to the prevalent evil of intemperance, and the duty of Christian people in regard to it. He declared moderate drinking to be a sin, because it first created the possibility of drunkenness, and then gave countenance and support to the system which continued it; and he expressed the opinion that a respectable moderate drinker exerted a far greater influence to perpetuate the evil of intemperance than the drunkard. Prior to the delivery of that discourse he had enjoyed a popularity, enviable, because honestly acquired in the faithful discharge of what he believed to be his duty. His sturdy blow at a popular vice, however, instantly changed, with many, their opinion of their minister, and he was denounced beyond measure. For a time it seemed doubtful whether the more Christian part of his people could sustain him against the determined opposition of the infuriated lovers of the drink.

The noise of the battle reached me in East Greenwich, where, also, some members of his church resided. I at once resolved on my course, and gave public notice that in Exeter, on the very ground where he had offended, I would express my views of the matter in controversy in a public discourse. The announcement gave great alarm to many of my friends, some of whom thought it would expose me to personal violence, and others that it would lose me the good will and patronage of the people, which I had acquired by careful attention to the duties of my profession, and a kind and courteous deportment. I was not, however, frightened from my purpose, and the time was fixed for the promised service.

I had recently married, on the ever memorable fifth of May, and now, as soon as June 2d, was about to sacrifice my professional prospects, so far as that locality was concerned, by a Quixotic assault on the customs and habits of the people, whom it was clearly my interest to conciliate. Such was the talk of the people. I improved my leisure hours in the preparation of a discourse for the coming occasion, as I had then no experience in public speaking, and on the morning of June 2d rode to Exeter, reinforced by my young wife, who, the year previous, in joining a temperance society which had two pledges—one simply pledging abstinence from distilled liquors, which was designated the "Short Pledge," and another pledging the party to abstinence from all intoxicating liquors known as the "Comprehensive Pledge."—had put C. P. against her name. As a matter of course I was now quite sure I was right, and quite courageous, being *thus* supported. Reader, if you have not learned that a married man rarely succeeds in any important undertaking without the permission if not the aid of his wife, it is time you did.

The room in which the lecture was to be given was crowded to its utmost capacity, and as the weather was warm, the windows low, and the sash raised to give free admission to the air, my audience was increased by scores of citizens who backed their wagons against the building, and, mounting into them, filled the windows with their anxious faces. The principal liquor seller of the place, a very tall gentleman, placed himself in the door-way, directly opposite the platform, and thus confronted me with a defiant scowl, as much as to say, "I will see, sir, what *you*, a green, young doctor, dare say against the business of an influential, respectable, and, withal, very tall and good-looking merchant."

The discourse was listened to with the most respectful attention, for there was too much of real manhood and genuine Christian principle among that people to tolerate any rowdy demonstrations, notwithstanding many of the best men present were entirely wrong in their opinions and practice in relation to the subject under discussion. The sight of that tall, scowling liquor seller, spreading himself in the door-way before me, had an effect quite different from what he anticipated. It made me quite impatient to reach that part of my manuscript in which I had addressed some words to gentlemen of his craft, and when I did reach it I gave the words all possible emphasis. That the reader may judge of its adaptation to the case before me, I will transcribe a few sentences from memory:—

"To those who are engaged in the business of manufacturing or distributing among your fellow-citizens intoxicating liquors I would address a few words. Among a Christian people it is, I believe, a settled principle that men ought never to engage in any business upon which they cannot consistently ask the blessing of God.

I now ask you, if, when you take the jug or bottle from the hand of the poor little ragged son or daughter of the drunkard, and go behind your counter, and turn your faucet to draw for a drunken father his daily quart of liquor, you can, while the measure is filling up, improve the passing moment to lift your heart to God and crave his blessing on such a calling? You dare not do it. You would fear the vengeance of insulted Heaven against such high handed wickedness added to such daring impiety. But you may say, perhaps, that you do not sell to the drunkard. What then? You sold to him while he was a sober man. He was, perhaps, educated in the school of drunkenness at *your counter*, but when he had lost his property and could no longer meet his payments, all at once your conscience became exceedingly tender, and when the poor besotted victim of depraved appetite begs you to furnish him but one glass to satisfy his insatiate longings, you can then vociferate in loud and determined tone, ' *You shall not have it*,' and the poor wretch, as he turns disappointed and unsatisfied away, mutters his curses against you as one of the prime authors of his destruction."

At the conclusion of the discourse Elder Meech grasped my hand, and, with a voice tremulous with emotion, thanked me for this timely and efficient support. "This," said the good man, "is friendship indeed, to throw yourself into the breach with me at such a time as this." Among the friends of the infant enterprise, one man, besides Elder Meech, was conspicuous. He was a man of large intellect, and a noble soul thoroughly imbued with the spirit of Christ. He had been greatly interested in the preparations for the meeting, active in extending the notice and in securing a general attendance, and with the most intense interest he now listened to every word of the discourse. It was but an utterance of his own thought and feeling by another voice, and both his intellect and heart responded. How that great, clear, and loving eye of his kindled as he saw that the truth was finding a lodgment in the minds and hearts of his neighbors and friends! It might have been truthfully said of him, as of the martyred Stephen, that "his face shone as the face of an angel." God be thanked for such men as Deacon Russell Jocelyn. It is with a thrill of pleasure that I write his name. For years I enjoyed his friendship and coöperation. But he has gone to his rest. He was a noble man by nature, made more noble, more efficient, and sweeter by the grace of God.

At the close of the public service I was solicited by a committee, just then and there appointed, to furnish a copy of the discourse for publication. My manuscript was placed in their hands, and a subscription raised upon the spot to pay for the printing of five hundred copies. It was printed and distributed, and no pamphlet ever circulated in Rhode Island was more carefully studied. The subject, however imperfectly treated, was entirely new. It interested both friends and enemies of the liquor system, and all were anxious to learn what could be said on the subject.

CHAPTER II.

Organization—A Commissary Department Wanting—Little Money but Rich—Ben Johnson Cures the Doctor—Cider Experience—Out of the Scrape—Rhymes and Retailers—Still Rhyming—Argumentum ad Hominem — The Winding Sheet — They Dislike but Patronize Him.

MY views in relation to the sale and use of spirituous liquors having thus become known, I began to receive invitations to address the people on the subject in different localities, and these invitations I generally accepted. Societies were organized at many points, and before the close of the year 1833 their numbers even in that little, but very wealthy and respectable, State of Rhode Island were very considerable. These societies had each a written constitution, the preamble to which briefly recited the reasons for its formation, and recounted the evils inflicted on society by the traffic in and the use of intoxicating liquors, and the danger to the habits of the people from their continued use, especially to the young. These societies were officered as other societies usually are which are organized and intended to advance special and important interests. They had each a President, one or more Vice-Presidents, a Secretary, and a Treasurer, and had some sensible plan been devised for supplying these organizations with the sinews of war, needed funds, it is doubtful if any other forms of organization would since have been adopted.

They would never have been needed, in my opinion, for those original societies would thus have been rendered as lasting as the system which they were intended to break down. And as they had no forms or features which were objectionable to any who were prepared to endorse their doctrines and adopt their pledge or bond of union, they might, to this day, have embraced all the real friends of abstinence, and given our forces the advantage not only of unity of sentiment, but *unity of organization*. The advantage of this is often seen in connection with political campaigns, where the primary organizations of a great political party are essentially of one pattern throughout the country.

My opinions in reference to the importance of a financial basis to the enterprise were given to the public in a pamphlet, published at Chicago, Ill., in the year 1864, with the following title: "THE TEMPERANCE CAUSE, PAST, PRESENT, AND FUTURE, or, *Why* We Are *Where* We Are." To that publication I would refer the reader for a more extended explanation of my views on that subject.

While the good work thus progressed in Rhode Island it was carried forward with even greater rapidity and energy in other neighboring States *because more liberally sustained financially*. I had no considerable share in the work outside of Rhode Island for years, as my temperance labor was entirely gratuitous, except in a few instances where my traveling expenses, merely, were paid by the societies before whom I lectured, and, in the meantime, I supported myself and an increasing family by my practice as a physician. As a matter of course I often lost professional business when abroad lecturing, and often resolved that under the circumstances I must decline future invitations; but committees would visit me and urge the needs of the cause in their several localities with such earnestness and persistence that I would consent to go just that once, and so it continued for years. In all this, however, I received a rich reward in intimate connection with the labor. The comfort of believing that I was thus lessening sin and consequent suffering, that I was thus, in a humble way, inducing my countrymen to honor the laws of God in their personal habits, and to secure their personal development in a right direction by laboring for the advancement of truth and righteousness in the world, and thus to come more into the spirit and the work of our Divine Master by active sympathy with the suffering, and by the practice of self-denial for the good of others.

How *rich* I often felt in seeing, at the close of an evening's service, twenty, thirty, and sometimes fifty names added to the pledge of abstinence, oftentimes embracing in the number some of the most honored and influential names of the community. How I rejoiced and gloried in the work; and often as I journeyed homeward from such labor late in the night, and alone under the silent stars, I devoutly thanked God that I was *permitted* to labor for so good a cause. It is a truth, with which I think the mass of mankind are not sufficiently impressed, that while we labor unselfishly for the good of others, we are taking the most direct and effective means for securing our own happiness and self-development in the highest and best sense of that term. Hence, really Christian labor brings its own exceeding great reward *now* and *here*, while engaged in it, and quite independent of any promised or anticipated rewards in the distant future.

In the autumn of the year 1835 I was invited by the leading citizens of Centerville, Warwick, to take the place and practice of a Dr. Knight, who, for many years, had been the principal and very popular physician of that village and vicinity, but who had decided to retire from business. I accepted the situation and removed my family thither. It was but five miles from my former place of residence, and as it was the center of a cluster of manufacturing villages, it offered a more extended field for professional labor.

Soon after my location at Centerville I was invited to address the people at the regular monthly meeting of the Centerville Temperance Society. I accepted the invitation and performed the service, getting more hearty thanks from the society than from a number of liquor sellers who were conducting a killing business in that and the neighboring villages, as, in the lecture, I expressed in not very complimentary terms my opinion of their traffic.

I mention the fact just here, for the sake of giving additional point to a brief narrative, of one of the most ludicrous and painful events which has ever occurred in connection with my temperance labor, and yet it was to me quite instructive. Hitherto I had not adopted the "Comprehensive Pledge," my warfare being with "spirituous" or "distilled" liquors. I had, however, stopped drinking wine, for Ben Johnson, to whom I had given a personal exhortation to relinquish his much-loved gin, had blunted the edge of my talk by asking me if I did not occasionally take a glass of wine, (the fellow knew I did,) and further, and worse still, had asked me *why* I drank the wine in preference to water. I had replied that when I had been riding in the cold, and was broken of my rest, &c., I had found the moderate stimulus of a glass of wine to be quite refreshing to me. "You are right," said Ben, "and when I have been out chopping all day, or sledding wood, and get tired and chilled, I find the moderate stimulus of a glass of gin refreshing to me." That speech had cured me of wine drinking, but still I occasionally drank at the tables of farmers a glass of cider. Not often, but occasionally, and I was not pledged against its use.

In removing my effects from my former residence to Centerville, a load or two of apples had been taken over —it was in the autumn—and a couple of barrels of cider, as I had owned an orchard in the country, and a neighbor had worked up my refuse apples "on sheers," as he termed it. The cider had been put into my cellar at Centerville and forgotten, for I did not care enough for it to put it on tap. Others, it seems, had cast affectionate glances upon it while it was being put into the cellar, and one morning a citizen of the village called and inquired if I had not a barrel of cider which I would sell. Just then I had use for every spare dollar, for I had bought the property of Dr. Knight, and my transfer to a new field of labor had taxed me pretty heavily. I remembered that there were two casks in the cellar, and concluded that one, properly cared for, would make all the vinegar we should need, and I therefore replied that I would sell to him the other barrel. The price was agreed upon, and he took it home on a wheelbarrow. He was a giant for strength, had a noble physical frame, and, as I afterward learned, was really a clever fellow and a useful citizen when free from the influence of drink. Of course, I knew nothing of the man's habits or history, when I sold him the cider, for I was a new comer in the village. Thus far it had not once occurred to me that I had been guilty of any impropriety, or had acted at all inconsistent with my profession as a friend of temperance.

A few days after the departure of the cider the superintendent of a factory in the neighborhood called at my residence, early in the morning, and requested me to go directly to a distant part of the village and see a Mr. Wilcox, who, he stated, was in a most deplorable condition. I inquired if he had been suddenly attacked, and what appeared to be the trouble or ailment. He answered that it was a sort of mania or drunken craziness. At the word "drunken" I started, of course, and inquired if he knew where the man got his liquor. In my thought I was after the rum-seller directly. "He has had no liquor," said my friend Allen. "No liquor! On what, then, did he get drunk?" "Why, somebody sold him a barrel of cider a few days ago, and he has been pouring it down ever since. He is not so drunk but what he can move about, but he is as fierce as a tiger, and the moment he is seen outside of his door the neighbors clap too their doors and bolt them that he may not enter."

What a revelation was here! Mr. Allen did not know that I had sold that barrel of cider, but I knew it, and if I ever felt like getting into a very small place and shutting the door after me it was then. Could I have been bought that morning at the then present valuation, and afterwards sold at former estimates, somebody would have made a speculation. I visited the miserable man, tried to purchase back what remained of the cider, offering for it all he had paid for the full barrel, that I might pour it on the earth at once ; but he refused to part with it. I assured him, however, that I should see him again the following morning, and if I found him in the same condition I would go into the cellar at all hazards and empty the barrel, for I was determined that it should not be true another day that a man in Centerville was drunk on an article which Dr. Charles Jewett, a temperance lecturer, had sold him. After my departure, his wife, at her own imminent peril, glided down the cellar stairs and drew the tap, and the barrel was soon empty. I certainly felt much obliged to her, and I can assure my readers that I have sold no cider since. That incident taught me that there was but one consistent course for any real friend of temperance to pursue, viz : To wage uncompromising and indiscriminate war on all intoxicating liquors, no matter by what *name* they may be called.

The second year I spent in Centerville, it was the year 1836, I believe, I wrote a rhymed address to retailers of liquor, a copy of which was solicited by my neighbor, friend, and faithful fellow-laborer, Rev. S. W. Coggshall, for publication in " Zion's Herald," the organ of the Methodist denomination for New England, and an earnest and able advocate of thorough temperance from that date to its last issue. It appeared in that paper, and as the friends of the cause in Rhode Island thought it contained some important truths, with which the public mind should become familiar, they caused it to be published in hand-bill form also, and thousands and tens of thousands of copies were distributed through that and neighboring states. I place it before my readers here, not for any literary merit it possesses, but that they may learn what were my views of the traffic at the date at which the article was written, and that they may also learn what instrumentalities were employed by the friends of the cause at that early period of its history, with which to mould the public sentiment, will, and action on this great question. Let it be borne constantly in mind that I am not giving a general history of the progress of the temperance enterprise throughout the country, but only such movements as occurred under my own observation, or so near to me that I became thoroughly acquainted therewith, and deeply interested therein.

AN ADDRESS

To Retailers of Intoxicating Liquors,

BY CHARLES JEWETT, M. D.,

of Centreville, Warwick, R. I.

Ye, who regardless of your country's good,
Fill up your coffers with the price of blood;
Who pour out poison with a liberal hand,
And scatter crime and misery through the land;
Though now rejoicing in the midst of health,
In full possession of ill-gotten wealth,
Yet a few days, at most, the hour must come,
When ye shall know the poison-sellers' doom,
And shrink beneath it for upon you all,
The indignation of a God shall fall.
Ye know the fruits of this accursed trade,
Ye see the awful havoc it hath made,

Ye pour to men disease, and want, and woe,
And then tell us ye wish it were not so,
But, 'tis a truth, and that ye know full well,
That some will drink so long as ye will sell.
But here that old excuse yet meets us still,
"If I don't sell the poison, others will."
Then let them sell and you'll be none the worse
They'll have the *profits*, and they'll have the *curse*.
Bear this in mind, you have at your command
The power to curse or power to bless the land;
If ye will sell, Intemperance still shall roll
Its wave of bitterness o'er many a soul.
Still shall the wife for her lost husband mourn,
And sigh for days that never shall return.
Still that unwelcome sight our eyes shall greet,
Of beggar'd children roaming through the street;
And thousands, whom our labors cannot save,
Go trembling, tottering, reeling to the grave.

Still loitering at your shop the live-long day,
Will scores of idlers pass their hours away;
And e'en the peaceful night for rest ordained,
Shall with their noisy revels be profaned.
The poisonous cup will pass, and mirth and glee
Gild o'er the surface of their misery;
Uproarious laughter fill each space between—
Harsh oaths, ungodly songs, and jests obscene.
And there *you'll* stand amid that drunken throng,
Laugh at the jest, and glory in the song.

How oft ye see the children of the poor,
With unshod feet, unwilling, throng your door,
And carry with them, as they homeward go,
The fruitful source of wretchedness and woe —
That which will change the father to a beast;
That which will rob a mother of her rest;
And take from half-fed children needful bread,
And give them curses, frowns, and blows instead!

* * * * * * *

Pour out your poison till some victim dies;
Then go, and at his funeral wipe your eyes.
Join there that mourning throng, with solemn face,
And help to bear him to the burial-place.
There stands his wife, with weeping children round,
While their fast-falling tears bedew the ground.
From many an eye the gem of pity starts,
And many a sigh from sympathizing hearts,
Comes laboring up, and almost chokes the breath,
While thus they gaze upon the work of death.
The task concludes; the relics of the dead
Are slowly settled to their damp, cold bed.

Come, now, draw near, my money-making friend;
You saw the starting—*come and see the end;*
When first you filled his glass, *one* would suffice;
Next *two* were wanting; and now, *here he lies.*
Look now into that open grave, and say,
Dost feel no sorrow, no remorse, to-day?
Does not your answering conscience loud declare,
That *your cursed avarice* has laid him there?

Now, since the earth has closed o'er his remains,
Turn o'er your book, and count your honest gains.

With these lines I purposed to close the article; but circumstances occurred which rendered it quite convenient for me to add a few lines. A Mr. Kilton, residing in Washington Factory Village, had been requested to purchase for his sisters some trifling article of dry goods. The merchant, of whom he purchased it, used as a wrapper, a leaf torn from an old account book, in which accounts had been kept years before, when liquors, as well as dry goods were retailed at the store.

When Mr. Kilton reached home, the purchased article was called for. He delivered it, retaining in his hand the paper in which it had been wrapped. Glancing his eye over the paper, he observed, that upon that leaf had been kept the account of the last week's purchases of a family by the name of Briggs. He remembered the history of poor Briggs; that he died suddenly, after a week's debauch. The entries on the leaf were as follows: —

"Monday, Sept. 5th. To one quart of gin. Price, —
Tuesday, " 6th. " " " " —
Wednesday, " 7th. " " " " —
. Thursday, " 8th. " " " " —
Friday, " 9th. " " " " —
Saturday, " 10th. To five yards cloth, for
                                winding sheet, " — "

Thus it appeared from the account that poor Briggs had been regularly furnished with a quart of liquor per day for five days in succession; that during the night of the fifth day, Friday, he had died, and that on Saturday the family had been furnished, at the same store, with his winding sheet, or the cloth of which to make it. As in the last line of the " address," I had bidden the liquor seller return from the grave of his victim, and look over his account-books, it seemed quite proper that I should inquire what he found written there, and I, therefore, added the following lines: —

    How doth the account for his last week begin?
    "Monday, Sept. 5th, one quart of gin,"
    A like amount, for each succeeding day,
    Tells on the book, but wears his life away.
    Saturday's charge makes out the account complete,

To cloth, five yards to make a winding-sheet.
There, all stands fair, without mistake or flaw,
How honest trade will thrive, UPHELD BY LAW!

It will doubtless interest the reader to know that by such plain utterances of truth, I did not lose the patronage of the liquor traders. They knew that I was right and that they were wrong, and they seemed to have more respect for me, the more distinctly I set forth the wickedness of their course. Beside this, I think they preferred the services of a physician who never swallowed the villainous compounds they sold. They saw, every day, in their places of business, the effects which liquors produced upon the reasoning powers of those who drank them, and they shrewdly enough concluded that the use of their liquors would not materially aid a man in the investigation of the causes and nature of disease, and in the choice of means for its removal.

REV. THOS. P. HUNT.

CHAPTER III.

A Visitor—Thomas P. Hunt—His speech at Aponaug—" An excellent sentiment, madam"—Facing the question—Yes or no ?—He loves but votes against it—A victory for rum—An " Open House " —A song furnished gratis.

During the year, I was strengthened and comforted by a visit from the Rev. Thomas P. Hunt of Pennsylvania, who had become quite distinguished as an advocate of the cause in that and other of the Middle States. I was most happy to entertain and confer with him. I arranged appointments for him at a number of points in my neighborhood, and was delighted to find the views I had taken of the whole liquor system so ably defended by this devoted and excellent man. There are few men living in our country who have considered the whole subject so thoughtfully and earnestly as this early advocate of our cause. His visit to me, and the long and earnest discussion we had in relation to the various phases which the enterprise then presented, constituted an era in my life, as an humble worker in the cause. His personal influence was more potent with me than that of any other man, I had almost said of *all* other men, in inducing me, at a later period, to abandon my profession, and devote myself to the public advocacy of abstinence from intoxicating liquors.

That the reader may be able to form some idea of the manner in which the subject was treated in public by

"Father Hunt," I will report the introductory portion of his lecture at the village of Apponaug in Warwick, R. I. I only regret that with the words, I cannot give his appearance before the audience, the expression of his countenance, especially of the eye, than which few keener are ever set in human heads, and the tone of his voice, at once *very* peculiar and very impressive. There are doubtless many citizens of Warwick living, who heard the address, and I am very certain they would, if required, testify to the accuracy of my report, made after the lapse of thirty-five years.

"Ladies and Gentlemen: I, last evening, delivered a discourse at Washington Factory Village in the town of Coventry. As I was quite at leisure during the afternoon preceding the lecture, I proposed to walk out for a little exercise. A friend suggested that I might do some service to the people of the village, perhaps, by calling on Mr. Capwell, the keeper of the hotel, and having a talk with him. He was represented to me as a very clever sort of a man, good natured, not at all inclined to be abusive, and it was thought my words might be of service to him. I called upon him; introduced myself as the person who was to speak on temperance in the evening, and found him disposed to listen to me with patience and candor. I told him I had been informed that he was the possessor of considerable real estate in the village, and assured him that whatever should have the effect to lessen the intelligence of the people, and to lower the standard of public morals, as I was quite sure his traffic would do, though he might not intend it, would most certainly diminish the value of his real estate, as it would render the village a less desirable place of residence. And I suggested to him that, in the long run, he would lose more by this depreciation of property, than he would gain, directly, by his traffic. He was listening to me with evident interest, and I could not but hope I was making a favorable impression on his mind, when, all at once, a side door opened, and a little bit of a woman rushed into the room so swiftly, that her cap border was turned back on her head by the current of air she created, and in a very excited manner and with a very shrill voice, she exclaimed, 'I *do* wish that people would mind their own business.' Taken quite aback for the moment by this startling introduction and speech, I replied, 'Well, madam, and so do *I!* I agree with you exactly, madam. That is an *excellent* sentiment of yours. I approve of it everywhere and always. I am a temperance lecturer, madam, and you see now, that while I am persuading this gentleman, your husband, very likely, madam, to abandon the sale of liquors, which make men drunk, I was laboring right along in the line of my business. You see I agree with you entirely. That is an excellent sentiment of yours. One reason why I labor to persuade men to leave off drinking, is because the use of liquor does, notoriously, lead men to *neglect* their business. For instance, here is a carpenter. He has a fine shop and good tools. He is himself a good workman, and has not only apprentices to aid him, but also skilled workmen. He ought to do a large business, but he does not. What is the trouble? The public know that he is a free drinker, and that he has, frequently, in the midst of an important job, gone off on a spree, and the work has stopped in consequence. Business men don't like to intrust him important jobs on that account. Now don't you see that if I could induce that clever carpenter to leave off drinking, he would, thereafter, *mind his own business.* You see I agree with you, exactly, madam.' Just here she turned upon her heel and rushed out of the room, not even stopping to bid me good afternoon. I felt aggrieved at it. I naturally like the ladies, and love to be in agreement with them always when I can. And when, as in this case I take great pains to prove that I am in accord with them, I like to have the fact appreciated, and to be treated with courtesy." By this time, my readers will believe me that all eyes were riveted upon that little crooked man, with the large mouth and the lightning eyes, and that all ears were open to hear words of instruction from him.

The public mind had, by this time, become so far enlightened in relation to the liquor traffic, that the people of Rhode Island clamored for the abrogation of the license system. The question of license or no license was referred to the several towns by act of the Legislature, and was to be decided by the popular vote. That style of legislation, whatever may be said against it otherwise, brings to the masses of voters, very directly, a sense of their individual responsibility, which is apt to be lost sight of when they act on this question through others, who are elected as party men, and may, perhaps, have other important duties to perform besides deciding for or against license. There is no chance, however, for casting on others the responsibility of the voter, when the vote is not for or against certain men, but directly for or against licensing liquor shops. When a man, about to vote on that question, writes "*yes*" on his ballot, he *knows* that he is to become in part responsible for whatever mischief the liquor traffic may cause during the year; and if he votes "*No*," he feels that thus he rids himself of personal responsibility for the continuance of the traffic so far as voting is concerned. It was interesting and instructive to see how different men deported themselves at the polls in reference to this matter. Mr. A. loves his glass, but last week his daughter came home to her father's house with two or three helpless children, as she dared not longer live with her drunken husband. How does he vote to-day? Watch him. Good! He decides *for* the loved ones at home, and *against* the liquor shop. Mr. B., who has one drunken son, and two others rapidly approaching the same condition, goes the other way and votes for license. God have mercy upon him! What will the poor man do or say when he follows that eldest son, the drunkard, to the grave, as he probably will very soon? Can he, by any sort of reasoning, bring himself to believe that he had no hand in the ruin of his son, when his example, arguments, and vote, all helped to fasten the chain upon him, and to sustain the system which put the cup of poison to his lip? Perhaps he may. When men reason with the stomach instead of the brain, there is no knowing what conclusions they may arrive at. It is well to have the line drawn so that every man may know exactly where he stands in relation to this as well as other important matters. So thought Elijah, "How long halt ye between two opinions? If the Lord be God, follow him, but if Baal then follow him." So in relation to the liquor system. If it be a blessing, sustain it, if a curse, destroy it.

Thus in Rhode Island, for a time, we had a clean issue. In some towns we were beaten. Warwick, the town in which I resided, was one of them, but in almost every case where the liquor party prevailed, its leaders made such use of their victory as to disgust the more decent part of the voters who helped them to secure it. Some liquor dealer would keep open house for the day or evening after the victory, and with free liquor the drinking and rejoicing would extend far into the night, and end, perhaps, with a row, thus uttering the condemnation of the liquor traffic in a language quite as emphatic as could be employed by its most sturdy opponents. The evening after the triumph of the liquor party in Warwick, a portion of the rank and file had a jollification at a certain establishment in Centreville. The presiding genius, who there dispensed liquors, on returning from the town meeting, sent out word that he should keep open house that evening, and that there would be a free drink for all. Wishing to aid my neighbors in giving a fitting expression to their joy on this occasion, I hastily penned a few stanzas, and sent a copy over by a friend for the use of the company. It was entitled

THE GROG-SELLERS' INVITATION.

Ye friends of grog, rejoice, rejoice!
The work, the glorious work is done,
Raise high each trembling stammering voice,
The battle's fought, and *we have won!*

Ye old established bruisers come,
With purple blossoms on each nose,

A SONG FURNISHED GRATIS. 47

> My house this day shall be your home,
> Rejoice with us o'er fallen foes!

Other stanzas of kindred character followed, and my contribution to the interest of the joyful occasion, closed, I remember, as follows:

> What though our wives should scold and fret,
> Blows, well applied, will cool their spunk,
> While rum our parching throats can wet,
> Rejoice and be exceeding—drunk!

CHAPTER IV.

A CONTROVERSY.

A "Plucky" Wholesaler—Retreating, he gets "a shell"—A retailer hit—Rinsing the glasses—Providence votes down the traffic—A laughable incident—The way to do it—A shot that hit—Enlisting a Sharp Shooter—He hits the "bull's eye"—"Crack up"—Shoot, but don't hurt folks—"Father Bonney's" Prayer—First extemporaneous Speech.

While residing at Centerville, I had a controversy with one of the most respectable of the liquor traders in Providence—Capt. Samuel Young—in relation to the character of that traffic, whether beneficial and moral or otherwise. Its origin was as follows:

A resolution of the Providence Temperance Society, urging all friends of the cause to withdraw their patronage from grocers who sold liquor, provoked the ire of Capt. Young, and through the columns of the "Providence Courier" he attacked the society for passing that resolution. Some friend sent me a copy of the "Courier," and directed my attention to the communication of Capt. Young by marking the article. I replied to it over my own signature, and in the conclusion of my communication, invited him to a further discussion of the subject. I had long desired an opportunity of presenting my view of the liquor system to the public through such a channel and under such circumstances as would insure the thorough perusal of what I should write. Here, now, was the opportunity, if Capt. Young would but stand fire. This, I feared, he would not do; but I was mistaken. He was an honest and earnest man, and believed he was quite right in selling articles which more than half the community consumed, and should he fear to defend his business when assailed? Not he. The controversy continued for some weeks, and the editor and proprietor of the "Courier" remarked to me, years afterwards, that his paper was never in such demand as during that discussion.

At length the liquor dealers of the city began to complain, as I was informed, that the discussion would do more harm than good, that is, to their interests, and for Capt. Young's spirited advocacy of the traffic they were not disposed to be grateful. He proposed to drop the subject, and designated a certain article as the last he should write. In that article he had resorted to a style of discussion which fairly absolved me, as I judged, from any obligation to treat him or the subject, in closing the controversy, with special delicacy. I therefore bore down on the retreating enemy with the heaviest guns at my command, and some of my friends fancied that they saw splinters fly. It may have been a mistake, however. At any rate, the brave captain survived, and for some years continued to deal in liquors. Although most of his sales were in quantities to be taken at once from the store, he sold some by the glass, and there was in the young doctor's concluding article a malicious fling at the glass-trade. After having spoken of the retail liquor trade in terms which many men thought abusive, he grew poetical, and added:

> "I'd sooner black my visage o'er
>   And put the shine on boots and shoes,
> Than stand within a liquor store
>   And rinse the glasses drunkards use."

The conclusion of my last article, as nearly as I can recollect, was as follows: "I have sought to present to your mind, in their proper light, the inevitable results of the terrible business in which you are engaged. If, in view of those results, and from a proper regard for the welfare of the community of which you are a citizen, you will now abandon that business, all may be well. God may forgive, and an injured people may forget, the past. But if you shall still determine to distribute maddening poisons among the people, to scatter firebrands, arrows and death around you, what I have to say to you in conclusion is this:

> "Go on, be rich, even to your heart's desire,
>   And grasp with greedy hand each worldly good;
> But know, thy God will at thy hands require
>   Thy brother's blood."

Writers on war tell us that not one bullet in a hundred of those hurled in battle hits or kills a soldier. How that may be I know not, but I was gratified that one of my shots at the liquor traffic in this controversy (I had not discharged an hundred,) brought down one of the enemy's infantry. A young man engaged in keeping a drinking saloon, was led by reading my concluding article, to abandon the business, and told his friends what particular missile it was that hit him. It was the line about rinsing tumblers for drunkards. He said that when he first read those words (it was in the evening,) they filled him with rage. On the following morning he went to his saloon as usual, brushed down the shelves, saw that the decanters were all filled, and waited for customers. Presently a poor degraded wretch walked in and wanted a drink. He furnished it, dropped the price into the change drawer, and set up the decanter. But there was something more to be done to complete the operation. That glass must be rinsed and set up. He grasped the tumbler in the usual way, with the fore-finger pressing the inside and the thumb and middle finger the outside, and with the customary flourish, rinsed it in the water in the little tub on the counter. He said that no sooner had the glass touched the water than the troublesome line, "And rinse the glasses drunkards use," rushed through his memory. "Alas," thought he, "it is too true. I am, indeed, a tumbler-washer for drunkards! Great business, that! How elevating, how ennobling!" Another toper came in, and the operation was repeated. "And rinse the glasses drunkards use." Every time he put a tumbler into that little tub, those words would sing themselves through his brain. The dinner-hour at length arrived. He closed the saloon and started for his boarding-house, first brushing his hair and coat and pulling up his dickey, for who could tell but that he might meet a certain very pretty girl in his journey. As he tripped along with nimble step and head erect, that mischievous line dashed through his brain again, and down came his eye to the flag-stones. He felt so ashamed, he said, in reviewing the labor of the forenoon, that he could scarcely hold up his head or look a friend in the face. He saw, at once that he could not follow the business longer and preserve the smallest particle of self-respect, and he resolved immediately to abandon it. He sold out directly, and told a friend what it was that opened his eyes to the ineffable meanness of such a calling.

The contest for and against license in the City of Providence was a memorable one, and the anti-license party were victorious. The dealers in liquors and their most devoted adherents were sorely disappointed by the result, as, before the day of voting they felt quite sure of carrying the city. After the decision was known there was a manifest depression of spirits among them. They were less defiant than before, and, had the proper measures been adopted then to keep in active exercise the spirit of hostility to the liquor traffic which had thus been distinctly manifested, and to increase largely the educational branch of the enterprise as distinct from the legal or repressive, I doubt if there could ever have been any serious movement of a retrograde character in the State.

The difficulty lies in making the influential and business men of the community feel that this great and needful enterprise has a just claim upon a portion of their time, their thoughts and the contents of their purses as much, aye, far more, than any other benevolent enterprise of the age, inasmuch as it has to do, not only with the public health and public morals, with the interests of education and religion, but is a needful protection for their own sons and daughters, as well as their business interests. In some particulars the advocates of license and free use of liquors have the advantage of us. The public meetings in which we educate and press forward our friends to more vigorous warfare on the

A LAUGHABLE INCIDENT.

liquor system, rarely occur oftener than once a week; theirs are held daily, and *nightly* as well. Where we have rarely more than one gathering in a village at the same hour, they often have a dozen. They advocate self-indulgence; we preach self-denial.

A laughable incident occurred in Providence growing out of the decision adverse to license which should not be forgotten. A poor fellow was seen on Christian Hill, in the western part of the city, and near the old Hoyle tavern, digging industriously at the foot of a certain pole, just at the forks of the street.

"Halloo! What are you doing there?" asked a gentleman who happened to be passing by.

The poor fellow, who was very much excited by recent events and the free use of rum, looked up sadly in the face of his questioner, and replied:

"Our liberties are all—hic—taken away, and it's only a mo—mockery to have liberty-poles sticking up about the—hic—city, when we have got no liberty, and I'm going to dig 'em down."

"Liberty-poles, indeed! you blockhead," replied the gentleman; "why, look up and see what is over your head."

The digger turned his face upward, and lo! there swung the tavern sign. He had mistaken its supporting post for the liberty-pole. The digging was, of course, suspended, and the poor afflicted apostle of liberty found some other way, probably, by which to express his grief. The event was celebrated in some temperance rhymes which found place in the next number of the Rhode Island Temperance Herald.

"Yes, dig it down, ply well the spade,
And make it bow its haughty head."

The article is hardly worthy of insertion here entire, but is referred to, to make my readers acquainted with an important part of the policy of the temperance workers of that early period. It was, to seize upon and employ every local occurrence which could be used to interest the popular mind in favor of temperance, and make a little capital against a ruinous system.

That mode of warfare on the liquor system, or its active supporters, is not, I think, practiced so extensively now as at the period referred to. Firmness, fearlessness, a good share of practical wisdom, and considerable caution, is needful to render it safe and effective. Of course, there are no good reasons why a dealer in liquors should not be held responsible before the community for the influence of his traffic, and he has no just grounds of complaint when one of his customers butchers his neighbor, or, it may be, his wife, or cuts his own throat in the frenzy of drunken delirium, if, in giving the facts to the world, through the press, or otherwise, the public are informed that *he* filled the jug, or bottle, for the murderer or suicide a few hours, perhaps, before the terrible event.

Yet nothing troubles a rum-seller in a country town or village more than such an exposé of his heartlessness. In such localities each man is known to every other, and to have the indignant gaze of every decent and moral man in the neighborhood turned full upon him as an active and guilty agent in such bloody work, and that, too, while perhaps the unburied dead is still above ground to confront him and sear his eye-balls, it is terrible to a man who has left to him even the shred of a conscience, and who has not utterly lost, as few indeed have, all regard for the good opinions of those around them. If we except legal prosecutions, which, when frequent and successful, take from the liquor-seller his ill-gotten gains, and thus make his traffic a losing business for him, and sometimes shut him up in the House of Correction, no measures, which I have ever employed to induce men to abandon the liquor traffic, have been so frequently effective as those above indicated.

To illustrate further my own method of personal labor for the furtherance of the cause, the following incidents may serve:—

Journeying across the State on a cold winter's day, I stopped at a public house to have my horse fed. While warming myself by the bar-room fire, I noticed within the bar, on the edge of a shelf loaded with decanters and bottles of liquor, the following words. They had been printed with full-faced type on a strip of paper, and the paper pasted on the edge of the shelf:—

NO CREDIT GIVEN HERE.

After reflecting for a while on the matter, and arranging in my mind some thoughts concerning it, I addressed myself to the landlord, who was the only person in the room beside myself, thus:—

"Landlord," said I, pointing to the inscription above, "I see that you bring your customers right up to the chalk, and don't plague yourself with book-keeping."

"Oh, yes," he replied, and added: "In the sale of liquors these days it won't do to give credit. If you don't get your pay down, from the class that buy liquors now, you will never get it."

"I think you are right, *there*," said I, "but you

might add a few words which would improve your inscription, and render it more striking and impressive."

"What would you add?" inquired he, apparently quite interested.

"Give me a pen and paper," said I, "and I will show you."

"Just step to the desk within the bar," said he, "and you will find paper, ink, and pen."

I followed his suggestion, wrote out in a single line his inscription, and adding three other lines I laid down the pen, leaving the paper on the desk, and returned to my seat near the fire somewhat curious to know how he would receive my proposed amendment.

He walked into the bar, and resting his arms on the desk, (it was a high one,) he bent over the writing for some moments, and when he turned away it was with a subdued and saddened countenance. The shot had evidently struck the target, his conscience. The inscription, as improved, read thus:—

"No credit given here,—
But *I* have cause to fear
That there's a day-book kept in Heaven,
Where charge is made and credit given."

When, from lack of time or ability, I could not make recent occurrences available to create a spirit of hostility to the liquor traffic, it has ever been my policy to employ as far as possible the leisure or larger abilities of fellow-laborers for that purpose. A successful move of that sort occurred as follows:

One of the churches of Providence proposing to build a new house of worship, sold their old one. It was purchased by parties who had less regard for proprieties than for the gains of a ruinous business, and they converted the building to a brewery. I stated the facts by letter to a young friend of mine, George S. Burleigh, residing with his parents at his native place, Plainfield, Conn., and requested him to give fitting expression to the feelings which such a sacrilegious act would naturally create in the heart of any well constituted individual, not case-hardened by the worship of Mammon, or the practice of degrading vices. I received directly the following poem, which for justness of sentiment, power of thought, and true poetic expression, will bear comparison, I think, with any poem produced on this continent by a writer of equal age, seventeen. Equally with the older and more widely known members of that talented family, he has by example and precept, by tongue and pen, given steady and substantial support to every genuine reform of our time and country. God bless the Burleigh family, and grant that their posterity through coming generations may never dishonor their ancestry of the nineteenth century. That is as much as we need ask or hope for.

THE CHURCH POLLUTED.

[Written on the sacrilegious conversion of a Church into a Brewery, in the City of Providence; and the first published poem of the author, GEORGE S. BURLEIGH.]

God of the holy, pure, and just,
  How are thy courts dishonored now,
Thy altars trampled in the dust,
  Where holy men were wont to bow,
And praise was heard and thanks were given,
And supplications rose to Heaven!

THE CHURCH POLLUTED.

Hushed is the voice of warning there,
    The swelling song, the spiritual hymn,
The morning and the evening prayer
    That rose above the arches dim,
And sacrilegious ruin smiles
Amid the desolated aisles.

Rude hands have marred the hallowed walls
    Where loud Hosannas oft have rung,
And sons of Belial crowd the halls,
    And work those holy things among;
And fires of death are burning on
The fragments of thine altar-stone.

There man shall hear no more again
    The voices of thanksgiving rise;
That "house is made the robber's den,"
    Those courts "a place of merchandize;"
And vile blasphemers gather where
The holy man once bent in prayer.

The losel song, the scoff and jeer,
    Shall rise with sounds of drunken strife,
And bitter curses greet the ear,
    Where once were heard the words of life,
And praise was given from heart and lip,
By men in holy fellowship.

And where the child was taught to go
    To taste the streams of mercy flowing,
Will pour a tide of death and woe
    More blasting than the siroc's blowing,
And burning as the lava-tide
That sweeps down Ætna's groaning side.

And will ye all in silence now
    The weapons of your warfare bury,
Nor stamp the shame upon his brow
    Who thus pollutes the sanctuary?
Nay, rather with new zeal press on
Until the victory be won.

> And speak for yon dishonored hall
>   Where fast will pour the tide of woe,
> Or even the stones beneath its wall
>   Will frown upon ye as ye go,
> And every tile upon its roof
> Will thunder out its stern reproof!

The following incident, and the use I made of it, may serve to illustrate further my method of turning passing events to account for the furtherance of the cause and the instruction of the parties immediately interested. While serving the public in Rhode Island, I had occasion to spend the night at the village of Woonsocket, and as there was no public house kept in the village on temperance principles, I was under the necessity of taking lodgings at a hotel where intoxicating liquors were furnished to all who desired them. Just after the clock had struck the hour of nine, some very respectable looking gentlemen who were sitting around the bar-room fire, engaged in an exercise which they called " cracking up." The object of the game seemed to be to determine which of the individuals should pay for the drink of the company. The important question was decided by the tossing up of a piece of coin and its fall near or remote from a certain crack in the floor previously designated. The services of the bar-keeper were then required to prepare for the party some intoxicating compound, of which each swallowed his glass with evident gusto. It was suggested to the mind of the writer, while the scene described was passing before him, that the individuals thus engaged did not, in their minds, associate their practices with the probable consequences to those connected with them by the most tender ties. The following article, which was written in the bar-room immediately after witnessing the interesting ceremony, and which found place in the village paper the following day, was intended to suggest to them the probable consequences of their recklessness and folly.

  Crack up! crack up! the clock strikes nine,
   We have not drank for half an hour;
  Say, will you choose, or rum or wine,
   Or brandy's stimulating power?
    Come, fill the glass
    And let it pass,
  Till sorrow, care, and thought are gone,
  And exiled reason quits her throne.

  Come, jovial boys, crack up! crack up!
  And fill again the maddening cup.
  What though our wives sit quite alone,
  And muse on hopes and pleasures gone?
  Though bitter thoughts their bosoms burn,
  The while they wait for our return.
    Let all that pass,—
    Come, fill the glass;
  We'll drink to love that never dies
  Till from *our* hearts affection flies.

  Crack up! crack up! come, fill again
   The accursed cup with liquid fire;
  And now, its contents let us drain
   To sleeping babes and hoary sire;
  To mother dear, though drowned in tears,
  And bending with the weight of years.
    Bid sorrow flee
    And drink with glee,
  Though babes may need a father's care
   From wretchedness and want to save.

And though we bring the time-bleached hair,
  Of parents sorrowing to the grave.
Come, fill again the accursed cup,
And let us drain; Crack up! crack up!

My first extempore speech was made in Warren, R. I. It is quite an era in the life of one who is destined to devote years to the business of public teaching from the platform or desk, when surrounding circumstances enable him, for the first time, to emancipate himself from the slavery of notes. While acting as agent of the Rhode Island State Society, I visited the town of Warren. I was entertained at the home of a clergyman, the pastor of a large church in town, whose congregation embraced a number of men pretty largely engaged in the liquor business. If my memory is not at fault, one of them was a distiller. With the business, which I should be likely to condemn, so largely represented in his flock, he was deeply anxious, of course, to have the lecture of the most unexceptionable character.

The hour for the meeting at length arrived, and during our walk from his house to the church he took occasion to express to me, in the kindest possible way, his views as to the proper manner of handling the subject. He thought the conciliatory method the best; that severe denunciation of men, even manifestly wrong, rarely benefited them or others.

I was troubled. I did not wish to stir up a tempest in his congregation, and yet there was a great duty to be performed, to set forth the truths of this important subject faithfully. I repeat, I was troubled and not a little embarrassed. The church was crowded, and a superannuated clergyman of the Methodist church, good old Father Bonney, was requested to offer prayer. He ascended the pulpit and prayed; and it was a prayer indeed, such as sometimes lifts a man off his feet to an elevation from which he seems to see the earth and its little ant-like inhabitants and insignificant affairs as a sort of dissolving view beneath him. He asked his Father and our Father for just what he wanted and for nothing he did not want. For the poor drunkard he besought restraining and reforming grace. For the suffering wife, the grace of patience and a Christian hope for a more happy future. For the neglected, shamed, and abused children, that God would, in mercy, preserve them from the contaminating influence of a wretched father's example. Nor did he forget the distillers and liquor sellers of Warren. It was a sensible prayer for just those blessings which all praying people in that assembly had just then in mind, and, of course, their hearts responded to the words of the supplicant. No mention was made in that earnest petition of the Sandwich or the Fejee Islands, of the missions in heathen lands, or of any matter entirely foreign to the occasion, as there generally is in the prayers of men who have no hearty interest in the cause of temperance, and yet are asked to pray for it.

The voice of the old man ceased, and all my trouble and embarrassment was gone. I arose to address the congregation with my manuscript before me. Something, however, I wished to say on points of local interest, which were not touched in the manuscript. I would, therefore, say a few words on these by way of preliminary. I became interested in the points I was considering, and exceedingly anxious that the congregation should see them in precisely the right light, for they were of immense importance, at least, so it seemed to me, just then. A few words more on another important point, and then I thought I would resort to my manuscript. But the important points multipled as I discussed them. The machine was fairly under way, and ran on and on, and I could not get on the brakes, could not even get to them. I spoke for nearly an hour and a half, and never turned a page of my manuscript.

I was instructed by that experience, that what is really wanting to success in extemporaneous speaking, is that a man discuss a subject in which he feels a deep interest, and one concerning which he has acquired some positive knowledge *which he feels anxious to impart to others;* that he have a tolerable acquaintance with the language he is about to use, and that he shall be so intent on accomplishing some desirable, practical result by his efforts, that he will forget himself, and have not a thought of what his audience may possibly think of his performance. Under those conditions, a man who has good digestion may venture to dispense with notes.

Some friend sent me a copy of a local paper containing a notice of that lecture which pleased me not a little. It was nearly as follows: "The State Temperance Agent, Dr. Charles Jewett, delivered a public discourse on that subject in the Baptist church during the past week. Our opinion of his lecture our readers will gather from a brief anecdote. Two gentlemen were once watching with considerable interest the evolutions of a dancing party, and as the dancers successively whirled past these observers, they compared opinions relative to their several performances At length, one stalwart fellow possessed of uncommon energy, and a very stout pair of cowhide boots, passed them, and the way those boot-heels came down upon the floor was a caution. 'What do you think of that style of dancing?' asked one of these gents of his companion. 'Well,' replied the other, 'he doesn't dance so handsomely as some men but he does dance confounded strong.'"

CHAPTER V.

A COWARDLY ATTACK.

"Smith's hat"—Giving up the lancet—My co-workers—A sick wife—Trouble—A visit to Boston—Dreaming in Rhyme—Laugh and be fat!—Encouraging progress—Doubt and uncertainty—A wife's counsel—A timely suggestion—Seventy Dollars!

The condemnation of the liquor traffic by the popular vote in Providence, the largest city of the state, and in many of the country towns, and a pretty vigorous effort to inflict the penalties of law on shameless violators, roused the wrath of the liquor sellers, and led to a most cowardly assault, under cover of darkness, on one of our prominent and very faithful fellow-laborers, Judge William Aplin. He was assailed on his way home from his office at about ten in the evening, by two ruffians, with the evident intention of getting him into a sack and taking him—we know not where. An accomplice was near with a horse and carriage, who, on the failure of the ruffians to accomplish their purpose, drove rapidly away. The Judge, though not a large man, was a very active and energetic one, and taught the scoundrels that there is vigor in the muscles of a cold water man. His assailants were never legally identified, although there was little doubt in the minds of the people as to one of them. He lost his hat in the struggle, and when compelled to fly on the approach of parties, whom the shouts of the Judge for help had called to the spot, he was unable to recover it. Many gentlemen who saw the hat next morning, exclaimed at once: "That is Smith's hat." The Smith referred to was the landlord of one of the city hotels. Others said, "Let us see whether Smith comes abroad this morning with his usual head dress." The landlord appeared with a new hat. It was whispered that Jewett's turn would come next; but I was never assailed, though some of my personal friends felt some anxiety for my safety. Parties offended by my course, however, relieved themselves by growling and scowling, and by the utterance of big oaths on the sidewalk in front of my office.

During the year 1837, I had relinquished my practice as a physician, and accepted an agency under the Rhode Island State Temperance Society, to travel through the state and devote myself to the instruction of the people in reference to the great points at issue between that organization and the advocates of license and the drinking customs—to aid in organizing the friends of temperance, where they were not already organized; and, in general, to labor for the advancement of the cause. The executive committee of the State Society had been instructed by a vote at the last annual meeting, to employ an agent; and under those instructions I had been engaged.

Pledges had been given at that annual meeting by delegates representing the local societies in all parts of the state, of financial support to the State Society in carrying out the policy decided upon, of employing an agent, liberally scattering through the state temperance publications, and in extending their operations generally. I was not so well acquainted with the value of such pledges, in general, then as I am now, or I should never have ventured on an agency, relying for support on a treasury to be thus replenished. The great crash of 1837 had shut down the gates of many of the manufacturing establishments, and the laboring population, very many of whom were owing me for past professional services, scattered, during the year of my agency, in all directions, and left quite too poor to pay their bills to my collectors.

This was a sad blow, financially, to lose thus the results of years of service, while every bill I owed was quite sure to find me. Still, I kept at work in the lecturing field, not doubting but that before the year should close the local societies would redeem their pledges, and I should receive the very moderate salary stipulated. They failed to do so, however, and so much of my salary as was paid was mostly raised by a few friends in the city of Providence. A very considerable portion of it, however, remains unpaid to-day. I do not chronicle these unpleasant facts in a complaining spirit or with a view to reflect on the good people of Rhode Island.

Of my fellow laborers in Rhode Island, a great proportion of whom have passed away, I could never speak but in terms of respect and affection, while I remember their personal kindness to me and their great faithfulness in the cause. I despair of seeing any better men in the world than good Dr. Clark, Peres Peck, Daniel Anthony, Peleg Wilbur, and John Kilton of Coventry; than good Deacon Brown or William Green of East Greenwich, or that band of noble men who, in our long and stern war with a wicked system, stood at their post of duty in Providence like oaks rooted by the sunshine and the storms of a hundred years. Oh, what men they were! William Peabody, Henry Cushing, S. S. Wardwell, John C. Nichols, James Eames, Willis Ames, Judges Aplin and Branch, Samuel Wheeler; and some of the younger who still survive, Amos C. Barstow, Sylvester Salisbury, and others. How freshly memory brings their familiar faces before me, and how I love to record their faithfulness and unselfish devotion to the work of reform!

At the close of the year I resigned my agency and purposed to return to the practice of my profession. Friends in the city urged me to locate *there*, as it was thought I could not fail, with nearly ten years of professional experience and troops of good friends in the city, to secure, at least, a fair practice, the avails of which would support my young family. I opened an office on Christian Hill, and began to receive a fair share of professional calls, when the severe illness of my wife kept me at home for weeks. It was an attack of hemorrhage from the lungs, and for a time I feared a fatal issue; but a kind Providence otherwise ordered. She recovered, and during her convalescence events occurred which resulted in sending me once more into the temperance vineyard. Those events seem to me worthy of narration with some degree of particularity.

During the preceding winter, that of 1839, I had been sent as a delegate to represent the Rhode Island State Temperance Society in a convention held in Boston. It was one of the largest and most enthusiastic I have ever attended. Thinking it possible that I might be called upon to make some slight contribution to the interest of the occasion, I jingled some thoughts in rhyme, in which I gave a historical account of a wonderful dream which had recently visited me. In this dream I had seen some queer things, and heard very remarkable utterances in the vicinity of Still-House Square, in Boston.

It had been arranged to have the convention continue in session two days, and on each evening to have a great popular meeting, addressed by gentlemen selected by a committee for that service. It happened that I was among the number selected, and when called upon to address the convention, I concluded my speech, which I had purposely made very short, with the recitation of "The Dream, or The Rumseller's and Rumdrinker's Lamentation." In one part of the recitation I personated an irate rumseller, and gave utterance to the usual sentiments of that class of persons. After him came the poor drunkard, and in a style peculiar to the most noisy and uproarious of that class, I gave expression to *their* sentiments, objections, and wrath in view of the measures of the temperance party. How the exercise was received by the vast audience it is not proper for me to state. The reader shall learn from the statement of a very excellent man and popular writer who was present, and whose peculiarities qualified him to appreciate fully the hits that were given to the opposition in that rather novel way. The only apology I had then or now have for the very extraordinary course I pursued on that occasion, is found in the fact that the notion was becoming prevalent that to those not especially engaged in the enterprise, temperance conventions were very dull, necessarily so. It seemed important to dissipate such a delusion, else we should soon lose the public ear, and thus a serious blow would be struck at the reform. I honestly think that, at the time, the exercise was useful in the way indicated. There was no literary merit in the article. It was its adaptation to the peculiar circumstances by which we were just then surrounded, with perhaps a tolerable personation of character, that gave it effect.

In an article published in the "Sons of Temperance Offering," from the pen of Rev. A. W. M'Clure, occurs the following passage:

"We have seen some laughing in our time; but decidedly the most extravagant, uproarious, and ecstatical burst we ever witnessed was at Dr. Jewett's recital of his poem, 'The Rumseller's and Rumdrinker's Lamentation,' as given at the great Convention held at the old Marlboro' Chapel in Boston, January, 1839. In reading this effusion in cold blood, at this distance of time, and under great change of circumstances, it is difficult to see anything about it sufficient to cause that deafening cachinnatory explosion, and its long resounding reverberations. But, at that time, when the 'fifteen-gallon law' was in all its glory, the satire was most ticklishly *apropos;* and never did ridicule seem keener, or more free from venom. Above all, the doctor's delivery justified what the ancient rhetoricians have said of the importance and effectiveness of *manner*. The whole densely-crowded audience was thrown into a paroxysm of laughter such as can never be exceeded in the same length of time. The fat man rolled in his seat like a pudding in a boiling pot. The lean man doubled himself up into a hard knot, then threw himself back in a rigid spasm, and at last twisted himself into a corkscrew, undergirding his poor ribs with both hands to keep himself from being shaken to pieces. The tremendous roar burst up into yells of delight, and shrieks of orgastic merriment. When the most furious stamping and clapping seemed too tame an expression of applause, men seized hold of each other, and exchanged mutual thumps of congratulation. Even grave doctors of divinity took to thwacking the pew rails with their stout walking-staves, leaving lasting mementos of their uncontrollable mirth. For many a day after did the intercostal muscles of the company retain the sorest reminiscences of that season of unparalleled drollery. We never expect to see the equal of it; nor do we wish to. One such laughing-spell is enough for a lifetime, and affords ' a joy for memory.'"

The representatives of the press who were present reporting the proceedings of the convention, obtained copies of this rhymed trifle, and it got a pretty extensive circulation through the Boston papers as well as through the country journals. It was also struck off in handbill form and sold by the newsboys. "Buy a Lamentation, buy a Lamentation, sir?" constituted a considerable part of the sidewalk music for a day or two. The convention was notable for the character of its material as well as its numbers. It was estimated that over three hundred of the clergy of the state were present. It was presided over by the Hon. John Tappan, one of the earliest and most devoted friends of the reform in the Eastern States.

Some of our younger brethren, who now manifest a commendable zeal for the advancement of the cause in connection with the temperance orders, Sons of Temperance, Good Templars, Temples of Honor, &c., seem to entertain the opinion that little or nothing had really been done in the good work of reform, until the Orders were established and the Washingtonian movement was started in Baltimore. I beg such to remember, after reading the preceding sketch, that we are still in the thirties, and that the Order of Sons of Temperance was not established until the year 1840, and that the first meeting of the five original Washingtonians at Baltimore, was on the eve of the 5th of April, 1840.

As early as 1839, there existed in the United States and the Canadas fifteen temperance papers, ably conducted, and all advocating the comprehensive pledge, *i. e.*, the pledge against *all* intoxicating liquors, by whatever name called; and in many of the towns and villages of the New England States more than half the entire population of the town were members of temperance societies pledged to abstinence. Men are liable to err, sadly, in connection with the movements of the present time, if they hold incorrect notions as to the history of past operations intended to secure the same end.

For special reasons I dropped the history of my labor in R. I., to give the history of the convention at Boston, and my connection with it. Returning in thought to my humble home in Providence, I resume the history of events in 1839, which had an important bearing on my future, as connected with the temperance reform.

My wife was slowly recovering from the very threatening illness I have before described, and was able to sit up for some hours each day. I was thus enabled to attend to the few professional calls I was then receiving, hoping in time to extend my practice, and expecting to devote myself to it for life. But "God's ways are not as our ways." I had other service to perform, it seems, in connection with the temperance reform, and was introduced to it as follows. I received, one evening, through the mail, an invitation from a committee, signed by Moses Grant of Boston, chairman, to prepare and recite, before a convention to be held in that city, a temperance poem.

"Will you undertake the service?" asked the sick wife. "No," I replied. "I cannot spare the time. I have a bill of $70.00 to pay in about four weeks for my small stock of medicines," (I had opened a small drug store in a part of my house,) "and must bestir myself and raise the money, which I cannot do if I sit down to write poems."

She urged me, notwithstanding, to comply with the invitation, suggesting that the Boston committee would, probably, pay me something for the labor, and expressing the belief that, somehow, a good Providence would provide if I set about the required service with an earnest purpose to help forward a good and great cause. Long before this I had learned that it was sometimes good policy for a man to listen to the counsel of a good christian wife, if he had been fortunate enough to obtain one. I yielded to her persuasion and set about the work. I was hard pressed for time, and wrote the last eighteen lines of the poem in the library of my excellent friend, Dea. Moses Grant of Boston, after reaching that city, and the evening before the day of the convention. This great gathering of good men, like that of the previous year, was to continue in session two days; the evening of each day to be devoted to public addresses, and other exercises. The recitation of the poem was advertised as a part of the exercises for the first evening.

4

The president of the Mass. Temperance Union, Hon. John Tappan, presided both day and evening. The poem, which had the merits of being *understandable*, and having *a practical aim*, if no other, was well received by an assembly of more than three thousand people, numbering some hundreds of the clergy, and very many men of the other liberal professions, justly distinguished for great learning, and the possession of the Christian virtues. Immediately after the recitation of the poem, a gentleman in the audience arose, and inquired if it would be practicable to have it printed, so that delegates to the convention could obtain copies to take home with them. Deacon Grant replied that the poem should be printed during the night, and be ready for delivery at the door of the convention room at ten o'clock, the following morning. Just here, Rev. T. P. Hunt, whom I have before introduced to my readers, sprang to his feet and made the following brief, but very pertinent speech:

"Mr. President, I am glad that poem is to be printed. I think it is worthy of publication, and hope, when printed, that the gentlemen delegates present, will buy, not a single copy each, but half a dozen each, to distribute among their friends, and that they will be willing to pay a good price for them, and in that case, perhaps our friend, the doctor, will obtain some reward for his labor, more substantial than the thanks of this honorable body."

It was a timely suggestion, and, from what followed, I have no doubt that hundreds of generous brethren acted upon that hint. I read the proof-sheets before two o'clock in the morning, and on the meeting of the convention at ten, A. M., the pamphlet was on sale at the door. A good friend of mine, Rev. L. D. Johnson, of Rhode Island, attended to the sales, and twelve hundred copies were disposed of before the close of the convention. After the final adjournment, and when, worn with protracted excitement and the broken rest of the preceding night, I was about to retire, friend Johnson came in, and requested me to go with him to his room, where he counted out to me, as the net profits of this hurried publication, $70.00, the *exact* sum to a penny, needed to pay *that bill* at home, which had so troubled me, and to meet which I had been advised to trust in Providence while I should perform what was regarded as a pretty important service to a great and good cause.

CHAPTER VI.

INVITED TO A WIDER FIELD.

Packing up—" Cast down but not destroyed "—A dialogue—Was it brotherly or wise ?—A christian hero—A clergyman and three churches—The poor house preacher—" If I had let rum alone "—Rum and horrors—We "went for" the buckwheat cakes—Crane's store—" What'll you have"?—" Didn't I call for't, ha ?" " You can't cheat me "—Doubted!

Soon after my return from Boston, I received an invitation from the Executive Committee of the Massachusetts Temperance Union, to serve them as a lecturing agent. I declined the invitation for the reason which I distinctly stated, that past experience had taught me not to trust for the support of my family to the treasury of an organization, which had no proper financial basis, but relied for its support on occasional donations from its friends, and collections taken at the close of public meetings. I was answered by an inquiry as to whether I had any plan to propose for the financial support of temperance organizations, and, if I had, to communicate my plan to the committee. I suggested a plan which, with its working, I shall presently describe more at length. It was adopted with slight modifications, which did not, in my judgment, improve it, and I was then invited to assist in carrying it out. The salary offered me was twelve hundred a year, or a hundred per month exclusive of traveling expenses. I accepted the invitation, fixed the time for commencing my labors, and appointments were at once arranged for me, commencing with the ancient town of Dedham, since celebrated in connection with the striped pig exhibition. The losses I had sustained through the financial crash of '37, the stopping of work in the factories, and the sudden dispersion in all possible direction of those indebted to me; as well as by my failure to receive the whole of the salary promised me for service in Rhode Island, had sadly embarrassed me, and now came the unpleasant task of settling up matters with very limited means, and of providing for my family, while I, by honest service, should earn something on another field with which to commence the world anew. I provided for my family a temporary home among my relatives in Connecticut. My personal property, even furniture, the gift of relatives to my wife before her marriage, was, at her request, sent to the auction rooms and sold, that the avails might aid in paying debts which I had contracted while serving the cause of temperance. The time for the commencement of my labor in Massachusetts had arrived, and yet, after employing all available means, I was unable to pay all my debts before leaving.

That was a gloomy hour. I went down to old India Point to take the cars for Boston, and reached the depot twenty minutes in advance of the time of starting. I had thus time to ruminate. In connection with the practice of my profession and as a laborer in a great work of reform, I had served the state faithfully for ten years, and now must leave it with a wife and four children to care for, with but little more money than would pay my fare to a new field of labor. I paced the platform, and presently extended my walk along the lengthened piles of pine wood near by, and for a moment I was quite unmanned. I may as well confess it; the boy, Charles Jewett, got the better of the man. I sat down behind a pile of pine wood, and wept. The warning bell of the waiting engine soon roused me. I took a seat in the cars and was off. In due time, I reached Dedham, Mass., and before a good audience got another fair opportunity to assail the wicked system I had long been fighting, and in the labor forgot personal griefs and embarrassments.

While on a brief visit to Rhode Island, a few months after leaving it under the trying circumstances already recorded, a friend reported to me a conversation he had had with a very wealthy and excellent citizen of Providence the day previous to my departure for Massachusetts, and I will here relate it, as it may give point to some suggestions of a practical character. I shall call the wealthy gentleman Mr. X., although that was not the initial letter of his name.

X. "Well, they tell me that Dr. Jewett is about to leave us."

F. "Yes; he goes to-morrow, having been engaged to serve the people of Massachusetts."

X. "I am sorry he is going. We could far better spare some others I could name; for, although his counsel has not always been wise, nor his measures such as I could altogether approve, yet, really, he has been a very useful man among us. I think he has done more to advance the temperance cause in this State than any half-dozen of us."

F. "He leaves us, I am told, under very straitened circumstances."

X. "Yes; it could hardly be otherwise. He is not a good financier. A man who mounts some reformatory hobby, and undertakes to revolutionize opinions and customs which he thinks wrong, is not likely to get very rich in the operation."

Reader, Mr. X. was reputed to be worth a million. He was quite an active member of one of the churches of Providence, a man of strict integrity, and, withal, a a thorough temperance man so far as his own habits were concerned. He was a *liberal* supporter of Christian missions, foreign and domestic, and, in fact, of every other benevolent movement of the day except the temperance enterprise. He had given to that, indeed, but should you multiply his gifts to that cause by ten, the product would not equal what he annually gave to some other enterprises. You will say, perhaps, that he lacked confidence in the permanency of the reform, or did not approve of all the measures which the state or local organizations adopted to advance it. Very likely. But why should a wealthy and Christian gentleman condition his support of the temperance cause on the perfection of the measures adopted to promote it? He is not thus critical and exacting in relation to other enterprises which he liberally supports. Ask such a man if he expects an exhibition of faultless wisdom in the management of the foreign missionary cause, of home missions, or the bible or tract societies,—he will answer you in the negative. Why then does he demand perfection in temperance operations as a condition of his financial support of them? Reader, perhaps that question may with great propriety be addressed to you. Will you consider it?

The words of that Christian and temperance millionare, Mr. X., as reported to me by my friend F., wounded my feelings at the time beyond my power to express. The unruffled composure with which he had seen me leave the state penniless, with a wife and four children to provide for, I should have been able to excuse if he had been silent on the subject, or if his words had not been reported to me, for I should have concluded that amid the multitude of his cares he had not become fully acquainted with my condition, or that he did not fully realize the amount of service I had rendered the state by ten years of hard labor. But when his words were reported to me I became convinced that he knew all, and yet,—— Oh, the miserable selfishness that could clutch a million and see a fellow laborer whose services to the public he fully appreciated go empty handed out of the state! If such selfishness comes of the possession of wealth, God in mercy grant I may never be rich!

Before considering further the history of the cause in the glorious old Bay State, I will take a parting glance over the field in Rhode Island, and see what memory can gather up worthy of record.

And first, it brings before me the name and valuable services of my successor in Rhode Island, the Rev. Thomas Tew. He was the agent of the State Temperance Society for many years, and was one of the most devoted, untiring, and energetic laborers in the work of reform I have ever known. He not only contributed by his public discourses and the distribution of temperance publications over his very limited but important field of labor, to correct and elevate the public sentiment in relation to the use of intoxicants and the liquor traffic, which he heartily hated, but he prosecuted violators of the law in the courts, and in short by every proper means within his reach he sought to crush a wicked system and to promote not only the virtue of temperance but all those Christian virtues which constitute the brightest ornaments of personal character and the strongest bulwark of the state. He literally wore himself out with hard and continuous labor. Friends who enjoyed the privilege of personal intercourse with him when he was no longer able to labor, have assured me that, worn and wasted as he was with disease and stretched upon a bed from which he had no expectation of rising, he retained to a wonderful degree his wonted cheerfulness, and while with feeble voice he discoursed with them of the future triumph of the cause, which revealed itself to his faith and hope, his eye would kindle with excitement, and then only would he express a wish, if it were possible, for continued life, that he might still further contribute to hasten on the blessed consummation. In answer to the inquiry of a friend as to the state of his mind and feelings, only a brief period before the spirit passed to its everlasting rest, he answered with a smile and the words, HAPPY, HAPPY!

Although, in general, the results of the liquor system are of like character everywhere, yet in certain places it gives us peculiar manifestations of its power, which are worthy of special consideration. The town of Foster, in Rhode Island, is one of those localities. I was informed while laboring in that town that in three different sections of it attempts had been made in time past to build a church, and that such was the low state of morals in those places at that time, induced mainly by intemperance, that the parties engaged in building had fallen out by the way, got into a bitter quarrel, and that, as a consequence, work on the church had, in each case, been discontinued; and the frames, partially enclosed, had been left to rot. Three frames in that condition had at different times proclaimed to passers-by the state of morals in the town of Foster.

Another result had been the drunkenness of a clergyman, on a funeral occasion, so that all recollection of the mournful occasion had been obliterated from his poor addled brain before he left the stricken home. At the period when this happened, the decanter was brought out at funerals, as well as at weddings and other joyful occasions. This versatile agent could help men to weep as well as to laugh. The clergyman referred to had drank when he first arrived, because he had been riding in the cold and was chilly. He had drank again before the funeral service, which was held in the house, to give him inspiration for that service. Before leaving for the grave-yard, a mile or more distant, another glass must be taken to guard against cold and *anticipated* fatigue. On returning from the cemetery, another drink must be had, because he had been exposed to the cold and *was* somewhat fatigued; and now they sat down to dinner. His reverence, by this time in a very sad condition, was placed at the head of the table, and not seeing the wife, whom he had just helped to bury, in her usual place at the table, he turned his glazed eyes to the bereaved husband and asked, "Why, where is your wife? isn't she at home?" That, I was told, was the last of his public services as a minister.

A citizen of Foster, when drunk, fell with his head on the hearth and so near the fire that the heat spoiled both eyes, destroyed the vitality of the nose so that it sloughed entirely off, leaving only a couple of unsightly holes in the face where a nose had been, burned the parts about the mouth, so that in healing all that was left of that very essential organ was a small hole into the buccal cavity, through which food could be introduced, and this hole was not central, but quite on one side. Besides this, the scalp had been so heated on the top of his head, that not only did it slough for a space as large as the palm of one's hand, but even a portion of the bone exfoliated. These losses of structure were replaced, in the healing process, by a sort of gristly or cartilaginous substance, and a permanent discharging ulcer remained on the top of the head for the rest of his life. He had been, I was told, an inmate of the poor house for fourteen years, and all this time, when the weather was warm and favorable, they would, at his request, place him outside the door where he could *feel* the influence of the sun and the fresh air. There this wretched remnant of a man sat and preached temperance to everybody that would pause and listen to him. "I don't know who you are, for I can see nothing; but whoever you are, I want you to look on me and be warned to let rum alone. Look at me now. This is all the work of rum, and you see there is no chance for me ever to be any better. I shall never see the sun nor the faces of men any more. I must go to my grave as I am; and yet I might have been as well off and as happy as you, as any one, if I had let rum alone."

And thus he was exhorting as long as I remained in

Rhode Island. What may have been his history since I left the state I know not. Was not this pretty powerful preaching to the eye as well as to the ear? and yet, reader, if you *habitually* use intoxicating liquors, you are probably so blinded and influenced by that terrible habit and the deceptive power of the drink, that you could have looked on that wretched object, listened to his touching appeals, and gone directly back to your home or hotel and taken another drink.

I will here record still another result of the liquor traffic in Foster. A poor fellow, naturally kind hearted and well disposed when in possession of his reason, under the bewildering, maddening influence of liquor, commenced a quarrel with his wife, and soon became so terribly excited that she, in alarm, fled to a neighbor's for safety, leaving behind a fine little boy about four years old, their only child, who was the very idol of his father, and on whose account, therefore, she had no fears. Seeing that his wife, the object of his blind rage for the moment, had escaped him, he seized the child by its limbs and dashed its head against the granite jambs of the fireplace, causing its death. He was immediately arrested, securely bound, and placed under the care of keepers.

A reliable gentleman, a leading friend of the cause, who subsequently resided in the house where the deed was done, gave me the information, and added, " When the remains of his child were about to be buried, the wretched father, now thoroughly sober, begged to be permitted to look upon its face once more before it should be forever hidden from his sight." The request was granted, " and," said my informant, " I never pitied any human being as I did that man. I forgot his cruel act in his present agony. As he looked into the coffin upon the bruised and discolored features of his once beautiful boy, he bent forward and placed first one cheek and then the other, now wet with streaming tears, upon the face of the child, and moaned and groaned as though his very heart would break."

Few of my readers, who are *habitual* and *pretty free* consumers of intoxicating liquors, would have drank a glass the less after witnessing that scene. Not that I suppose them to be heartless or unfeeling men, or deliberately and consciously wicked and brutal; but because the terrible agent which you have allowed to obtain a ruling power over you, has *deceived* you and accustomed you to *reason falsely* on this one subject, so that facts seen or arguments presented do not, generally, lead you or others similarly situated, to sound and logical conclusions.

A pleasant incident occurred at Pawtucket, while I was serving the R. I. State Temperance Society, the relation of which, in a brief chapter, may carry with it a valuable moral, or convey valuable hints to the reader. I had just reached the village, and was in consultation with that stern old veteran in the cause, Abraham Wilkinson, a very belligerent Quaker, who never knew the meaning of the word fear, and whose hatred of the whole liquor system was so intense that, had he been Autocrat of Rhode Island, he would have roasted a rumseller as readily as a Thanksgiving turkey, i. e., unless the fellow would solemnly promise to quit the destructive business. While conversing with the old patriarch, a gentleman, his nephew, came in, who seemed to have some private business with him, for, taking him to a distant part of the room, he conversed with him for some minutes in an undertone. I heard enough to convince me that some movement was on foot for the enforcement of the penalties of broken law on a liquor seller. My ear caught the words: "We want just one man more, and one who can be relied on."

I stepped across the room, and addressing the stranger said: "Please accept my services, sir." He looked at me doubtingly. Uncle Abraham said: "He'll do," and then introduced me to the gentleman as Dr. Jewett, the temperance agent. He was satisfied, and we crossed the street to a store in which a convicted rumseller was under keepers. An effort was to be made to convey him to the jail in Providence, and a mob of perhaps a hundred of the liquor fraternity were gathered about the door, declaring in language more emphatic than elegant, that there was not enough of the — cold water fanatics in town to take that man to Providence; that blood would be spilled if the thing were attempted, &c.

Here, now, was a predicament, with a very few men in it. What was to be done? There were five of us, all told. Jencks the officer, the two Wilkinson's, one other man (name forgotten), and the writer. We made our way through the crowd into the store where the culprit was in custody. Three stout wagons, previously engaged, just then were driven up in front of the store by men who knew how to handle the reins, and when all was ready, we took the convicted seller of illegal drinks by the collar on each side and cleared our way through that swearing, sweltering crowd, helped him to a seat in the middle wagon with a sufficient guard, while other friends occupied the front and rear wagons. It was the work of less than half a minute after we left the store. Just as we leaped into the wagons some of the rowdies sprang for the wheels to upset the vehicles, but the drivers were too quick for them. Crack went the whip, and those who would have whole bones must clear the track. Away we went at a pretty rapid pace for four miles, over one of the best roads in the United States, followed a part of the way by a number of wagons loaded with brutal men, swearing vengeance. We lodged our prisoner safely in jail, and prepared to return. For one, I expected a battle on our way back, and for lack of a breech-loader or a Remington six-shooter, I helped myself to a three foot oak club of reasonable size from the jailer's woodpile, and so we started. Instead of going back by the way we came, however, our drivers took the old road for Pawtucket, and in about forty minutes we were eating buckwheat cakes and honey at Uncle Abraham's, while the poor satellites of the liquor sellers, who had followed us half way to Providence, were still lying in wait by the turnpike road-side to pelt us with stones on our return. The usually stern visage of Uncle Abraham took on quite an amiable expression as he passed us the buckwheats, and remembered that there was just one rumseller less in Pawtucket.

About this time another incident occurred in Pawtucket, which caused considerable swearing but a great deal more laughter; for when a practical joke is played on even a bad man, his most attached friends will often join in the laugh at his expense. Crane's liquor store, on the Massachusetts side of Pawtucket bridge, (the river constitutes the line between the states there,) was regarded as a destructive place, and yet as he kept his liquors in a back room, into which none but the right sort were admitted, it was difficult to prove him a violator of law. To the proper understanding of the story it is necessary that the reader should know that Dr. Jewett, the temperance lecturer, *can* personate character pretty accurately, so his acquaintances will tell you. He can, when he chooses, be as drunk, to all appearance, in one minute or less, without drinking, as most men can with free drinking and the lapse of considerable time. The imitation is so accurate that the most practiced eye cannot detect the counterfeit. I was in a barber's shop, near Pawtucket bridge, conversing with the very intelligent and gentlemanly barber, when two young men, gloriously drunk, rushed in with, " How are ye, Joe? Give us the time o'day. Ha! what's up? Put 'em through my boy! Go it boots! ha!" That was about the style. To print the talk of men under such circumstances soon uses up your interrogation and exclamation points. I saw my game at a glance, and tipping a wink to the barber to "keep dark" and "lay low," I instantly assumed the disguise of drunkenness, and began to complain to them that the Pawtucket folks had got to be so mighty temperate that a poor fellow who's a stranger in the place couldn't get a glass o' grog to wet his whistle for love nor money.

These generous fellows assured me in a very sympathetic way: "There's liquor enough in Pawtucket, if you know where to find it."

"Jest so; but there's the trouble, you see. I'm a stranger in the place and how should I know?"

"Come along," said they, "and we'll show you."

So away went the trio, arm in arm, over Pawtucket bridge, the doctor in the middle, and a roaring, shouting rowdy on each side. Reader, had you been there, as a stranger, and looked on, it would have bothered you to have decided which was the drunkest of the three.

They are at Crane's door, and one goes on up the street; the other volunteering to do the honors of the city.

The rowdy and the doctor, both pretty well "set up," walk right in with the dash peculiar to men in their condition, and the young rowdy who "knows the ropes," pushes right along to the rear or liquor room, his much obliged friend, the doctor, being just at his side. Young rowdy draws for himself (he is a regular customer) and drinks.

"Now stranger, what'll you have?"

Thinking to call for something they had not got, the doctor answers: "If I take anything, I'll take a glass of ale."

There was no ale in sight, and he supposed there was none in the building.

"Sartin," says rowdy, "all right, the ale's in the front store." So Crane and rowdy lead on to the beer pump.

"Now," says the doctor, with an occasional hiccup, and an amazing amount of particularity: "I want you to understand, now, that I don't go none of your swill stuff. If your beer's all right I shall go it, and if it isn't I shan't."

"It's all right," says Crane, and he pumps up a full glass, the foam piling up on the surface as big as a teacup or a cat's head, and passes it to the boozy doctor. With that careless disregard for all else but the drink, usually manifested by such as he appeared to be, he lifts the glass to the level of his mouth, and with a tremendous puff blows the foam into Crane's face, and all over his vest. He took it in good part, simply brushing off the foam, for such blundering heedlessness is expected of men half drunk. The doctor tastes the beer.

"It's sour."

"No it isn't," says Crane, "it's first-rate."

"You lie," roared the doctor, "I guess I know beer, but" (dropping his voice,) "never mind, we won't quarrel about it. But what do you say *now*—on the whole ; had I best drink it or not? You see how it is with me; what do you say? Speak it now like a man, what do you say?"

Thus appealed to, Crane replied, "On the whole I guess I would not drink any more to-night. I think you have got enough."

The doctor concluded he was right, and set down the glass.

"But I'll pay you for it."

"No," says Crane, "if you don't drink it you needn't pay."

"But look here," says the doctor, "didn't I call for't, ha?"

"Oh, yes! of course you did."

"Well now, I want you to *understand* that I'm no sneak, anyhow, and when *I* calls for things I *pays* for 'em; what's to pay?"

"If you pay anything, it'll be three cents."

"All right," and fumbling in his pocket the doctor

drew forth the three coppers with his right hand, and counting them out with great precision, one by one, into the open palm of the left hand, he exclaimed:

"There you have it. That's right, ain't it? That makes it all square 'twixt you and I, don't it?"

Crane, glad, no doubt, to get rid of so irritable and awkward a customer replied, "Yes, all right."

"Well, then," said the doctor,. "good bye to you," and out he went.

In half an hour he was before a large audience in one of the churches, and while commenting on the then present status of the liquor system, told the audience *where* he had been and *what* he had seen.

The talk of the village, the following day, was largely on Mr. Crane, Dr. Jewett, the beer and liquor trade, and the practical joke played by the doctor on the old veteran liquor seller. Crane insisted, however, that there was no counterfeit about *that* drunk, that it was the genuine article; and he asked, "Do you think I don't know when a man is drunk? You can't cheat *me* there. A man may reel and pitch about like a drunkard, but he can't make his eye drunk. That man's eye was drunk. Why, I stood close to him when he was fretting about the beer, and my eye wasn't more than two feet from his, and that eye of his was drunk. You can't cheat me."

When Crane found that it was quite impossible to make even his own customers believe that the doctor was drunk (for the barber, at the shop, saw him put on the disguise of drunkenness in an instant, and so stated to all inquirers), he became very wrathy, and declared that any traveling humbug of a lecturer who would play such a game on a decent, respectable citizen, deserved a thrashing, and he swore by all current oaths that he would "pound that scamp to a jelly" if he could get his eye on him before he should leave Pawtucket.

The doctor heard of his terrible threats, and took his next morning's exercise in front of Cranc's store, pacing backward and forward, and affording the dispenser of rum and *beer* all the opportunity he could have desired to execute his threats. His courage, however, was, like much of his beer, only foam or froth. He wisely kept his head within his den.

CHAPTER VII.

REVIEW OF THE PAST.

The Convention of 1838—The great petition—A committee worth remembering—Looking ahead—Hats off, gentlemen!—The law of 1838—Wholesale dealers to the front!—They meet—A Paixhan shell—The lesson of past events—Study and reorganization.

My readers, who were not residents of Massachusetts from the year 1835 to 1840, will better understand the history of my labor in that state, with that of the leading friends of the reform, and the events which followed, after the perusal of a brief chapter on the progress of the good work during the period intervening between the dates above given, and on the condition of the cause in the state when I commenced my labor in May, 1840.

Prior to the year 1838, the power to grant licenses for the sale of intoxicating liquors within the State of Massachusetts, was vested, by law, in a Board of Commissioners for each county, whose term of office was three years. As the temperance sentiment of the state grew stronger, and hatred of the liquor traffic more intense and universal, the people began to clamor for the abrogation of the license system. As the law stood, the end they desired could only be attained by electing County Commissioners who would refuse to license. The triennial election of those officers, therefore, turned on the temperance question, or rather on the known views and purposes of the nominees in regard to license. Many sharp battles had been fought at the polls in the election of these officers before the year 1837. In a majority of the counties, anti-license Boards had been elected, and as a matter of course, the prohibitory clauses of the law alone were operative. Violators of the law were very generally prosecuted, and as a consequence, the open traffic had, in some of the counties, ceased to exist. The law was occasionally but secretly violated, like all other laws, but the penalties were too severe to be surely incurred by open violations. Thus, on a part of her territory, Massachusetts had a trial of prohibition before the year 1837.

Everywhere the results were satisfactory, not only to those whose active efforts had secured the change, but to all lovers of good order and good morals.

The immediate diminution of crime and pauperism was perhaps the most striking result of the new order of things, but its influence to increase productive industry and thrift among the people, to promote domestic and social happiness, and a more general attention to religious observances, were features scarcely less marked.

These results of *partial* prohibition converted thousands to our doctrines and practice who had resisted all our arguments, or who had been too indifferent to the whole matter to listen to them, and greatly stimulated effort to secure, to the entire state and all its interests, the benefits certain to result from general prohibition.

At a State Convention, held in Boston in February, 1838, it was resolved that an effort should be made to

JOHN PIERPONT.

secure, from the Legislature of the state, at its next session, a law prohibiting the traffic. A form of petition had been prepared, to be circulated through the state for signatures. Though not at that time a citizen of the state, I was present on that occasion, and heard the form of petition read to the convention, by its author, the Rev. John Pierpont. It is too important a portion of the literature of this great reform to be forgotten. For clearness of statement, strength of argument, and rhetorical finish, it has never been equaled by any form of petition presented to any legislative body in this country, since we were a nation. My readers I am sure will thank me for giving it place in this connection. They will find it profitable reading. If read in every family, in the presence of all its members, on New Year's day of each coming year, it would conduce far more to the happiness of our families than the custom of New Years' calls, with their usual concomitants. It is much to be regretted that there are so few in our land, with all our colleges, capable of reading *properly* such a document in public. John Pierpont was one of the most impressive readers to whom I ever listened. All eyes of that immense audience were riveted upon him, while reading, and so perfect was his enunciation, that not a word or syllable was lost by any individual of the throng, whose organs of hearing were not defective.

To the Honorable the Senate, and House of Representatives of Massachusetts, in General Court assembled.

The undersigned, citizens of Massachusetts, ask leave to call the attention of your honorable body to the laws now existing in this commonwealth, licensing the sale of intoxicating liquors, for drink, to the injury, as your memorialists conceive, of the individual,—both buyer and seller—and to the serious detriment of the best interests of the State.

It is not the purpose of your memorialists to call into question the patriotism of those men by whom, in former days, those laws were first made, or of those by whom they have since been modified. In their day, they, doubtless, acted according to their light. We wish that they who shall come after us may be able to bear witness for us that we have acted according to ours.

We do not propose to exhibit to your body a picture of drunkenness, in any of its degrees, or of its effects upon the miserable victim, or upon the often more miserable ones who are bound to him by the ties of the family, or of society. Your own eyes, when directed to the subject of human misery in this community, to its objects and its sources, will be struck by more appalling scenes than any that we can paint;—nor when you see and consider them, will you ask us for evidence that, with comparatively few exceptions, misery flows, directly, or by necessary consequence, from intoxicating drinks. These, the laws of our Commonwealth allow to be sold for the express purpose of being drunk; and this, too, now that we know, as our fathers did not, that they are always poisonous to the human system; and that, in just the degree in which they are drunk, they are destructive to the bodily and mental energies, the moral character, the highest interests of every one who drinks them. Can it, then, be for the best interest of the community that they should be drunk? Can it consist with the character of a highly moral community that they should be sold by permission, and under the protection of its laws? That a priesthood should be ordained for the very purpose of pouring this poison into the veins of the body politic—a priesthood, whose only office, so far as it is recognized by the laws, is exclusively a work of destruction, without one healing tendency, one salutary influence—a priesthood, who, if not engaged in this work,—not laboring " for the public good " in *this way*—are faithless to the ministry to which they are elected and anointed by the law!

We respectfully ask—Is it RIGHT to license man thus to mar the image of God in his brother man? right to give him authority thus " to sell insanity," and deal out sure destruction? If it *is* right, why should *any* man be forbidden to do it? If *not* right, why should any be permitted? Why forbid all but " men of sober life and conversation" to do this if it is right. Why allow " men of sober life and conversation" to do it, if it is wrong? Will the poison be less active or less fatal, if it is dealt out with a *steady* hand? Will the buyer be the less a drunkard, because the seller is a sober man? May this pollution be poured out upon society only by clean hands? Or, is it the presumption of the law that, in such hands, it will do no harm?—that a man " of good moral character" will sell, not to drunkards, but to sober men like himself! Is it, then, more " for the public good" that the sober men of the Commonwealth should be made drunkards, than that they who are already drunkards, should remain such? Can that which always works private evil, conduce to the public good? Can that which is bad for all the parts, be good for the whole? Can evil be converted into good by multiplication? Can wrong be legislated into right?

Under the laws of this Commonwealth, the *body* of the citizen—unless, indeed, he be poor and in debt,—is jealously protected. Not a hair of his head can, with impunity, be harmed. The law lifts up its trumpet voice against personal injury, so long as it is *merely* physical. But, when the physical evil becomes linked in with moral,—when the destroyer takes hold of soul and body together, to drag them into the pit,—then, the arrows of the law are returned into their quiver—its thunders are laid aside, and its shield is spread over the pit into which they both go down!

It may be too much to expect, from human laws, that they protect the morals of society from corruption, and even from temptation. But *is* it too much to ask that they will not *throw open* the doors of temptation, and hold them open, that the "simple ones" may go down through them into the chambers of death?—Is it too much to ask that the sale of intoxicating drink may be prohibited by penal laws? It is said, we are aware, that this will be an infringement of the citizen's rights. We answer,—then are those rights already infringed. All, but a few, are already forbidden, by penal statute, to retail ardent spirits. Is it a greater infringement of rights, or a bolder stretch of power, to restrain the few, of "good moral character," than it is to restrain the many of an opposite description?

Again,—may not our neighbors—our children—be protected by penal statute, from "practices against their health" and life, as well as the lower orders of creation? By penal statute we protect our *fish* from poison, why not our *men?* By penal statute—by a thousand dollars fine, and a year's imprisonment in the county jail,—we punish the man who shall "expose *any poisonous substance* with the intent that the same should be *taken and swallowed* by a neighbor's cattle." Why not, then, if "with the intent that it be taken and swallowed" by the neighbor himself? So that sickness, delirium, death ensue, what matters it by what name the draught be called? To the sufferer, or to society, is the injury the less, because the delirium is longer continued, and the death-pains more protracted? If I be willingly accessory to my brother's death, by a pistol or cord, the law holds me guilty;—but guiltless if I mix his death-drink in a cup. The halter is my reward if I bring him his death in a bowl of hemlock;—if in a glass of spirits, I am rewarded with his purse. Yet, who would not rather die—who would not rather see his child die, by hemlock than by rum? The law raises me a gallows if I set fire to my neighbor's house, though not a soul perish in the flames. But I may throw a torch into his household—I may lead his children through a fire more consuming than Moloch's—I may make his whole family a burnt-offering upon the altar of Mammon, and the same law holds its shield between me and harm. It has installed me in my office, and it comes in, to protect alike the priest, "the altar, and the god." For the *victims* it has no sympathies. For them it provides neither ransom nor avenger.

But there *is* an AVENGER. While these sacrifices are smoking on their thousand altars, through the length and breadth of our land, The Ruler of the nations is bringing upon us the penalties of his laws, in the consequences of breaking them. Even now, He who renders to every land, as to every man, according to its works, is showing us that He is as strict to visit with suffering those who violate His organic and moral laws, as He is ready to accumulate good upon those who observe them. The fields of our great country, which He has charged with the elements of plenty,—which are, every year, waiting to be bountiful,—which He waters "that they may bud and bring forth, and give seed to the sower and bread to the eater," are becoming like the field of the slothful man of old. They are "overgrown with thorns;—nettles are covering the face thereof;—and the stone walls thereof are broken down." The hand and the mind of the cultivator are struck with the palsy of intemperance.—A great portion of the bread corn which the land—grateful for even niggardly culture—pours into the husbandman's bosom, is snatched from his children's mouths for the craving maw of the distillery;—and when that, which God gave as the supporter of life, has been converted into its destroyer, the vessels that waft the destruction to the nations on the Baltic, the Mediterranean, and the Black seas, bring back from those nations, and at their own price, the very bread of which we have first robbed ourselves, in order that we may ruin them.

Nor does the temperate and industrious citizen who sees the execution of these laws of a Righteous God, escape his full share of their penalties—for, while his heart is made to bleed at the sight of the sufferings which the demon Intemperance is scattering broad-cast around him;—while he feels himself discouraged and humbled that while his own hand and voice are lifted up against the destroyer, they are lifted up in vain, for that the destroyer is still upheld by the laws;—his purse is made to bleed as freely as his heart, in the form of "poor-rates," and augmented prices;—he must feed a drunken neighbor's family, and at the same time pay double price for the bread that feeds his own.

Your memorialists feel that, on this subject, it is not more their right than it is their duty to remonstrate. Would those who throw this stumbling-block in their brothers' way, take care of such as fall over it—or could the curse of drunkenness be confined to its own ranks, and the dead be made to bury their dead,—the evil *might* be borne; though borne, even then, with a profound sorrow, with a divine pity, for those who had fallen under the curse. Even then, philanthropy, which is but another name for the christian spirit, would prompt us to intercede for our suffering brethren, and to plead with those who legislate for the *common* weal, intreating them to interpose all the barriers in their power to keep back the waves of this destruction. But, so it is not— so it cannot be. In the body politic, "if one member suffer, all the members suffer with it." If the laws of a Christian state *will* open these seminaries of poverty, vice, and sorrow, the same laws *must* open, near them, to receive their graduates, alms houses, criminal courts, penitentiaries, prisons, and sepulchres. And, while these are fitting up, and filling up, the earnings of the industrious, the savings of the prudent *must* be taken from their pockets, by the hand of the same laws, to guard and support them.

Is it necessary " for the public good" that these fathomless fountains of sin and misery should be everlastingly kept open? that the few should fatten by feeding on the many? that the whole head of the state should be kept sick in the paralysis of its industry,—its whole heart faint in the corruption of its morals,—that the whole body should grow leprous, though it yet may live? Is the life which would be left in the body of this Commonwealth, after intoxicating drinks shall have done their work upon it in taking away its strength and soul, such a life as God breathed into it at its birth, and designed for it at its maturity? We cannot but think that the Sovereign of all States designed for this a nobler life than Intemperance, aided by law, will leave it—a higher destiny than such a destroyer, with such support, will ever allow it to fulfill.

Your memorialists are aware—we use the words of the chief magistrate of a sister state—that "The cause of Temperance, and that philanthropic movement which has already done so much to check the ravages of that fell destroyer of individual health and happiness, and that prolific source of crime and misery, Intemperance, depend mainly, for their ultimate and perfect success, upon moral causes; but, they may, yet, receive aid and support from legal enactments." Your memorialists believe that such enactments would now be regarded with favor by the great mass of this community; and, even if they are not in all cases, enforced, that they would, yet, do much to check the evil which all good men deplore. Your memorialists, therefore, pray that *all* laws, authorizing the sale of intoxicating drinks, within this Commonwealth, may be repealed; and that such sale may be made penal with such exceptions, and under such conditions as to your honorable body may seem good. And your petitioners shall ever pray &c.

That form of petition was extensively circulated through the state, and received many thousands of signatures. When the Legislature assembled, these petitions were poured in upon it from every section of the state, and were referred to a joint committee of the House and Senate. The entire membership of that committee I am unable to state, but with two of its members I afterward became personally acquainted, and for reasons which I am about to state, they should be had in lasting remembrance by all friends of temperance and sound legislation. The Hon. James G. Carter, of Lancaster, and Samuel B. Wolcott, of Hopkinton. My information concerning the action of that committee, I derived from the gentleman first named, with whom I had the pleasure of laboring for years in the good cause, after I became an agent of the Mass. Temperance Union. The Committee held repeated consultations in relation to the matters submitted to them, and finally agreed to report in favor of the legislation petitioned for.

Mr. Wolcott, who was distinguished for his skill in drafting bills, was requested by his associates to draw up a bill in conformity with their joint conclusion. He did so, and at the next meeting of the committee, he submitted his draft. It was read, its various sections subjected to the most careful scrutiny, after which, the committee unanimously voted to report it to the House. When the committee were about to append their names to the report, Mr. Wolcott remarked in substance as follows. "Gentlemen, in accordance with your wishes and opinions, in which I entirely concur, I have drawn that bill. I fully believe it to be in accordance with the principles of right and justice, and as a committee, and as conscientious men who have had assigned to us a specific duty, I see not how we can do otherwise than to report it, or some bill aiming at the same result. As an individual I am prepared to sign it, but before doing so, or inviting you to do so, I wish to express my opinion very decidedly, that in signing it, we, individually, sign our political death warrants. Should the bill become a law, as I have no doubt it will if we report it, it will bear heavily on a large amount of capital invested in the liquor trade, and it will interfere indirectly with the indulgences of many of our people; indulgences hurtful to the parties, and injurious to the public, but to which thousands will cling with great tenacity. The law, though just and right, will therefore encounter a storm of opposition. The party in power, to which we belong, will suffer from its passage, as the party in minority will seek to make out of it capital against us. Our party, to save itself, will repeal the law, and we shall be regarded as having done it great injury, and they will probably find it necessary to sacrifice us to appease the wrath of the opponents of the law.

It is an unpleasant dilemma, gentlemen, for those of us who may have political aspirations, but I see not how, as honest men, we can do other than to report to the legislature a bill in exact conformity with our convictions of right and justice. I shall therefore sign the bill." "He did so without the shake of a single nerve," said Mr. Carter, " and inspired by his noble example, we followed him, and the bill went to the house with our unanimous approval." "I did not," said Mr. Carter, "share his opinions or fears in relation to the fate of the measure, for I thought it would commend itself to the good sense and justice of the people, and that the law would stand." The result, however, proved the sagacity of Mr. Wolcott, as the reader will learn from the perusal of these pages, and the entire transaction bears testimony to the possession, on the part of Mr. Wolcott, of an old fashion devotion to principle, never more conspicuous in the case of any legislator with whom ancient or modern history has made us acquainted. Reader, let us thank God that the race of heroes is not yet extinct, or, at least, that it was not in the year 1838.

As an important item in the history of the reform in this country, I place before the reader, in this connection, a copy of the law of '38. It was enacted in the month of April, and was something more chilling than an "April shower" to the rum interests of Massachusetts.

AN ACT TO REGULATE THE SALE OF SPIRITUOUS LIQUORS.

Be it enacted, &c.

SECTION 1. No licensed innholder, retailer, common victualler, or other person, except as hereinafter provided, shall sell any brandy, rum, or other spirituous liquors, or any mixed liquor, part of which is spirituous, in a less quantity than fifteen gallons, and that delivered and carried away all at one time, on pain of forfeiting not more than twenty dollars, nor less than ten dollars for each offence, to be recovered in the manner and for the use provided in the twenty-sixth section of the forty-seventh chapter of the Revised Statutes.

SEC. 2. The county commissioners in the several counties may license, for their respective towns, as many apothecaries or practising physicians as they deem necessary, to be retailers of spirituous liquors, *to be used in the arts,* or for medicinal purposes only; and the mayors and aldermen of the several cities may, in like manner, and for like purposes, license apothecaries as retailers for their several cities; and the court of Common Pleas in the county of Suffolk, in like manner, and for like purposes, may license apothecaries or practising physicians as retailers in the town of Chelsea, which licenses shall be granted in the same manner and under the same restrictions now provided by law for licensing retailers; provided that the number of persons so licensed shall not exceed one for every two thousand inhabitants, and in towns containing less than two thousand inhabitants, one person may be licensed; and provided, further, that in such cities and towns where there is no apothecary or practising physician, such other person or persons may be appointed as aforesaid, as may be deemed proper by said county commissioners, and no person so licensed shall sell any spirituous liquors, to be drunk in or about his premises, on pain of the forfeiture provided in the first section of this act.

Sec. 3. All licenses hereafter granted to innholders, retailers, and common victuallers shall be so framed as not to authorize the licensed persons to sell brandy, rum, or other spirituous liquors; and no excise or fee shall be required for such a license.

Sec. 4. The provisions of all laws now in force, inconsistent with this act, are hereby repealed.

Sec. 5. This act shall take effect on the 1st day of July, 1838, but shall have no operation upon any licenses granted previous to that time.

Approved by the Governor, April 19, 1838.

Prior to the passage of this law, the magnates of the liquor trade, the distillers, importers, or wholesale dealers, had been content to keep in the back-ground, and let their subordinates, the retailers, occupy the front rank in the defence of the trade. Only when the latter had violated grossly the restrictive provisions of former license laws, or sold without license and were about to suffer imprisonment for the non-payment of fines and costs, did the aristocracy of the trade ever appear at the front, and then only to go bail for their servants the retailers, as otherwise their shops would be shut up, and some of the pipes through which the heads of the liquor department were wont to irrigate a drunken world with rum and whisky, would be choked up.

Although these honorable gentlemen, lords of the brandy pipe, the wine butt, or the money bags, often expressed, in the hearing of respectable citizens, their profound contempt for the petty dealers, knights of the toddy-stick, they would, as stated, back them in the courts, because they knew quite well that they were a necessary part of the machinery—the finger ends of an organization of which they constituted the head, trunk, and limbs, and they understood that it would go hard with the said head and trunk if the fingers should be cut off. Now that a blow had been struck in the passage of the new law which threatened the entire retail trade, the dealers in liquor by hogsheads and cargoes saw the necessity of coming to the front. They held meetings in Boston for consultation, and prepared an address to the public, which was signed by Daniel L. Gibbins, a millionaire, who had accumulated his wealth by the liquor trade, and eleven others, all wealthy men and in good repute, except as connected with their traffic. We cannot afford space here for the very plausible and ingenious document sent forth by these twelve liquor dealers, or for the courteous but scathing and exhaustive review of it by L. M. Sargent in a series of letters which appeared in the columns of the Mercantile Journal. The friends of temperance in Massachusetts had great reason to congratulate themselves on such champions as God had given them in John Pierpont, Lucius M. Sargent, and others, at this important period of the reform. These men hurled no pebbles into the camp of the enemy, but great explosive shells, which made terrible havoc where they fell; and in those days, bad men, who with their bad hearts had sound heads, did not, without great inducements, place themselves within the range of our reformatory artillery.

The ten letters of Mr. Sargent to that committee of liquor dealers, and his twelve letters to the Hon. Harrison Grey Otis of Boston, who, in Feb. of 1839, headed a petition for the repeal of the law, together constitute the most trenchant and exhaustive discussion of all important points at issue in this warfare that has ever been given to the public. I purpose soon to reprint them, with what I hope will be regarded as a fitting introduction; and I know that all who are now engaged in earnest efforts for the prohibition of the liquor traffic, will thank me for placing in their hands so complete an armory of keen and polished weapons.

The law was repealed in 1840, and the state fell back, so far as legislation was concerned, on the law of 1837, leaving the question of license or no license with the county commissioners. There was, therefore, no general throwing open the flood-gates to a deluge of rum on the repeal of the law of 1838, for in a large majority of the counties our commissioners still refused to license the traffic, and only the prohibitory part of the law of 1837 was, therefore, operative. The friends of the cause were in no wise disheartened, and at the annual Convention which immediately followed the repeal of the law, expressed in no doubtful terms their determination to battle with the wicked liquor system till its annihilation should be secured.

This speedy repeal of a law which had been passed

by overwhelming majorities, and hailed by good men everywhere as the harbinger of unnumbered and inestimable blessings, certainly must have some lessons of wisdom to teach us if we are but tolerable scholars. What are they? First of all, the necessity of such thorough organization of the friends of temperance where we seek improved legislation, that we can, if need be, make ourselves felt in the acquisition or retention of power by the great political parties, without which they can neither help their auxilliaries or save themselves. The liquor party are always organized, and at a word from their leaders, every liquor store, dram shop, saloon, or bar-room in a county or state, becomes a recruiting station for any party to which the liquor interest may for the time ally itself. *These* " head-quarters" are always open for six days and nights of every week, and at least one-third of the number are open also on the seventh day—the Sabbath. They need no famous orators or bands of music to attract a crowd, for they have other unfailing attractions,—their liquors. They *have* their orators and often their music, and these are always welcome; but they are by no means dependent on these adventitious aids, as they have, as before stated, attractions which will draw many men from their homes who are miles away, and detain them there often for the entire day and evening, waiting, like Mr. Micawber, " for something to turn up." That something turns up often —the bottom of the glass, as its contents are poured through dry throats into inflamed stomachs. Whatever issues may divide the parties of the day, there is one object, the attainment of which such a company always regards as of, paramount importance—the continued sale of intoxicating liquors, with the least possible restrictions. Nine persons in ten of such a company will sacrifice every other plank in their political party platform to the prospect of securing a full supply of liquors for the future. No matter whether our immense interest in the production of iron be up or down,—whether commerce prosper or be annihilated,—whether the credit of the government be preserved or destroyed,—whether its debts are paid or unpaid,—whether the cotton crop be one or ten million bales,—all these, with the added questions relative to the public health and morals, the interests of education and the wise or unwise government of the country, are, in the estimation of the crowd in a liquor saloon or beer shop, as nothing to the great question relative to an ample or short supply of stimulating, maddening drinks for the future. The settled purpose to secure a full supply of drink overrides all other questions. Shrewd politicians know this, and do not fail to respect an end or object which such masses of our voting population have so much at heart.

Our wishes and purposes as friends of abstinence and prohibition are directly opposed to those of the class we have named. Politicians who may sit in legislative halls, executive chairs, or on the judges' bench, cannot please them and us at the same time. They, therefore, being intent on retaining power and place, look sharply at both parties to see which it is safest for them to displease. Our opponents are thoroughly organized, we are not; they place the support of the liquor trade *first* on the list of objects to be attained through their political action; we put the attainment of other ends before the annihilation of the liquor traffic, in the use of our franchise. While matters stand thus, ought we to wonder that the wishes of the liquor folks are respected before ours? It is idle and worse than idle to complain of the inevitable, and our defeat at the polls and in legislative halls *is inevitable* until the conditions are altered; until politicians clearly see that they will lose more by offending us than the opposing party.

Thus much we are taught, not only by the repeal of the law of 1838, but by many events which have since transpired.

Beneath all this, we come upon another great truth, incidentally taught us by the events we have contemplated, which must receive more attention than heretofore, viz:—The power of alcoholic liquors or other stimulant-narcotics, over men who become addicted to their use, is wonderful, almost unlimited. No other class of substances ever brought to bear upon the bodies, and through these on the minds, affections, and morals of men, can compare, in the measure of their influence, with intoxicants. That power must be studied, not only by all who would be successful reformers, but it must be better understood by the masses. It is not enough to know that it exists. We must have the philosophy of it. The minds of men must be as familiar with it as they are with the laws of gravitation. To this end, and for the attainment of knowledge on many other important points, our local or primary temperance organizations, must, even on our most advanced fields, such as Maine, Massachusetts, and Vermont, become schools of instruction, not in rituals and points of order merely, but in relation to great fundamental principles, to the everlasting God-ordained laws which underlie the whole subject of intoxicants, with their attendant mischiefs and miseries. This reorganization of our forces, and the progressive education of the elements which compose them, is a work which no legislature can do for us; nor any other body or class of men outside our own ranks. It is a work which *we* must do, or the great movement in which we are engaged will never be consummated. We should bring to its consideration the best talent we have among us, a burning zeal for the advancement of the cause, united with and tempered by a spirit of forbearance and conciliation, which shall result in crystallizing as it were, into organizations and modes of procedure, all the wisdom of the temperance host from all sections of our country. Thus and thus only can we organize victory.

That series of victories which was gained by the Prussian armies over the French forces, during the late Franco-Prussian war, was the result not of their courage or of their heroic endurance alone. These qualities were, during the struggle, frequently exemplified in a splendid manner by the French forces which were beaten. The result was due to the skillful plans perfected by master minds before a blow had been struck; to the perfection of their organization, their admirable drill, and the precision and celerity of their movements, guided all through by some master minds which originally planned the campaign. Courage and heroic endurance on the field of battle will be unavailing to those who are carrying out a badly planned campaign.

CHAPTER VIII.

TREASON.

Robert Rantoul and Massachusetts Democracy—" Up guards, and at them "—A political illustration—A shallow Trickster—A laugh out of place—Hard at work, but happy—Judge Crosby—Wise counsel.

THE loss of the law of 1838 was not effected without an example of treason on the part of a professed friend of our cause which should not be forgotten, lest the truth which Shakespeare puts in the mouth of Mark Anthony, should come to be questioned.

" The evil that men do, lives after them ;"

Gov. Morton, (for so I must call him, though he occupied the Executive chair but one year)—had been the President of the Massachusetts State Temperance Society at one time, and was supposed to be in perfect accord with the friends of the reform as to withdrawing sanction and support of law from the liquor traffic. He had been the standing candidate of the Democracy for some years, and seemed likely to *stand* for the remainder of his life, for any chance he was likely to get to *sit* in the Governor's chair. As soon, however, as the law of 1838 was passed, and a pretty decided opposition to its continuance on the statute book, had developed itself, it began to be whispered that Judge Morton was opposed to the law, and would lead the opposition against it. This was at first regarded as incredible, by those who had labored with the Judge, in the cause of reform, years before. It proved true, however, and with ninety-nine hundreths of the Democratic vote of the State, and the votes of the sellers and lovers of liquor who bolted from the whig party on account of the passage of the law, he was elected, and in return for the help of the grog-shops in his election, he, in his message to the Legislature, recommended the repeal of the law. He did not, however, enjoy long the fruits of his treason to the cause, for the good sense of the people, at the very next election, sent him into that retirement from which he never afterwards emerged. While on the Judges' bench he had been much esteemed, as also for his private virtues, but he could not withstand the temptation which prospective official honors presented, and so he fell, as thousands have done before him.

How striking the contrast between his course and that of another distinguished democrat of Massachusetts, who was, at the time, the most popular man of the party, the Hon. Robert Rantoul. He was a member of the Legislature when the law was passed, and it not only received his vote, but his hearty advocacy. No voice pleaded more eloquently than his, for that protection to the wronged and the suffering from the liquor traffic, which it was believed that law would afford them. The party subsequently committed itself squarely against the law and to the support of the claims of the liquor party, and it has maintained that position ever since. The result has been what the clear-headed and warm-hearted Rantoul predicted, it sunk the party to such a depth that for the last thirty years they have never come to the surface. Their championship of the grog-shops lost them Rantoul and others of the best men of their party.

I have before stated that the friends in Massachusetts were by no means disposed to abandon the work before them, on account of the defeat they had encountered in the loss of their law. In addition to the regular system of educational operations which the Massachusetts Temperance Union were at the time adopting, and which will be more fully described hereafter, they determined to secure practical prohibition, if possible, in those counties of the State, where under the old law of 1837, which was now again in force, the County Commissioners still granted licenses, and hence, when and where, in a county, a new Board of Commissioners were to be elected, they made special efforts to secure an anti-license law Board. Where neither of the political parties put in nomination men pledged against license, the friends of the cause called a convention forthwith, and nominated an independent ticket, whom they could trust. Repeatedly they elected their ticket over the nominees of both parties. Thus by the vote of the people, and generally by large majorities, *the licensing of the retail liquor trade had been condemned in every county of the State before the close of the year* 1846.

It astonished professional politicians and wire-pullers very much, to discover, as they did about those days, that the people, when sober, were learning to dispense with their services, and to transact their own business in their own way, by open, manly, and direct methods, that required no tricks or cunning contrivances of theirs.

They found themselves ignored altogether. When I commenced my labor as an agent of the Massachusetts Temperance Union, in April, 1840, I found the friends engaged in the efforts I have before described, to secure the election of anti-license commissioners throughout the State. This was, of course, in addition to the usual educational efforts of the Union. A short time before leaving the State of Rhode Island for my new field of labor in Massachusetts, I caused to be published a lithographic print, intended to convey through the eye to the minds of those who might study it, my view of the then existing state of the temperance cause. It was entitled,

DEATH ON THE STRIPED PIG.

Some words of explanation will be necessary to the proper understanding of its aims and character.

By reference to the law of 1838, found on a former page, the reader will perceive that thereby the sale of liquors, in quantities *less than fifteen gallons*, was prohibited. *That* Legislature would not have made even that exception, had it not been for the fact that the laws of the General Government allowed the importation of certain liquors in fifteen gallon casks. To avoid any conflict, therefore, with National Legislation, that exception was made. The opponents of the law called it, in derision, "The Fifteen Gallon Law," and, led on by unscrupulous and contemptible demagogues, the meanest variety of the genus homo now in existence, they made a deal of capital against the law, by asserting that it was hard on the "poor man," and "hard working classes," who must be deprived of their accustomed stimulants, because not able to buy fifteen gallons at a time, while the favored and petted rich, who could buy from the importers, could revel in unlimited luxury in the highest heaven of fuddledum, which is certainly not very high.

When the law went into operation, all sorts of devices were adopted to neutralize its provisions and avoid its penalties. At a military muster held at Dedham, in Norfolk county, some mercenary and lawless wag had arranged to evade the law by giving a drink to all who should patronize a certain wonderful exhibition he was prepared to make; nothing less than a pig striped like a zebra from snout to tail. A picture of the wonderful animal adorned the tent under which it was exhibited. A four-pence-half-penny, or six cents, was charged for admission. Of course the pig had been striped for the occasion with a paint brush, and the trick was rendered perfectly transparent by the first glance. The patrons of the show, however, after learning the cheat, were solaced by a glass of grog, for which they were not required to pay, and all went on " as merry as a márriage bell," until the sheriff, with his posse, gobbled up the whole concern, tent, pig, and exhibitor, and took them from the field. This despicable device of the liquor seller, however, afforded much merriment to that large and thoughtless class who will have their laugh, even though it be at the expense of a good man or a good cause.

> " The watch dog's voice, that bayed the whispering wind,
> And the loud laugh, that spoke the vacant mind."

Even a very loud laugh, is not, of itself, by any means, evidence of a " vacant mind," but a laugh at the manifest discomfiture of a good man, or a good cause, is a square blow in the face of virtue, and a rich contribution to the joy of Hell. I would bite my lip until the blood flowed, if I could not otherwise suppress a laugh, under such circumstances. The press of the country, especially that portion of it controlled by whiskey-drinking editors, told the story of the Striped Pig with great eclat. I determined to turn the popularity of the pig to account, and make it, if possible, contribute to the advancement of the temperance cause.

I also published, soon after, a print, which was intended as a blow at the License System. Large numbers of both were sold, and for many years copies might be found pasted up in the various workshops of Massachusetts, the study of which has, I trust, helped to fix in many minds, just views of the liquor traffic, and of the iniquity involved in licensing it.

At no period of my life have I labored with more pleasure to myself or, in my judgment, more to the profit of the enterprise than for the first year of my service in Massachusetts. I had not then, to be sure, the experience which I now have, and could not *then* discuss certain phases of the subject with so much ability as I think I could now, after a further study and discussion of the subject for thirty years. I was, however, more hopeful then than now of a *speedy* triumph of our cause; not because I had more confidence in the soundness of our principles, or a higher estimate of the benefits which would result to all the interests of society from their general acceptance and from the practice of abstinence by the masses, but, because I gave credit to the friends of the cause, in advance, for more wisdom and

perseverance than they have manifested. I could endure
more labor then than now. In fact, during the period
referred to, I was scarcely sensible that there was any
limit to my power of endurance. I could then address
public assemblies every night of the week, put in an
extra service or two on the Sabbath, when required, and
make any number of short addresses to the advanced
classes of our schools and academies. I wrote monthly
reports of my travels, and the state of the cause in the
places visited, for the Massachusetts State Journal,
besides a great deal else for the press, generally, both
in prose and verse. With a love for my work which
made it easy, treated with great kindness by the friends
of temperance and Christianity everywhere, my labors
generously appreciated and promptly rewarded, and
most encouraging evidences that the good work was going
rapidly forward, what was wanting to render my work
pleasant? Nothing. I had not been laboring thus six
months in Massachusetts, when my salary was raised to
$1500 a year, without any solicitation on my part, but
because I was dealing with generous, noble-minded men,
who believed that I earned it, and therefore, ought to
receive it. Besides this, I had the happiness to labor
with a gentleman, my senior in years, and in the service
of the society, who commanded my highest respect, as
he did that of all who knew him, and whose superiority
for ability to plan, and skill, and vigor in executing
reformatory movements, I have not known, the Hon.
Nathan Crosby; since then and for many years a Police
Judge in the city of Lowell. With all this, my domestic
relations were as pleasant as they could well be. I was
happy at home, happy in my work, and rejoiced greatly

in the evidence everywhere observable that the cause of temperance was advancing.

As an evidence that I am not mistaken in the opinion I have expressed of the ability and tact of Judge Crosby as a practical worker and guide in connection with reformatory labor, I place before my readers a copy of a circular which he penned just after the passage of the law of 1838, and of which he sent copies to leading friends of the cause in every town of the State. I ask my readers to study it with attention, and observe its practical character. Would it not be well if the friends of the cause everywhere would heed his counsels and act in accordance therewith.

To the Friends of Temperance.

Permit me to call your attention to a few things of immediate importance to our cause. We call for *immediate*, *united*, and *decisive action*. The prospect was never more cheering, or right effort more successful. The Law now forbids the sale, and no longer stands in the way of the application of moral means to banish the traffic or use. We are no longer to be told in answer to our remonstrances and entreaties, that the statute authorizes it, and says the "public good requires it." Let us then awake to new zeal and put forth *moral means* as they have heretofore not been known among us in the promotion of this great and glorious cause. Our opponents profess to approve of *moral* suasion. Let us then use all *moral* appliances to the *utmost* of our power—early and late—at home and abroad—monthly, weekly, and daily—by conversation, social meetings, lectures, papers, tracts, and song—by associations and individual example—by preaching, by exhortation and prayer, and the *traffic will cease*—drunkenness will be known no more—rivers of tears will be dried up—scattered families will be gathered together again, and songs of praise and deliverance will break forth from every family and every house in the land.

Let me urge immediate attention then, to accomplish all this.

NATHAN CROSBY.

WISE COUNSEL.

1st. To your organizations to promote this cause—awake them to effort—reorganize—or press onward as the case may require.

2d. Hold frequent meetings—divide your town into small districts and assign to each active man a small territory, or a few families—and to 15 or 20, each seller and each inebriate—and *let every man be faithful to his charge.*

3d. Never let a seller or drinker meet you without some friendly admonition.

4th. Take measures to put the Temperance Journal and Almanac into all families where instruction is needed to break or soften down prejudice; in fact every family should have the paper. It costs $12 per 100 copies, monthly, per year.

5th. Remember that all your labors in this cause—all your sacrifices in time, in money, in mind or sympathy, go for the preservation and happiness of your own family and neighborhood, and for the benefit of those who need such aid above all other—the mortified, desolated, wretched victims of intemperance.

6th. Remember too, that deliverance from the evils of the rum traffic and use is *too great a blessing* to be obtained without *great labor.* Would you have angel's joy? Do angel's work—visit the sick—feed the hungry—clothe the naked—bind up the broken heart, and wipe away the tear of the drunkard's wife: and will not the laborer have his hire?

N. CROSBY, *agt. M. T. Union.*

CHAPTER IX.

Money, how will you get it?—Financial Plan—Duties of Agents—The way our Plan worked—Illustrative Reports—The Washingtonian movement—The Temperance Union breaking down, why? An explanation—Local organizations essential—Washingtonianism, its errors—Washingtonianism, its power—Summing up.

In a former chapter, I have referred to a plan of operations which, when invited to accept an agency under the Massachusetts Temperance Union, I ventured to suggest to the Government of that organization. The history of subsequent events in connection with the cause cannot be clearly understood by the reader without a more accurate knowledge of the plan under which we were working. It was founded on the theory that all genuine reform had for its basis certain great truths not understood by the masses whose habits and customs the reformers sought to change. To instruct the people in relation to those truths was therefore the first work to be attended to. But how was this to be done? The *example* of those who had become acquainted with those truths and were living in conformity therewith would be instructive to a certain extent. But the influence of individual example is limited to a narrow circle, except in the case of persons of great distinction, and other agencies would, therefore, be needed. The living teacher must be sent abroad to proclaim reformatory truths to the people in popular assemblies, and the printing press must be employed extensively. Tracts, pamphlets, and newspapers must fly abroad as on the wings of the wind for the public enlightenment. These instrumentalities would cost money—they could not be extensively employed by an organization which had no reliable financial basis. To secure such a basis was therefore a matter of primary importance. All benevolent or reformatory organizations of which I had any knowledge, had been sustained by one of four methods:

1st, By the Government of the country—the public treasury.

2d, By occasional subscriptions or donations from interested parties.

3d, By collections taken at the close of public services; or,

4th, By small sums, received at regular intervals, from all the friends and supporters of the enterprise, whatever that may be.

The first named method was out of the question, for the Government patronised and licensed the evil we sought to destroy. To the second plan there were serious objections, as it placed the burden of sustaining the new movement, beneficial to all, on the shoulders of the few. They would soon weary of this, and any system of operations based upon their support entirely, would be a failure. The third plan had been tested pretty thoroughly and been found unreliable. The fourth seemed to me the only feasible and reliable one, yet it could not well be applied to the local organizations then existing, as the only condition of membership in those, was the pledge of abstinence from the manufacture, sale, and use of all intoxicants. To impose on their members *new* conditions, would very likely excite rebellion in our ranks, lessen our numbers, and perhaps demoralize the whole movement.

But what was to be done? A reliable financial basis must be secured or a speedy failure was inevitable. The plan I suggested, and which was finally adopted, was to secure *an extensive, paying membership to the parent society* direct, rather than attempt to remodel the local societies, and add the payment of a certain sum at stated periods, to their other conditions of membership. The fee of membership of the state society was fixed at one dollar annually. There were about four hundred towns and cities in the state, and an average of twenty-five members from each would give us ten thousand dollars. In addition to this, certain wealthy friends had given to the society annually sums varying from twenty-five to five hundred dollars each, and we judged that when they should see the list of state members carried up to five or ten thousand, and the operations of the society extended and more and more efficient, they would most gladly continue their support, and perhaps increase it. We might therefore reasonably calculate on an annual income of from ten to fifteen thousand dollars, advancing from that to twenty and still higher, as the friends and adherents of the reform multiplied, as they certainly would under such a system of operations. It was arranged that each "dollar member" should receive, in part pay for his dollar, the "Temperance Journal," a monthly paper, the official organ of the Union, through which he would be kept thoroughly informed of the operations of the Union, the labors of its agents, and the measure of success which might attend their labors. It was arranged that each agent of the society should make a report of his labors in the towns he visited, the number of lectures given, the additions secured to local societies, and the number of dollar members obtained in each town. All this, appearing in the "Journal," would give it a real practical interest to every friend of the cause, and through its columns every member of the Union could judge whether the dollar he contributed to its support was judiciously expended.

Besides the circulation of the "Journal" among the members of the Union, efforts were to be made, in each town, to have a copy supplied to every family in the town. For such general circulation, the paper was furnished for $12 per hundred. If there were three hundred families in one of the rural towns, thirty-six dollars only would be required to furnish every family with the paper. The funds for this purpose were obtained generally by subscription, and oftentimes liberal-minded men who were not themselves tee-totalers, but were witnesses of the terrible results of intemperance, would give to that fund—judging correctly, that the placing of such a paper in the hands of every family in town, monthly, through the year, must soon work a desirable change in public sentiment. The distribution of the paper to every family was generally effected through the agency of the teachers of the district schools. With eight districts in a town, two hundred copies of the "Journal" would give a package of twenty-five papers to each district. There was thus a division of labor among our devoted brethren, by which this plan was carried out, very perfectly in some towns, less perfectly in others, and in some dark corners and sections of the state no interest was felt in the matter at all; though the places of which this could truthfully be said were very few.

As to the reception of this plan of operation by the people, and its prospective influence if carried out, the reader can judge from facts. I have before stated that an important feature of the new "Plan" which had just been inaugurated, was *a monthly report of labor from each lecturing agent*, which, given to the temperance public through the press, would enable the friends of the cause to judge whether he was the "right man in the right place;" in other words, whether his was a paying and a profitable agency. No provision had been made for sinecures. On the contrary, every salaried servant of the cause was to give his time and thought wholly to the work before him, of contributing by his lectures and through the press, to the creation of a sound public sentiment in reference to the subject of his mission, and at the same time, to secure financial support to the parent society. My first monthly report, with a few facts added, will give the reader a pretty distinct idea of the working of the "plan," and enable him, too, to judge what would have resulted if we had been left without interruption to work steadily on under it for the thirty years which have passed since it was inaugurated. I can never cease to regret its abandonment, which was necessitated by the introduction of other machinery or modes of operation. I religiously believe that carried out, in good faith, it would have crushed the system with which we are warring within half the time that has elapsed since its adoption.

> "Of all the sad words of tongue or per
> The saddest are these—it might have been."

My first report of labor in Massachusetts was as follows. I give it with but slight abbreviations because I wish the reader to have a very definite idea of our modes of operation in 1840, under the new plan.

GRAFTON, May 1st, 1840.

FRIEND CROSBY: In compliance with your request, I will proceed to give you a sketch of my adventures since I left the city of notions on the business of my agency. My first appointments were in the town of

LEICESTER.

My lectures were well attended. I laid before the people at the close of each lecture our plan of operations, and found the friends ready and anxious to coöperate in carrying it out. At the close of each lecture a goodly number gave their names as permanent members of the State Union on the conditions prescribed. The day following my first lecture, a Mr. Dewey, a staunch friend of the cause, volunteered to aid me in obtaining members. I obtained in Leicester sixty-three. The clergy of the town, Rev. Mr. Nelson and Rev. Samuel May, are tried friends of the cause, and exert a most salutary and extensive influence. There is one place in the village licensed to sell liquors, but the authorities of the town have so much regard to the welfare of their townsmen, that they have limited the operations of the establishment to the business of poisoning travellers—and have taken a bond from Mr. Bond that he will not under any circumstances sell to towns-people. This is tying the paws of the beast pretty effectually; for it is the neighborhood custom which mainly supports these nurseries of crime.

On Saturday I visited the town of

SPENCER.

Here an appointment had been made for an address to the children at three o'clock, P. M., and also for a lecture to the adult population in the evening. The occurrence of a fire in the village prevented the meeting of the children. (I omit here the account of the fire and some curious incidents in connection with it.) I obtained but few members in Spencer, for the lecture was not as well attended as it would have been had it not been for the fire, and the next day being the Sabbath, I had no opportunity of calling on the people at their homes.

This is all I can report from Spencer at present.

The town will do its part in the support of the good cause, financially and otherwise, when it has a fair opportunity.

On Sabbath evening I lectured in

BROOKFIELD, SOUTH PARISH.

The rain poured down in torrents, and but few, of course, came out. On Monday afternoon, I again addressed the people in the Rev. Mr. Nichols' Church, and obtained a number of members to the Union. On Monday evening I addressed a fine audience at

BROOKFIELD, WEST PARISH.

The following day, Tuesday, through the active co-operation of Mr. Joseph A. Sprague, and Mr. Harrison Barnes, whose kindness I shall long remember, I obtained additional members to the Union, swelling the list to thirty-six for Brookfield. These gentlemen assured me that the town should number its fifty members, and I doubt not they will secure that number, with the aid of Rev. Mr. Nichols, and Wm. Howe, of the South Parish, both of whom volunteered to secure, as members, the names of some friends whom I could not see. They have one tavern in the South Parish, where they carry on the business of drunkard-making pretty extensively. Do not misunderstand me. I do not say that they sell to drunkards at this place. Oh no! they only sell to sober men until they become drunkards, which is infinitely worse. In the West Parish too, there is one establisment that Hath-a-way to change sober men into sots; and still another near by, of the same sort. A man was found drowned in a mill pond near the village a short time since with a bottle of RUM in his pocket. He had long been noted for his intemperate habits. I regret exceedingly that I am not able to give you the name of the heartless wretch who filled that bottle, for *that* I consider the most important fact to publish in connection with the affair. Could I have obtained the name, I would have written it out here in staring capitals, and requested your printer to have set it in large full faced type, so that it might have looked as black as possible.

NORTH BROOKFIELD.

This town I visited on Tuesday evening, and enjoyed the pleasure of an introduction to that veteran in the cause of temperance, Rev. Thomas Snell, D. D. I received from him and other friends, a cordial welcome, had a fine audience in the evening, and obtained *on the spot* at the close of the lecture, *sixty members* to the State Union. The cause is safe in N. Brookfield. To Mr. Batchelder, I am under many obligations for his kindness and hospitality.

I took the cars on the Western R. R., on Wednesday morning and came to Worcester, and dined with Porter at the "American Temperance House." If any man wants a good dinner in Worcester let him go to Porter's. If he would have splendid accommodations he should go to Porter's. If he wants to find a gentlemanly and obliging landlord, let him go to Porter's.

The stage which leaves Worcester for Millbury at five o'clock P. M., (except when it gets started about six,) took me to

MILLBURY.

A rainy and dark evening prevented many from coming out to the meeting, and the audience was not therefore large. I received, however, at the close of the lecture the names of eighteen persons as members of the State Union, and with the co-operation of Dr. Amory Hunting, the following day, I swelled the number to *fifty*. If I may not credit a portion of the Doctor's kindness to the circumstance of my being a brother Pill-Box, there are few more earnest friends of the cause than the Doctor.

A friend from Millbury visited Worcester a short time since, and as a man and wife who formerly hailed from the Emeral-Isle, but recently from a Worcester grog-shop, were passing him, he heard the following language—which is full of meaning—addressed by the wife to her husband. " Sure, Pat, and they're all timperance folks jist about here, so keep that bottle out o' sight, darlin' dare."

I am now at

NEW ENGLAND VILLAGE IN GRAFTON.

I have lectured here to an attentive and respectable audience, and obtained here last evening and to-day, over *thirty* members to the State Union. This evening I am to lecture at the centre of the town, and I have no doubt I shall swell the list of members to *fifty* for Grafton.

Thus far, Dear Sir, *the plan works well*; and if I in concluding this long epistle, may be allowed a Yankee guess, it shall be this, That we will give the moral suasion party in Massachusetts, as much of that article as they can conveniently digest during the year eighteen hundred and forty.

CHARLES JEWETT.

My second report of labor in Mass., with its results closes with the following paragraph: "During the first month of my engagement, ending May 23d, I delivered twenty-eight public lectures, and obtained 715 permanent members to the State Union, and thirty-three donors,* who will together pay into the treasury the sum of $760. All, except forty-four, were obtained in sixteen of the fifty towns of Worcester county. That county alone will give over *two thousand* members to the State Union." The report of my labor for June of the same year (a bad month for public labor, the evenings being short, and the people busy on their farms,) closes as follows: " I have delivered thirty public lectures, and added 400 to your list of members during the past month.

But little more than a year had elapsed since we began working under the new plan of operations, when the influence of the Baltimore, or "Washingtonian" movement, began to divert attention from our efforts, to a novel and more exciting mode of operation. When the new movement reached Mass., our State Union sought to make of it an efficient auxiliary in the work before them. They secured, at considerable expense, reports of the speeches of the most prominent of their

---

*Persons who were not prepared to adopt the pledge of the State Union, but would give their dollar and receive its publication, were enrolled on its records not as members, but donors.

speakers, and published them in tract form for general distribution. Thousands and tens of thousands were scattered over the state, and everywhere much curiosity was excited to hear the reformed men. Our local societies, auxiliary to the State Union, anxious to meet the wishes of the people, would often secure a visit from some of their prominent speakers, and these everywhere insisted that the intemperate could not be got to join existing organizations, and that a new "Washingtonian" society must be formed in each town, and the more surely to interest the intemperate, some of that class, if they could be persuaded to sign the pledge, must be placed at the head of the new organization.

Grave and thoughtful men hesitated. It seemed such a perilous proceeding to give up an organization which, in some localities, had existed for ten years, was officered perhaps by some of the most reliable men in town, and numbered its hundreds of pledged members, and go into a new society with a recently reformed man at the head of it, who *might* make a life-long and successful struggle against his old masters—depraved appetite,—habit,—and the dram-shop, and *might* possibly fall off in a month and bring reproach upon the organization. But clamor, and a love of the new, and the sensational, carried the day, and thus, all over the state, the local societies were re-organized, and the *State Temperance Union lost its auxiliaries.* The agents of the "Union" counseled against this re-modeling of our organizations and the turning of all public efforts into that channel, but their counsels were in vain. Heartless men charged their honest efforts to mercenary motives —to a desire to maintain an order of things by which their salaries were secured—and so the work of disorganization went on. In July, 1842, the Senior agent of the "Union" and the Editor of its publications wrote thus in a leading article of the state paper:

"Our plan was favorably received, and our agents were carrying it forward with all practicable despatch through the state. Under it the circulation of the Journal had risen to nearly 25,000 copies monthly, the Almanac and Tract to 70,000 more. More than 6,000 members and donors have been obtained, the 'Cold Water Army' paper established, and the whole operation of banners, badges, songs, &c., gotten up. The committee and friends who had watched with much interest and care the successful influence of the plan, were buoyant with hope that we were now to have a somewhat more *systematic* and *permanent* effort in our great enterprise than had ever before been made in the state. It was anticipated that we should soon have 10,000 men and women in the state who would, by the payment of a single dollar annually, secure the regular advancement and ultimate triumphs of the cause. We cannot with integrity conceal the cause of our embarrassment. We should be false to the cause and to ourselves were we longer to remain silent upon a matter of such vital importance to both. Stating the cause of our empty treasury must not be taken or understood to be any evidence of complaint against the movement which has occasioned it. Our John Hawkins' tract* of 80,000—the uniform aid and sympathy of our agents, will establish our zeal in the Washingtonian efforts; and yet our empty treasury is owing to the diversion of our funds from us to them. The answer to our calls for accustomed aid

---

* A tract in which reports of his speeches were published.

comes up from most of our towns,—'we are doing so much for the Washingtonians, you must excuse us this year;' or, 'must delay,' or, 'be content with half as much as last year,'—till we are *compelled*, &c., &c."

Another extract from the same report says:

"In the midst of unprecedented and most heart-cheering success in our efforts, we were suddenly cut off from the means of proceeding on our triumphant way. We were receiving assurances enough from all quarters that our labors and operations were neither misapprehended nor undervalued, and we were as often pressed to move onward with all our instrumentalities. At the same time, our accustomed support was *suddenly* and most unexpectedly withheld; and of course, we became as suddenly involved in obligations to agents, printers, paper manufacturers, rent, &c., &c."

The magnitude of the calamity which overtook the temperance enterprise in the way I have described, cannot be properly estimated without considering carefully the work the Temperance Union was accomplishing. The extracts I have made from the reports of agents, and the general summary of its work embraced in the statements already given by the senior agent through the editorial columns of the Temperance Journal, will give the careful reader a tolerable idea of the influence it was exerting. The following sketch of its modes of procedure and the hold it had on the public confidence, may not be amiss in this connection:

"Four agents were handsomely supported in the field, visiting, instructing, and building up the local societies and scattering over all parts of the state the publications of the 'Union.' Their official organ, 'The Temperance

Journal,' had, at one time, a circulation of over twenty thousand copies monthly. Besides this, they published a paper especially for youth—a 'Temperance Almanac,' songs and hymns for the use of local societies—and not content with these means of influencing popular sentiment, the glorious old 'Temperance Union' printed the saving truths it taught on *banners* and *badges* for festive occasions, on fans for the use of our temperance girls, and even on the *handkerchiefs* of the children. With steady step Massachusetts advanced, under that system of operations, straight toward the final overthrow of its worst enemy. A public sentiment was everywhere being formed adverse to the use, and sternly opposed to the traffic in, intoxicating liquors. County after county successively elected commissioners who refused to license the sale of liquors. Our temperance constituencies began to be represented by temperance men in the state legislature. At one time we had even a majority of staunch temperance men in the National Congress. It came to be understood that, to find favor with the people of Massachusetts, it was needful that a man should favor the great social reform whose blessed influence was everywhere so manifest, not only officially but *practically as a citizen*. The agents of the state society were everywhere welcomed by the clergy of the state, who, with rare exceptions, admitted them to their pulpits, often yielding to them the time usually devoted to ordinary pulpit instruction. The usual social religious meetings of the week would be. so arranged by the clergy of the town where an agent of the society was about to visit it, that the whole population could hear him if they chose without neglecting other important meetings.

The *pledge* was presented at the close of our meetings, and numbers were usually added, at each meeting, to the pledged sworn foes of the liquor system."

I have already recorded the fact that one of the practical results of the Washingtonian movement was the crippling of the "Massachusetts Temperance Union" by revolutionizing and ultimately destroying that multitude of local organizations which were its auxiliaries, the elements of its strength, the active agents through which its publications had reached the people, and by the aid of which measures planned by its executive officers and agents had been carried out and rendered effective to the extent we have seen. Let your thoughts, dear reader, dwell for a moment on that calamity. What can a state organization or a state central committee accomplish without the aid of local organizations to receive their suggestions, make provision for the proper reception of their agents and secure them a hearing in public assemblies, carry out their plans, circulate among the people the publications of the parent society, and aid in securing for it needful financial support. How will you Christianize a state without *local* churches, or educate its people without *local* schools? Could a State Central Committee conduct to a successful issue a political campaign without local clubs or organizations to carry out their measures? Shrewd politicians understand these matters, and hence we hear their constant exhortations to their partisans in every political campaign, "Organize! organize!! everywhere," and, "Circulate the documents." Take away regiments with their colonels, companies with their captains, and sergeants with their squads, from a group of general officers, and their courage, tactics, and strategy will cover no field with dead or wounded enemies. Oh! it was a stunning blow to the most effective temperance organization which ever existed in this country, when the friends of temperance in all the towns and villages of the old Bay State, through an honest but mistaken zeal in behalf of a popular but necessarily partial and ephemeral movement, consented to the abandonment of tried, reliable, and well officered organizations, and the substitution therefor of Washingtonian societies, officered, generally, by men but recently reformed.

Nor was this the only mischievous influence of the new movement. Some of the most prominent of the new disciples, although they advocated total abstinence, held and advocated zealously, doctrines utterly unsound in many important particulars. Mitchell, one of the original five, and the leading spirit of the group, held that, as Washingtonians, they should have nothing to say against the traffic or the men engaged in it. He would have no pledge even, against engaging in the manufacture or traffic in liquors; nor did he counsel reformed men to avoid liquor sellers' society or place of business. He would even admit men to membership in his societies who were engaged in the traffic, and in my hearing he admitted that he had paid for liquor, at the bar, for *others* to drink after he signed the pledge. *He* would not drink liquors, but if others chose to, that was their business. Of course, with these views he was decidedly opposed to all legal measures for the suppression or restriction of the trade. Our business was, so he argued, to get everyone to sign the pledge of abstinence, and then, of course, grog shops would do no harm, as they would have no customers. To shallow reasoners, or men of little observation, this was very plausible, and great numbers accepted the doctrine as sound and adopted it as a plank in their temperance platform. A division was thus effected in our ranks, and papers were started to advocate the *new* temperance doctrine as distinct from those of the Temperance Union, and there were large numbers of men in various parts of the state who labored very industriously for a time to widen the breach between the Washingtonians and the old advocates of the cause.

The embarrassments created by the new order of things, the false doctrines introduced with it, and the bitter controversies which grew out of them, imposed a heavier tax on my brain, nerves, and power of endurance than my public labors, which were unintermitted for years. Among the other false notions advocated by Mitchell was, that religious exercises of every kind were out of place in temperance meetings, even prayer.

This notion, however, was so preposterous, that but few of his followers accepted it, and it was pretty soon abandoned.

Looked at coolly, from this distance of time, that Washingtonian movement was a curious phenomena. It had elements of power in it, which will always be potent among men. The utter absence of all regard for station, social position, or distinctions created by wealth or superior education, was one striking feature of it. A man, with not a penny in his pocket, and who could neither read nor write, if he had once been a "hard case," and was now sober, and a member of the Washingtonian Temp. Society, was just as good a fellow, and was just as much honored as a reformed judge, statesman, or major-general, and was heard in the meetings with just as much attention.

Another important feature of it was, the retention by its individual members, of their individuality, if I may so speak. It was not a society, acting as such through its chosen officers, or certain committees, to whom certain duties were assigned, but rather an aggregation of individual reformers, associated by mutual sympathies rather than definite forms, each a missionary of the common faith, and so far from losing a sense of their individual responsibility in the association, that in the early history of the movement, each member was expected to work just as though he stood alone and was singly and alone responsible for the enlargement of the temperance Zion.

Suppose that element or order of proceeding, introduced into a church,—a benevolent organization,—a political party, or an army on the field of battle—and fancy the result.

The utter disregard, by its members, of all conventional notions of propriety, as to the detail of one's personal experience, was another element of its power, which can hardly be estimated. Some very fearful people are restrained from relating in public, very important and interesting facts in their own history, lest some fastidious critic should whisper the word egotism. That folly was utterly cast aside in the Washingtonian movement, and if the freedom these reformers took, sometimes degenerated into license and ran on to absurdity, it was not a novelty in the history of reforms.

While expressing my regret at the disorganization of

our system of operations by the Washingtonian movement, let me not be understood as claiming perfection for the system we were pursuing. Though a great advance on anything that had preceded or followed it, it had some manifest defects. Its financial arrangements were not the best conceivable, though they were the best I judge which could have been adopted at the time, and under the circumstances. The true method, undoubtedly, is that adopted afterwards by the Order of the Sons of Temperance, and subsequently by the Good Templars and other close organizations. *Small*, but *definite* sums, received at *regular intervals*, from *each* member of *the primary organization*, a certain portion of the aggregate amount to be employed for the support of local operations, and another portion appropriated to the support of a State organization. That is the true plan. It meets every necessity of the case, and is perfectly reliable. That excellent financial plan—with the blessed pledge of abstinence,—the fraternal kindness shown to the fallen, and to those striving for a better life, with the regularity of their meetings, constitute the real strength and efficiency of the Temperance Orders. The sentinel at the door, the trappings and the tinsel, the multiplicity of offices and forms, the engrossment thereby of too much precious time in their weekly and occasional meetings, and the tendency of the *social features* to engross too much attention, are their elements of weakness.

CHAPTER X.

The clergy and their general faithfulness—Mistakes and their results—"Experiences,"—their potency—More blunders—The clergy disaffected—Close organizations, their origin—Practical results—Different organizations compared—What is needed.

I have already stated that the great mass of the clergy of Massachusetts, coöperated, heartily, with the Temperance Union and its agents. Nineteen-twentieths of them were total abstainers, and besides occasional sermons, very many of them gave the wicked liquor system a blow, whenever and wherever they had opportunity.

In those days an orthodox minister who wished to illustrate the doctrine of total depravity, found convenient illustrations in the existence of liquor-saloons, bar-rooms, and drink-shops generally, and in the fact that men would engage in distilling and importing liquors, and in burdening public and private conveyances with huge hogsheads of rum, and other liquors, of which ninety-nine gallons in every hundred would contribute to the production of guilt and misery, or aggravate evils already existing. The wickedness of licensing such a traffic came in for its full share of denunciation. In the prayers of the church, the temperance cause was remembered, and earnest supplications were made in hundreds of worshiping congregations every Sabbath, for the special blessing of God on the enterprise. The

Unitarian clergy were very generally with us in the work, and the Universalists, believing that all men would be saved, labored in this cause as if they had fully determined they should be. Of course, there were here and there exceptions to the general facts I have stated. A few in each of the sects were cowardly, and dared not condemn a system, so largely represented in their pews, and others hurled their denunciations against the grosser forms and phases of the wicked system, while the champaigne bottle and fashionable revelry, or Satan in silk, were handled very tenderly.

As I have before stated, the clergy of the state were represented by hundreds in the annual meetings of the Union, or State Temperance Conventions, and at their homes, in their own parishes, they were among the very foremost promoters of the cause. If, within the last twenty-five or thirty years, large numbers of the clergy of Massachusetts, and New England generally, have not identified themselves so closely with temperance organizations and temperance efforts as formerly, it becomes all real friends of the cause to inquire, if there has been anything in the management of the enterprise, by which we have, in a measure, lost their sympathy and coöperation. That there has been, I am certain, and I should be false to my convictions of duty to the cause, and be guilty of the cowardice and time-serving policy I condemn in others, if I did not state the facts as I understand them.

A history of the reform, as *I* have seen it, and so far as I have been identified with it, and as I shall write it, shall include every *important* influence known to me, which has, in my opinion, been operating either to hinder or advance it, however the statement may effect the opinions or prejudices of fellow-laborers, or of the public generally. In other words, according to my under-standing of the facts, I shall write history and not a work of fiction. A series of events or unfortunate circumstances have, together, lost us, in part, the close coöperation of the clergy, as well as that of many leading members of the Christian churches, though they still sympathize with the enterprise, and approve of, and generally practice total abstinence from intoxicating liquors. The first of the series was the objectionable doctrines and peculiar style of teaching or lecturing introduced in connection with the Washingtonian movement. The peculiarities of that style gave it, as we have seen, wonderful popularity and considerable efficiency in certain directions for a time. I have already called attention to some of the elements of its power. There is still another worthy of remark.

From the commencement of that special movement, no fact concerning it was more obvious, than that the simple relation by reformed men of their past bitter experiences, and of the substantial happiness of the new life they were living, in the practice of abstinence, had far more influence with the drunkard who listened to their relation, than the arguments of the most able men on our platforms. In view of that fact many argued the uselessness of all other measures.

It is strange, indeed, that men should so blunder as to conclude that the greatest work we have in hand in connection with our enterprise, is the reformation of the drunkard. That is an important end to attain, but it is certainly of less consequence to save the *thousands* now intemperate, than by proper education and restraints to save from the pit-fall of drunkenness the *millions* now temperate, especially the rising race, for whom all good men and women naturally feel an instinctive and deep solicitude.

The reason why the relation of experiences had more influence over the drunkard than argument, may be readily understood from a few moments reflection on the obvious facts of the case. Under the influence of intoxicating poisons, the higher faculties, such as the moral sense and the reason, are the first to fail, while the imagination, the passions, appetites, and emotional nature, continue quite active, in fact they often exhibit a preternatural strength, even in cases of maudlin intoxication. Hence argument, appealing as it does to reason, *failed* with the drunkard, for his reasoning powers were for the time being paralyzed,—while the simple relation of personal experience, by a once fallen but reformed man, being every way calculated to excite his sympathies, and kindle anew his failing hope of a better and happier life—found often a ready response, and hence that instrumentality has been blessed to the salvation of thousands.

Again, the recently reformed man told the story of the grog-shop, and the drinking saloon, as it had never been told before. They had seen the inside, and the working of these establishments, when there was no restraining influence operating upon their keepers, or the company; at ten, eleven, or twelve o'clock at night, and often during. the wee small hours, when the sober and Christian portions of the community were in their beds. And what a revelation! There are no such terrible exhibitions of depravity elsewhere seen on this earth as are made in such places. Imaginations, depraved and phrenzied by drink, conceive all abominable things. A perverted will, and a devilish ingenuity, set to work to realize those conceptions, while conscience is drugged, and all sense of obligation to God or man, with all humane feelings are annihilated. The history of what may take place under such circumstances, may well startle the community, as indeed, it did. These revelations constituted no inconsiderable part of the discourses of these new reformers. They contained other elements quite unobjectionable, and often exceedingly touching, and well calculated to make a most salutary impression on the minds of hearers.

But there was much in the discourses of that class of men, or many of them, calculated to corrupt the public taste, and render excitable men, accustomed to listen to them. intolerant, afterwards, of more sober instruction. Some of the most influential of these reformed speakers, including Mitchel, one of the original five, seeing the extensive and growing influence of the new method of promoting temperance, came, honestly, no doubt, to regard all other efforts as useless, and did not hesitate so to express themselves. Temperance sermons, prayers, arguments, and exhortations, which were not *experiences*, were of no account. The clergy and their influence were ignored. All that was wanted of the ministers was, to become members of the Washingtonian Temperance Society,—officered, frequently, by recently reformed men—and to open their churches and vestries for a temperance meeting whenever an itinerant lecturer came along, of whom, perhaps the minister had never before heard. If he hesitated, or in any way thwarted the plans of the new apostle, he was sharply denounced. *This* was the first mistake or circumstance that lost us the co-operation of many of the clergy, and of many thousands of religious men, everywhere. As to whether the clergy were justified in withdrawing for a time from the field of active labor on account of the circumstances I have detailed, is a question about which men will differ. I think they erred; that the evils justly complained of, were aggravated thereby. Paul informs us that he had been "in peril among false brethren," but he did not abate his Christian activity on that account. Our clerical co-workers had less to complain of than Paul; for their brethren who created the trouble, were, for the most part, *not false*, but simply rough, rude men, who had been trained for years in a very bad school, had recently discovered, and heartily embraced some truths, by which they had been greatly benefited, but still held many crude and unsound notions. We should not have looked to them for examples of courtesy, hardly of fair dealing. They had rough work to do, and many of them executed it very roughly. Our New England clergy had always been treated hitherto with deference, even by irreligious and vicious men; and a little more friction, such as our western clergy get, would not have hurt them. Gradually applied, I am sure they would have borne it with Christian patience; but the commencing of operations with a horse-card instead of a hair-cloth mitten, exceeded their power of endurance, and very many of them bolted. Not all, by any means. I could name scores of excellent men of the finest culture, and of high standing, who still continued personally active in reformatory labors as distinguished from their ordinary parochial duties, who bore with all this rudeness for their great love of the cause; and their clear perception of its fundamental character. They were to be sure often grossly imposed upon by unworthy men, who, taking advantage of the new order of things, assumed the role of public lecturers, often from love of notoriety, and the small gain of "*a collection*," while many of them did not in their lives illustrate even the single virtue they recommended in their coarse harangues.

Some of the early trophies of the Washingtonian reform, were reliable men, and their style of public labor, though novel, was unobjectionable. A few became Christian men and treated the church and the Christian ministry with respect, and were everywhere welcome, where known. These however, were a small minority of the whole.

Another movement, which lost us the active co-operation of thousands of excellent and able men, was the substitution of close for open organizations. Prior to the formation of the order of Sons of Temperance, *all* our public meetings were open to the world. There was no Ritual to control the order of public services which was determined by surrounding circumstances. The opening exercises, after the president of the society had called the meeting to order, were generally, prayer, the reading of the minutes, or the record of the last meeting and the reading of reports, if special duties had been assigned to committees. These services did not usually consume more than twenty minutes of the evening. The remainder was devoted to a free discussion of the subject of temperance by interested parties, unless provision had been made for a regular lecture, in which case, of course, that service had precedence. But whether the evening hours were occupied with the lecture or a general discussion, all was in the hearing of the masses. In many places it had been found difficult to maintain for any long period, a regular organization; as they had no financial basis, and consequently could not maintain an aggressive war, than which, nothing is so well calculated to preserve the efficiency of organizations, and the proper discipline of their members. The want of a financial basis and the Washingtonian tornado had sadly demoralized the movement; and it was in that condition when the order of the Sons of Temperance was instituted. Some of the brethren who originated that order had long been familiar with initiation fees, and ceremonies, rituals, regalia, emblems of office, sentinels, conductors, &c., and no doubt honestly believed that they were rendering the cause of temperance an essential service by incorporating these features into temperance organizations.

What seemed to them wanting in our former organizations was a closer bond of brotherhood, financial support, and forms more imposing, and these they thought would give strength and permanency to our societies. An organization with which they were familiar, having all the features before named, and doubtless others with which the public are not acquainted, had existed for ages, and why should not temperance organizations, if rightly constructed? Thus they undoubtedly reasoned, and the result of their consultations, their organizing talent, and their devotion to the cause of temperance, is before the world, and has been, for years, in a powerful organization, the influence of which has been blessed to the reformation of thousands once intemperate, and to the benefit of thousands of young men who have been saved from falling into habits of intemperance by its teachings, its pledge of abstinence, and the fraternal influence of the association. I do not make that declaration unadvisedly. I know whereof I speak, for I have labored in and with the organization, and shall in the future, while it shall continue to be, what it now is, one of our principal instrumentalities for the advancement of the cause; still I earnestly long and devoutly pray for the coming of that time when not only the leaders, but the masses who are now zealously laboring through the orders for the advancement of the temperance cause, shall clearly see what many have perceived for two decades, at least, that a triumph of the cause, as I have before stated, is simply impossible while our primary working organizations are, in so many of their features, objectionable to so large a portion of those whose coöperation we wish to secure.

In the New England states, where the question of the continuance or annihilation of the liquor traffic is most warmly contested, not half our strength is, at this moment, organized, and it never can be under existing forms. Let a friend of the cause, with intellect sufficient to draw sound conclusions from obvious facts, in any case, and anxious to arrive at the truth and the best way of doing a desirable thing, go to-day into almost any village or town of New England, and thoughtfully consider the facts which will there come under his notice. He will find the people divided in opinion and practice relative to the drink question and the liquor traffic. The Protestant churches of the town or village are, generally, in sentiment and practice, strongly opposed to the liquor system; not all their members, by any means, but an overwhelming majority. Will it do, now, to trust to these churches as our primary organizations in the battle we have to fight with the rum power at the polls, finally, as well as elsewhere? *No.* Emphatically and forever *no*, and for reasons obvious. Its members are not unanimous in their opposition to the liquor system, and an organization to answer our purpose must be. Again, *the terms of admission to the churches, any one of them, will exclude large numbers of earnest friends of our cause,* who, though not professing Christians, hate and purpose to war with the liquor system, not from the motives which mainly impel the earnest Christian, but because it is a deadly foe to the peace of their families and their business interests, to the security of life and property, to the social and moral wellbeing of society, to education and civil government. For all these reasons, thousands, aye, thank God, millions of our countrymen and countrywomen hate the liquor system and will join us in our war upon it, who could not join the church. They do not consider themselves now proper subjects for church membership. The churches, then, will not answer our purposes as primary organizations, for, I repeat, their terms of membership will exclude a multitude who must go with us, or we cannot secure controlling majorities. Still, the question returns, how shall we organize our strength in the town or village of ———— ? Organized it must be, or we cannot employ it effectively, for unorganized opposition to the Devil and his plans and servants, never amounts to much. Suppose we establish there a Division of the Sons of Temperance, a Lodge of Good Templars, or a Temple of Honor. We know beforehand, all past experience and observation tells us, that we cannot organize, under those forms, but a portion of our real strength in that locality. Yet, knowing this, many will insist upon a close organization, and will have nothing else; and if a few urge that an open organization, such as we worked under prior to the year 1840, can be made to embrace *all* the real earnest friends of total abstinence in the town or village, certain parties, zealous friends of close organizations, declare that open organizations are "played out," that "they cannot be sustained," that "the young people will not take any interest in them," and that "it is the young, mainly, whom we wish especially to influence," &c., &c. The older portion of the people, the clergy, the leading members of the churches, and other influential citizens, seeing and hearing all this, and fearing that if they press objections to close organizations, which they honestly entertain, it may dampen the ardor of the younger portion of the people, who, for obvious reasons, generally manifest a decided preference for them, will waive their objections and allow the proposed new organization to take that form. A few of those who, at an earlier period, worked in open societies, and would much prefer such an one now, will yield their preferences and go into the new close organization. I did so, and thousands of others have done so, not because we prefer them, or believe them best, but because the popular pressure was in that direction, and I, for one, did not wish to make, what to many might seem factious opposition to the plans and purposes of my brethren. I have never, however, concealed my opinion, that before a triumph of our cause can possibly be reached, we must have forms of organization more acceptable to the grey-haired and the venerable, to the clergy and leading Christian men, who are active and influential in all other good enterprises that succeed; to our judges, bankers, merchants, and prominent business men generally, of whom we now number comparatively few in our close organizations, but of whom we had a full proportion in open societies, prior to the year 1840. We want in our organizations, the old men and the strong men, the Presidents and Professors of our colleges, our Christian Editors and Teachers; in short, all who love the cause of total abstinence and desire the downfall of the liquor system. We shall never get them while we have close organizations *only*, and they retain all their present features, because some of those features do not approve themselves to their judgment, nor accord with their tastes. I have said that it will not do to rely upon the churches as our primary organizations in the battle we have to fight with the rum power, because their terms of membership will necessarily exclude large numbers of the real earnest friends of temperance. Now the same objections, exactly, lie against close societies. They are, like the churches, agents or instruments of good to thousands, but *their conditions of membership will keep out a large portion of our friends.* "But what would you have us do?" asks the Son of Temperance, or the Good Templar. "Shall we abandon forms of organization to to which we are attached and which we believe, and you admit are instruments of good to thousands, because there are others who are friendly to temperance, who do not like our forms and will not join us?" No, I would not counsel that. What is really wanted or needed, is, that you shall see the facts as they are, perceive the necessity that all our strength should be organized if we would secure a triumph of the cause, that we can never organize it all in close societies, and therefore, that you should cease to regard the formation of open societies with disfavor or suspicion; that you should look upon such societies, when formed, not as the rivals of yours, but as auxiliaries, needful helpers in a common cause; that you should speak a kind word in favor of open societies, whenever you see there are elements of temperance strength which, after years of trial, you have failed to incorporate with close organizations. Do for temperance what thousands of good men do for the cause of Christ. Broad-breasted Christians often give their influence and money to build, for other religious sects, houses of worship in the very village where they reside, and perhaps on the same street where stands their own church. Do for temperance what I have done for years, and what thousands of total abstainers have done, especially in New England, where open societies were most numerous formerly, and were wonderfully effective. I have worked in good faith for years with and for Sons of Temperance and Good Templars, believing, all the while, that open societies would serve our purpose better, and that their reëstablishment, with the addition of a proper financial feature, would be found to be a necessity before a triumph can be reached. I saw, however, that close organizations must have a trial, and a thorough one, before the earnest and excellent brethren working in and through them, could be made to see the necessity of other forms. They have been tried for nearly twice the period during which we worked in open organizations, and for one, I think it time to look at the facts as they are, and, instead of an obstinate adherence to existing and partial methods only, see if some measures cannot be devised for bringing our whole force into the field.

CHAPTER XI.

Open Societies, their advantages — Discussion before the masses wonderfully effective — Comparisons — Our Progress too slow — Why I thus speak — Our younger brethren — Progress before the year 1840 — Some change essential to a triumph — Three classes will not join the Orders — Why ? — Regalia — They love the drink — Out of Date ? — No — How they work in California — A glorious success — A supposition — Policy our ground of choice.

THE advantages of the open society may be stated thus: their working involves less expense, so that with a similar system of quarterly or monthly fees, which may be readily incorporated into their constitution or working plans, they can expend more money in the educational work of the enterprise. A large portion of the money raised in close organizations is expended, necessarily, for the rent and furnishing of halls or proper places of meeting. Open societies used the churches, vestries, chapels, town halls, and court houses, and generally without charge except the expense of lighting and and warming in winter and the pay of the sexton. They could do it now in nine cases out of ten. Nothing is expended in open societies for regalia, staves of office, and emblematic decorations. As the opening exercises, prayer, singing, and the reading of the minutes of the last meeting, and occasionally the report of a committee, did not usually occupy more than a third part of the evening, more time could be, and was devoted to a discussion of the general subject, or those local results of the liquor system, often so terrible, and when properly discussed, so well calculated to awaken and keep alive in the community a spirit of hostility to the whole liquor system. In open organizations, no time is consumed by ceremonies of initiation, the installation of officers, &c., hence more can be given to the reading of instructive documents and the discussion of the subject before the masses. Still more important advantages were found in the attendance *of families as such*, comprising, often, the grey haired father and mother with their beloved offspring, the stalwart young man, the beautiful daughters, and even the dear little boys and girls, often very young. These all used to go to temperance meetings *together*. Fathers and mothers never listen to truths which concern the well being of their families under circumstances so well calculated to make those truths impressive and effectual, as when the dear ones are by their side and where they can watch the effect of the truths uttered on their young minds, as their influence may be seen in the agitated countenance, in the eye sparkling with interest, kindling with indignation at the recital of terrible wrongs, or dim with tears when human sorrows and sufferings are the subject of remark. Seven-eighths of our weekly temperance meetings now are held in private rooms. Few of the aged are there to give to the proceedings the dignity and gravity which their presence generally confers, and the children are left at home; and worst of all, the drinking portion of the community, the very portion which we wish to influence by our arguments and appeals, are excluded. *They* have not the pass-word.

What a blow would be struck at Christianity, if, from

the regular meetings of the sanctuary or the weekly meeting for religious conference, sinners were excluded, unless they came with the pass-word, or would declare beforehand their readiness to join the church. At the close of the exercises in open societies, you can take advantage of any good impressions made to get men to join the society, which they can do on the spot by signing the pledge of abstinence, it being a part of the constitution, and from that moment the pledged man is a member. In close organizations, considerable time must elapse and certain ceremonies intervene, before membership is attained.

Once more. Those petty rivalries which are now frequently occurring between the different Orders, where they exist in the same community, and often between subordinate and neighboring organizations of the same Order; and those unbrotherly strifes for offices and honors, which too often occur now, were *unknown* in the open organizations, *absolutely unknown*. No doubt, my brethren who have embraced the cause within the last twenty-five years, and never worked in open societies at all, will be surprised at these utterances; but men, past fifty, who worked in the open societies which existed in New England by thousands before the year 1840, will fully understand me; such men as Senator Wilson of Massachusetts, Gov. Buckingham of Connecticut, Neal Dow of Maine, and Amos C. Barstow of Rhode Island, and thousands of others past the age of fifty. Let our younger brethren, before they express their unbelief in the historical truth of my statements, ask such men, and I am willing that their statements shall stand, whether for my justification or condemnation. How far they were effective, let the facts tell. In less than fifteen years, the style of operations I have described, so far revolutionized the public opinion of Massachusetts that the license system was abolished in more than three-fourths of the counties of the State. The old style of operating gave place, in the years 1840, '41, and '42, to the Washingtonian System, and that very soon to the Sons of Temperance and other forms of close organization, and they have had the field almost exclusively for over twenty-five years; and what is the present status of temperance in that state as compared with what it was in 1843? It may be doubted whether we are stronger at the polls now than we were twenty-five years ago. If we have gained at all, it is but a slight gain to have been secured by twenty-five years of labor, even with whatever of hindrance may have fallen in our path. For myself, I believe as firmly as I believe any fact that I cannot absolutely demonstrate, that, had the work of reform been prosecuted for the last twenty-five years in New England in open organizations, with such added provisions as experience might have suggested, the liquor traffic would have been crushed before the public attention could have been diverted from that issue by the great struggle for the preservation of our Union.

I am censuring no one for the course which matters have taken. I have assumed that the changes in our forms of organization were made in good faith, and from the best motives, and yet I have ever believed it a sad mistake, and see no reason now to change my opinion. For the prominent brethren of those Orders, whose friendship I have enjoyed, and with whom I have labored for many years, I have the most profound respect, and deeply regret that the perusal of what I feel it my duty to write in this connection, may give them pain. They may think me sadly mistaken, judge it unwise that I publicly express such opinions at the present juncture, and may feel called upon to controvert them; but my motives they will never question. A nice regard for personal popularity with the thousands to-day most active in the temperance reform, and with the organizations by whom I am most frequently employed, would have dictated a very different course from that I am pursuing, and my fellow-laborers know that full well.

In those portions of our country, where existing close organizations did not supplant open ones, and where, not only our younger brethren, but even those in advanced life, now working through the orders, and zealous for their multiplication and enlargement, have had no experience in the working of open societies, I am not surprised that they cling with tenacity to existing forms, and deprecate any important changes. Why should they not? They know that by present modes of procedure great good is accomplished, and have had no experience of methods more simple, and yet more effective. In many portions of our middle, western, and southern states, open societies never existed to any considerable extent, and where they did exist never embraced so large a proportion of the population, or enjoyed the measure of popularity, they did in New England. Were our brethren throughout the country familiar with the working and history of open organizations, as they existed there from 1830 to 1840, and had they witnessed the wonderful changes wrought through their instrumentality during those ten years only, they could never speak of them in such terms as I *have* heard many employ. They would as soon lampoon their mothers.

In many towns a clean majority, even of the legal voters, were pledged to abstinence before the year 1840, and that pledge was against all intoxicating liquors. Thousands of our temperance fellow-laborers, now under thirty, of both sexes, erroneously suppose that until the era of Washingtonianism all our societies were under the old pledge—simply to abstain from *distilled* liquors. They are greatly in error. Most of our New England societies had discovered the defects of the old pledge, and had substituted therefor the pledge of total abstinence from all intoxicating liquors before the year 1838. As early, even, as 1833, the insufficiency of the old pledge had become apparent to many minds, and from time to time they communicated their thoughts to others. I am certain that at the first National Convention, held in Philadelphia May 24th and 25th, 1833, there were two men, perhaps more, on the business committee of that convention, who were *then* prepared to have taken the higher ground of total abstinence from all intoxicating liquors — the celebrated surgeon of N. H., Dr. Amos Twichel, and Gerret Smith, Esq. The majority, however, were not prepared for so long a step at the time, and so these brethren with their clearer and more advanced views of the subject, comforted themselves with the belief that the lapse of a little time would convince all of the propriety of taking higher ground. They were not mistaken.

At a meeting of the Middlesex County Temperance

Society, held at Charlestown, Mass., in the year 1836, the following resolutions were passed:

Resolved, That, in order to ensure the steady progress and final triumph of the Temperance cause, it be recommended that the principle of abstinence from all intoxicating drinks, as an article of refreshment or luxury, be religiously observed by the friends of Temperance.

Resolved, That we continue to regard the formation of Temperance Societies on the principle of entire abstinence from all intoxicating drinks, as the most efficient means of advancing the cause.

At a meeting in Woburn, Mass., Oct. 8th, 1835, the Hon. Samuel Hoar in the chair, the following resolution was passed:

Resolved, That it be recommended to all friends of Temperance to adopt the principle of total abstinence from the use of all intoxicating liquors, as a drink.

In some towns the transition from the old to the new pledge was gradual, as in the instance following.

The Springfield Temperance Society took action as follows in 1835:

Voted, That this Society do now adopt the pledge of abstinence from all intoxicating liquors as a beverage, to be subscribed by such of the members of the Society as may prefer it to our present pledge.

Voted, That hereafter, any person may become a member of this Society, by subscribing either of the above mentioned pledges.

The Springfield Gazette, which gave an account of the meeting, adds, that "130 individuals signed the new pledge at the close of the evening service."

The New Hampshire State Temperance Society, at

their annual meeting for 1836, held in Concord, June 1st, debated the question of adopting the total abstinence pledge during an entire day, and until ten o'clock in the evening, when it adjourned until the following day. Before the close of the second day the entire membership of the body had become so thoroughly convinced that higher ground must be taken, that the new or total abstinence pledge was adopted *unanimously*.

Nor was this advance to a higher pledge confined to New England, by any means.

More than one thousand societies existed in the State of New York, in 1837, with a membership of 80,000, pledged to total abstinence.

As early as 1836, the Pennsylvania State Temperance society, at its session in Harrisburg, passed the following resolution.

Resolved, That it is the deliberate judgment of this Convention, that all the friends of temperance should wholly abstain from all intoxicating drinks as a beverage, and should cease to furnish them as such for their families or friends, and that the Convention do earnestly recommend that Societies be formed hereafter on the principle of total abstinence from all intoxicating liquors.

In New Jersey, at a meeting of the Baptist Association, held at Burlington during the autumn of 1835, fifty of the fifty-one clergymen present, signed the total abstinence pledge.

The Maine Temperance Union, with its pledge of total abstinence, was formed in 1837.

The Massachusetts State Temperance Union, adopting the pledge of total abstinence, was formed in February, 1838.

The Baltimore Conference of the Methodist Church, the New Jersey Conference of the Methodist Church, the General Association of Baptists of Indiana, and the Baptist Convention of Ohio *all* endorsed the doctrine of total abstinence before the year 1838, as did many other religious bodies in different parts of the country, and there were not, I think, twenty-five protestant clergymen in the entire state of Massachusetts, who had not adopted the principle and pledge of total abstinence before the year 1840. Nor was the warfare of those years upon the license system directed simply against the traffic in distilled liquors.

At the March town meetings, for 1835, *thirteen* towns of Worcester county voted against licenses to sell distilled liquors, and *ten* towns gave majorities against licenses to sell any variety of intoxicating liquors. In North Brookfield the vote stood 165 against license to 40 for license. Holden gave against license, 115, for it 45. West Boylston, Westboro', and some other towns condemned the wicked system of license by large majorities.

This wonderful revolution in the sentiments, habits, social customs, and governmental affairs of the people of New England was wrought within the period of fourteen years, reckoning from 1826, by the efforts of an awakened and earnest people acting entirely through open organizations. Had all our temperance societies during that period had sentinels at their doors to keep out those whom they desired to convert to the faith and practice of abstinence, could such a revolution have been wrought, within the period named? That question

SOME CHANGE ESSENTIAL TO A TRIUMPH. 163

I respectfully put to all concerned for the advancement and final triumph of the temperance cause.

I have repeatedly expressed the opinion that a triumph of the enterprise is impossible until we shall be able to organize and effectively employ all our strength, all those who have been converted to the doctrine and practice of abstinence by some of the instrumentalities heretofore employed. Three classes are lost to us now, and will be hereafter, while our active organizations preserve all their present forms and features. The first class comprises a very large number of our strongest and best citizens, who are honestly opposed to all close, or secret organizations. I have heard the opinion expressed scores, perhaps hundreds of times, that such opposition to close organizations is a mere pretense, or excuse for non-action and neglect of duty. It is impossible. The general character of the class of persons of whom we are speaking, forbids us to entertain, for one moment, such an opinion. Let those who hold it observe critically the parties, who, though practicing abstinence and heartily hating the whole liquor system, still stand quite aloof from the Orders, in spite of urgent invitations, repeated for years, to join them, and who have, in many cases, resisted a good deal of pressure in that direction. Take either of the New England States, where close organizations have been almost the only ones existing for the last twenty years, and not one half the members of the Congregational and Baptist churches who are practical abstainers have been with us as members. What is there in the lives or characters of these men and women that should lead us to question their honesty and veracity when they tell us that they cannot join us, as at present organized, without violating their consciences? Nine-tenths of the clergy of both those denominations were members of the temperance societies in 1840, and were among our most efficient laborers in the cause.

Another large and influential class stand aloof from the orders because the wearing of regalia and emblematic decorations is offensive to their tastes. Members of the orders by thousands, who now wear regalia, sacrifice their tastes to their great love of the cause, and restrain all expression of their feelings in relation to the matter, lest they should be misunderstood, and wound the feelings of their brethren. But when the proposition is made in the Lodge or Division room to appear, on some public occasion, in regalia, how often we find objections urged against the measure, and that too, by some of our most active and worthy members. If they are out-voted, they submit and wear the regalia, and if need be walk in procession to the church to occupy the center of the house, or some conspicuous place during the services of the day or evening. To many such no sacrifice required of them and no labor they are called upon to perform in connection with the cause, bears so heavily upon them as those external adornments which do not together weigh four ounces. Many differently constituted may wonder and smile at all this, but these are stern truths, nevertheless. I happen to be one of the unfortunate ones, if the brethren so regard it, who have no taste for such adornments. I would rather the brethren would double or quadruple my regular fee or impose upon me any service which the constitution or rules of the order allow, than to hang on my neck, for a single evening, the very brilliant decorations which I have seen many excellent men wear with apparent pleasure, and which probably cost them not less than twenty-five dollars. Say, if you please, that it is *a mere matter of taste*. Granted. But why should we trammel our organizations with needless trappings, to wear which many of our educated and strongest men must, if they join us, crucify their natural or acquired tastes. If a ready mark of recognition is wanted, would not a modest piece of colored ribbon tied in the button-hole of a gentleman's coat, or a small rosette pinned on a lady's dress, answer the purpose as well? So small a change as that would, I honestly believe, have added during the last twenty years thousands and tens of thousands both to the Sons of Temperance and Good Templars; and if increase of numbers and influence is wanted, why should so much be sacrificed to a childish love of display. A glance over the world will show that it is not the educated and cultivated classes or nations who delight in trappings, gew-gaws, and glittering externals. Least of all does it become workers in a genuine reform to spend money and time in needless decorations. We are striving to impress the Christian world with the truth that true temperance is the handmaid of religion, and in that effort we shall succeed best, with the least possible display of tinsel and trappings.

A third class, which is by no means a small one, find in the peculiarities of our present organizations a convenient excuse for standing aloof and doing nothing to advance the cause, who would feel compelled to join and labor in an open society if one existed in their neighborhood, because, should they fail to do so, it would be at once suspected that they had private and very particular reasons for objecting to a pledge of abstinence. That is the *real* fact in *their* case. They have a secret love for the drink which they do not care to acknowledge, and which our present arrangements enable them to conceal while claiming to belong to one of the classes before described. Great numbers of such individuals joined open organizations prior to the year 1840. They were compelled to do so and to practice abstinence by the circumstances surrounding them. A great evil was abroad in the land, invading the homes of the people and warring on all public interests. But one mode of arresting it had ever been discovered—the organization of those opposed thereto, under a pledge of abstinence. No excuse was possible for not joining in a popular crusade against the common enemy, growing out of any peculiar or objectional features of our organizations, for they possessed none. They could not plead that associations of the people to accomplish desirable results were unnecessary, for most of them belonged to one or more societies—religious, political, or industrial. They wished to be reckoned among the friends and supporters of all good institutions and enterprises, and there was no way to manifest their concern for the removal of this great scourge, but to take their stand with the associated friends of temperance. *Now* such men find it quite easy to excuse themselves from any participation in the work of reform, on account of the peculiar features of our organizations. I want all reasonable ground of excuse removed, so that no respectable citizen shall be able to occupy a doubtful position.

But some reader may, perhaps, suggest that open organizations would not *now* serve our purpose as they did formerly; that they were adapted to a certain stage of the enterprize which we have long since passed. We have, however, satisfactory evidence that they can be rendered as efficient now as at any former period. In proof of that statement, take the following history of a late movement in California. It appeared in a religious paper published in Chicago, Ill.,—the "Advance"—for October 5th, of the present year, 1871.

HOW THEY CLOSED THE GROG SHOPS IN A CALIFORNIA TOWN.

There are different theories of temperance reform, but any of them are good enough that *succeed when put in practice*. Some object to "total abstinence" and temperance pledges, but they work well sometimes. As witness this record from California:

Santa Cruz, being one of the younger towns of the State, has but just now emerged from its era of grog shops, whisky saloons, and rum holes. Every new American town seems to be, somehow, condemned to start in this way. Some are burned to death, and ruined in the process. And some throw off these evils, and come out into a virtuous and prosperous life.

Santa Cruz has taken the latter course. Last New Year's, ten men, habitual drinkers, some of them just going into the embrace of delirium tremens, visited with a remarkable spasm of good sense, determined to reform! To reform, they knew very well, was to stop drinking. They could not "taper off." Some of them had tried that too many times to have any faith in it. They were in earnest, and determined to take a course that was sure to succeed. That course was the plainest thing in the world. *It was to stop drinking intoxicating drinks.* They did stop. *They pledged themselves, then and there, to one another, not to drink a drop of anything of the kind.* They were not religious men. But some of them were educated men. Some had not yet wasted all their substance, a few had handsome estates left, and all were in the prime of life.

Like other Americans, when they undertake to do anything together, they *organized,—they formed a society,—a total abstinence society. They opened it to all who would join them in their pledge, men or women.* Their wives joined, gladly enough. Many of their companions in drinking habits joined them. Many people of life-long habits of total abstinence joined them too.

The saloon keepers said, "Oh! yes, we've seen this tried before. It will last a few weeks, as long as the novelty is on." And so, with wise looks, they quietly waited for the reaction to come, and the brisk business that would return to them with it. Meanwhile, the new society grew. Members were proposed, and admitted every Monday evening,—they met weekly.

From the original ten they came to be fifty, seventy-five, a hundred, a hundred and fifty. And now their membership is two hundred. *The reform came to be the town talk.* Nothing could be said against it. Even the liquor-sellers, whose stocks were on hand, whose rents were running on, and whose bills to the wholesalers were coming due, could not say a word, for hadn't men a right to *stop* drinking, as well as to drink, if they wanted to?

The churches quickly and heartily seconded the movement. In fact, its commencement is probably owing to the private persuasion of one member of the Methodist church with one or two of the original ten, to stop drinking. *The ministers preached, and many of the Christian people joined the society.* There was joy in many houses, where there had been despair before. Not less than forty or fifty families are now temperance homes, with all the consequent thrift, comfort, and hope, which a year ago were threatened with the ruin so sure to come upon the drunkard.

The dram-sellers waited in vain. A majority of them got tired of waiting. They closed their doors, and went about other business. Instead of a reaction, came a grand celebration! The whole population, almost, turned out and held a celebration in a grove. It brought tears to many eyes to see the long procession that day, with its banners and its bands of music,—a spirited and noble celebration, in the interest of social order, domestic peace, and true religion. *The people who originated this movement were not church-goers, nor were their families. Nor are they now. But many of them begin to fall in.* Well known Christian families joined them in their reform society, and they are gradually becoming attendants at church. Three-quarters of a year have now passed away, and there has been no reaction. Very few have withdrawn from the society, and very few indeed have violated their pledge and been dropped. *The great object is to get in every drinking person, and save him by total abstinence, before it is too late.* They have succeeded in many cases, where success was a great victory.

This reform has put a different face on this community, you may be sure. We have just had our State election and every lady was surprised at its unusual orderliness in Santa Cruz. It was the theme of remark all day, and the papers of the next day commented upon it. Total abstinence made it so, nothing else.

I have observed this reform carefully all the year, and I believe it genuine, and likely to be permanent. It is a great pleasure to report it. It has not been my privilege to know of many of the kind in California, hitherto. I hope there will be more, hereafter, notwithstanding our wine-growing and brandy-making,—things greatly against it, to be sure. It this example of local, spontaneous reform suggests the trial of the same to other places needing the like, within the reach of your circulation, they may be assured, from our experience here, that the results will be eminently satisfactory.

It has already been imitated in our county. Similar societies have been formed in Soquel, and Watsonville, and elsewhere, embracing at this time a membership of about five hundred, including the society in this town.

S. H. W.

Could anything be more simple and satisfactory than the operation therein described? I would have the reader notice the period of time during which this desirable work was done. Ten months at the outside. Please notice also, that all who would sign the pledge of abstinence were admitted to membership—both sexes—all ages. There was no committee to consider and report on applications for membership, or balloting for or against their admission. No long ceremony of initiation, occupying precious time greatly needed for interesting and instructive discussion.

We would have our Christian readers also observe

especially the conduct of the clergy, and church members of Santa Cruz, in relation to the movement described. "Well known Christian *families* joined them in their reform society, and they are *gradually* becoming attendants at church." The italics are mine.

Suppose now some well meaning, but ill informed minister or layman had, at the very inception of this reformatory effort, suggested to the parties concerned therein, that intemperance was but "one shoot of the old root of sin," and that the true way to assail it was through the church, especially appointed for warring upon all forms of sin, and further, that no movement which does not aim directly at the thorough conversion of men, can be effective, or will reward the labor, &c., &c. Suppose, I say, that such nonsense had been industriously preached to the people of Santa Cruz during the month in which this society originated, and they had listened to and believed it, what would have happened? Satan and the liquor-sellers might have rejoiced over a grand work arrested in its forming stage, and the drunkards would most likely have remained drunkards still.

In the management of a farm rendered well nigh valueless through neglect or bad culture, the skillful and experienced farmer will not despair of success because he may not be able to effect the renovation of all its acres at once.

Oh, when will good men estimate the soundness and value of their theories and favorite methods of procedure, by honest comparisons of practical results!

Reader, if you would desire to be eminently useful to your generation and country in connection with the temperance reform, let me urge you to read over and over again that simple story of the reform in Santa Cruz, but especially ponder, and inwardly digest the sentences I have italicised. There are, in that brief history, texts for a dozen sermons or temperance lectures; and suitable matters for at least half a dozen lengthy and instructive essays.

The reader will perceive that I have discussed this question as to the choice of forms of organizations as one of policy simply. Had I believed there was anything morally wrong in the formation and support of close organizations, I certainly should not have joined and worked with them. My opinion of their moral character I have further indicated, by commending them oftentimes to congregations of the people at the conclusion of my public discourses, and urging them to connect themselves therewith. I have done so, not because I believed them the best calculated to serve our purposes, but because they were eminently useful, and the best existing at the time in those localities, and I did not feel myself at liberty to throw cold water on the efforts of earnest brethren by questioning, before a mixed audience, the wisdom of their choice as to the forms through which they would labor.

CHAPTER XII.

OPERATIONS OF THE MASSACHUSETTS TEMPERANCE UNION.

Sad results of wrong measures—Our temperance poets—Fourteen o'clock—A Cotton Speculation—Jimmy's Mill—The Distiller's Disaster—A grist from Jimmy's Mill.

It may be well to add a few words to what I have already written relative to the Washingtonian movement, and the action of our State Union in reference thereto, lest it may be supposed that its officers were indifferent to so striking a phenomenon. When it began to be influential, in cities south of us, our Executive Board and the agents of the Union sought to avail themselves of it, as an auxiliary to the system of operations they were so successfully conducting at the time, and my senior in the agency, Nathan Crosby, Esq., who was at the time editing the publications of the Union, managed the matter with that excellent judgment and tact which characterized all his movements. Some of the most distinguished of the new apostles were invited to the state, and opportunities were afforded them to address the people. Their speeches were reported for our papers, and John Hawkins, one of the most earnest and acceptable speakers among the reformed men, was for a time employed to visit certain parts of the state, and operate more especially with the drinking men, and those recently reformed. His influence was most salutary, and his discourses generally acceptable. While thus our committee endeavored to utilize the Washingtonian excitement, it made a very important movement in another direction.

A Mr. Stewart, an honest, earnest Irishman, heartily devoted to the cause, and a man of more than average ability, was employed to travel along the lines of railroad, then in process of construction, where large numbers of his countrymen were employed, to labor with them, both personally and publicly, where meetings could be held, and to form total abstinence societies among them, where practicable. He labored faithfully and judiciously, but the results did not seem to warrant the continuance of that instrumentality, and it was soon abandoned.

Although the Temperance Union labored to use the Washingtonian excitement, and the new elements of power it created, in a way consistent with the preservation and continuance of the regular system of operations they were conducting, they found it a very difficult matter. Some who had not been in love with the Union for various reasons, sought to create of the new element a rival to it, and a State Washingtonian Society was formed. Journals, in the interest of the new movement, sprung up in every considerable city in the state. These made strong appeals for local patronage, and thousands of our old and substantial fellow-laborers, all over the state, transferred their patronage from the publications of the Union to these ephemeral sheets. It soon became evident that the general movement had been so demoralized by the advent of this Washingtonian phase, and the use made of it by certain parties within the state, that it would be impossible for the Union, with its limited financial support, to sustain so extensive a system of operations as they had heretofore done, and greatly to my regret, my senior in the agency decided to resign his position. My earnest protest was unavailing, and in his retirement, the state lost one of the most able and judicious advocates of the cause I have ever known. He was not an eloquent orator, but an able and earnest man, who studied the subject thoroughly, discussed it kindly and logically, and the dignity of the enterprise was never lost sight of in his public efforts. In addition to my labors as the lecturing agent of the Temperance Union, I had now to edit their publications.

In my efforts to increase, if possible, the circulation of the Temperance Journal, a monthly paper, the official organ of the society, I promised its subscribers and the reading public, that each number through the year 1846, should contain an illustrated original poem, which should have reference to some phase of the temperance question, or to some feature of the wicked system with which we were at war. With the assistance of some excellent fellow-laborers, I redeemed my pledge, and this extra effort to give added interest to the paper, was rewarded by an increase of its circulation. Those twelve poems were, at the close of the year, published in a pamphlet, illustrated by the very expressive wood cuts which had served to give them added interest as they appeared in the Temperance Journal. Four of the twelve were from my own pen, and the other eight, far better, contributed by the pens of fellow-laborers. My readers who have kept themselves well posted in relation to our American literature for the last thirty years, will not be surprised that I speak of the other eight short poems referred to, as better than my own, or *some of them* at least, when I record that two of the number were furnished by the two brothers, William H. and George S. Burleigh, whose splendid intellects have been at the service of the temperance reform from their very boyhood. For one, I heartily thank God that some of the most distinguished poets of our age and country have never prostituted their powers by singing the praises of the filthy and obscene god, Bacchus. Every stanza and line of Pierpont, Whittier, and the Burleighs, have been consecrated to the dethronement and destruction of vice, the crowning and exaltation of freedom and virtue, and the purification, elevation, and advancement of our race, in all that renders men truly wise, good, great and happy. As a specimen of my lighter style of composition, by which I sought to give interest to our temperance publications, at that period of the reform of which I am now writing, I insert here two of the articles referred to. It should be remembered by the reader that these were written hastily, in the intervals of severer labor, and for the specific purpose before stated. No one can be more thoroughly aware of their defects than I am, but they certainly contributed to give added interest to reformatory publications, and thus to advance a great and good work, and that is more than can be said of very many of the more pretentious efforts of those who jingle words and syllables in rhyme.

FOURTEEN O'CLOCK.

Night o'er the earth her raven wing had spread,
Hens had retired, and men had gone to bed,
When two spruce dandies took it in their head
    To visit Sandy's shop,
    And take a social drop
Of whiskey-punch, spiced sling, or "Tom and Jerry;"
    And while with curious skill
      He mixed th' inspiring draught,
      They stories told, and laughed:
    Then did their glasses fill,
      And while they quaffed,
Cracked their coarse jokes, and made themselves quite merry.

Now, gentle reader, with your kind permission
We'll leave them there, and make a slight digression.

A little spark alights upon the ground,
And seizing on the dry leaves scattered round,
    Kindles at length a very pretty fire,
Which, having no respect for man's fine labors,
Burns up your house, then seizes on your neighbors,
    While to the very heavens the flames aspire.
        Burning roofs fall,
        For aid men call;
The fire, with blazing fury, still drives on,
Until (its work of devastation done)
    It leaves a heap of smouldering ashes there,
    Which Sorrow may extinguish with a tear.

Thus causes small, through folly or neglect,
Produce oft-times a terrible effect,
    Draining from mortal eyes oceans of tears.
Oft the deceitful, treacherous, sparkling glass
Has sunk the man of wisdom to an ass,
    Or something like one, all except the ears.

The rum goes in, and common sense goes out;
Genius and learning both are put to rout,
    And empty as his pockets leave his head;
Kindly affections hasten to depart,
    (Each grace and virtue dead,)
And hissing vipers nestle in his heart.
    With lustrous eyes, intelligent and keen,
    As slaughtered pigs, in Boston market seen;
    With fiendlike scowl or idiotic laugh,
    And tongue, for mouth like his, too big by half,
    He bawls as constant as a weaning calf;
A silly subject for contempt or pity,
Yet in his own opinion wondrous witty.

The fiend, who sneaks about, to get his claw
On thoughtless souls, wherewith to fill his maw,
    Whene'er he sees men in this wretched state,
Laughs as though he would split his sooty hide,

And all his black apprentices beside
    Shake their long tails, with fiendish joy elate.

Such man becomes, and such these tipplers were,
By frequent sips of Sandy's liquors rare.

Night's half-way house old father Time had passed,
    And left two milestones in his track behind,
And onward toward the third was journeying fast,
    When to their homes our heroes seemed inclined.
Sandy politely guides them to the door,
    And kindly held the light;
    For 'twas a very dark and dreary night,
And now the rain did like a torrent pour.
Drunkards need space to travel in, and they
Their zigzag journey took toward *Broad*way;
They reached it, and pursued their course along,
Cheering old night with fragments of old song.

We said the rain fell fast, and so it did,
    And down the gutter like a river flowed;
And as with gathering strength along it sped,
    Bore on its breast a very filthy load;
But whence derived, we shall not here declare,
    Lest we might give offence to ears polite;
    Yet to prevent mistake, and set all right,
We'll *hint* that hogs and horses travel there.

Into this Mississippi of Broadway,
    While city lamps did shed a fitful gleam,
Our drunken friends by some mischance did stray;
    And as they reached the middle of the stream,
    A church clock struck to tell how time sped on;
And to be sure and keep their reckoning good,
They halted in the middle of the flood,
    And stamping with their feet, they counted *one*.
Again it struck; they stamped, and tallied *two*,
While high above their heads the water flew.

Three, said the clock, and as their feet replied,
The filthy water splashed from side to side.

Another clock, behind the first in time,
From old St. Paul's, just now began to chime;
And while its tones reëchoed through the town,
Amid the flowing filth their feet came down.
Six, they exclaimed; when from a neighboring spire
Another bell rang out the alarm of fire.
This gave the drunken dandies quite a sweat;
For though from head to heels they now were wet
With mingled gutter-wash, a falling shower,
Which on their crazy heads did constant pour,
Yet there they stood, and stamped, and counted still,
And on their ears each stroke successive fell.

They reached, at length, *fourteen;* and quite amazed,
One thus exclaimed, while wildly round he gazed,
Through all my—(hic)—*life, some twenty years or more,
I never knew it*—(hic)—*quite so late before.*"

A COTTON SPECULATION.

In Bristol County, in a certain town,
  Not fifty miles from one they call Fall River,
A trader lived, a man of some renown;
  And though he peddled grog they called him clever.
He chanced to have a very worthy wife,
    Possessed of real nobleness of mind,
    Benevolent and kind;
And swayed by her he lived a decent life.
Upright in some respects, yet still for gold,
The devil's own elixir, *Rum*, he sold;
And while promoting thus the *public good*,
Took in exchange the cash, or—what he could.

His house stood distant from his store
  Some twenty rods or more;
And toward the close of a fair summer's day
A wretched beggar thither bent his way.

His eye was sunken and his look was sad;
  His beard, unshaven, o er his bosom hung;
While tattered rags, with which the wretch was clad,
  Stirred by the evening breeze, around him swung.
An old crushed hat protected his grey head,
  While his thin locks were streaming in the wind.
He moved along with tottering, feeble tread,
    Bending beneath a pack
    Which rested on his back,
While his lean dog was trotting close behind.

He mounts the steps and gently rings the bell;
  The wife invites him in and sets a chair,
And while the wretch his tale of woe doth tell,
  There glistens in her eye a sympathetic tear.
She offers food, but that he does not want—
  And seeing what a scare-crow dress he's got on,

Concludes of clothing he must sure be scant,
   Especially of that part made of cotton.
For through his tattered rags, all glazed with dirt,
   (Although she has a most observant eye),
  Collar or wristbands she cannot espy,
Or e'en the smallest vestige of a shirt.
    Then quick as thought she to her chamber flew,
       And from her husband's ample store
      Selected one he oft had wore,
And in the beggar's lap the needed garment threw.

He stammered out his thanks, and in his pack
He stowed the gift, and swung it on his back;
Then took his leave, and toward a neighboring wood
He bent his steps and made what speed he could.

There seated on a log he viewed his prize,
As any tippler would with gin inflamed eyes;
And thus communed he with himself: "Shall I,
To please the eyes of other people, die?
True, I am shirtless, but then, what's the harm?
We need more than our clothes to keep us warm.
To clothe the outward man is sure a sin,
If we neglect the better part within.
'Tis true "man wants but little here below,"
Yet wants that little often—*that* we know.
Rags will buy gin, and gin, I sure *must* have,
Without, though clad in silks, I could not live.
So here it goes!" The garment then he tore,
And with the rags he hasted to the store,
And had his empty bottle filled once more.

As out the wretch was passing with his gin,
By chance the merchant's lady happened in,
And to her husband thus: "What had he there
Within that bottle?"—"What? Some gin my dear."
"And could that wretched beggar thus deceive?
Can tears tell lies? What shall we then believe?

Stooping and sad, he tottered to our door,
And begged I would 'have pity on the poor.'
While like a child he wept, I could but heed
His prayer, and gave him what he seemed to need:
He'd not a rag of cotton on his skin;
And had he still the cash to purchase gin?
"He did not pay in cash," the man replied.
"Not cash!—and what had he to pay beside?"
"Why, rags." "He barter rags! What sort? Speak quick;
I fear the wretch has played us both a trick."
"Here is the bundle," said he, "if you doubt
What it contains, just pull the fragments out."
She drew them forth, and made the fellow stare,
By loud exclaiming, "Sir, see there! see there!!
There is your name—I wrought it there myself—
And that old ragged, dirty, lying elf,
As great a hypocrite as e'er was born,
Has sold you your own shirt, in pieces torn."

Then, staring in the face of her liege lord,
And suiting well her action to the word,
With bitter irony, she thus exclaimed:
"Dear sir, don't look confounded or ashamed;
For one of moderate means, and humble station,
You've made a splendid *cotton speculation*."

Another style of composition which occasionally served to relax a little the facial muscles, often made rigid by the contemplation of wrong and injustice, and to promote good nature among those engaged in war, was entitled,—"*Mechanical Rhymes for these Curious Times,*" or "*Grists from Jimmy's Mill.*"

It appears that Jimmy, who contributed to the work of reform by turning the crank of our printing press, (they are now worked by steam, in fact they were then, now that I think of it, for *Jim* was a steam engine of the most approved construction,) had become thoroughly disgusted with the newspaper poetry of the times, and one day declared that he "cud grind out betther poetry nor that on the machine which he tuck over wid him from the ould country."

"Jimmy," inquired I, "have you indeed a machine for grinding out poetry?"

"Troth I have, and it wud do your heart good to see it work when it is in order," said he.

I bade Jimmy brush up the machine, have its joints or journals well oiled, and promised that when I should get hold of some facts suited to the purpose, we would give the machine a trial. Many a grist was subsequently ground out on that mill, and so deeply did some of the dear children of the old Bay State get interested in these products of the machine and in the clever Irishman who they supposed worked it, that when Dr. Jewett was expected at a certain point, some of the children asked their clergyman if he supposed the doctor would "bring that funny fellow, Jimmy, along with him."

The following is hardly a fair specimen of Jimmy's work, as it will be seen that he got into the hopper some facts which seemed to have no very direct relation to the principal grist to be ground. It is *my* opinion, however, that Jim intended, in a sly way, to hint to the Boston Distiller that *he* was not the first individual who had had the honor of tumbling into a fermenting vat. In fact, that Sambo had been there before him. And I suspect that when he afterwards got in the facts about Haman, which seemed so inappropriate, he really intended to give the distiller a hint that *his* fate came very near being that of the Persian prime minister, who got hanged on a gallows of his own construction. Of course when the doctor got hold of the machine, it ground out more regular rhymes than under Jimmy's management.

THE BOSTON DISTILLER IN THE FERMENTING VAT.—A GRIST FROM JIMMY'S MILL.

A noted distiller of Boston fell into one of his fermenting vats a few days previous to the appearance of the following article, and was dragged from it by the hands of his workmen in the establishment, but for whose timely interference he must have lost his life by strangulation.

Doctor. "Jimmy, have you learned that a celebrated distiller fell into one of his fermenting vats a few days since, and came near losing his life by strangulation?"

Jimmy. "Indaad I did. I read it in the paper; and whin I told the matter to Michael McGowan's wife, she foch'd a scrame, and slapped her two big hands togither, and rin capering about the room like as if she'd been half mad. 'What ails you?' said I. 'What ails you?' said she, pouting out her lips and spaking my own words arter me, in a kind of mockin' way. 'Botheration to ye! Doesn't them same distillers make the vile crathur that pits strangulation down the necks of paple more dacent and honest nor themselves? Didn't my own cousin, Tim Taggerty, rest his sowl! drink the liquor till it made him crazy entirely, and then put a rope on his neck and hang up in the barn? and wasn't that *strangulation?* Didn't Betty Cragin, whin she was drunk, roll her baste of a carcass on her own swate baby, that wasn't more nor sax weeks old, and smother the life out of it? What was it but *strangulation?* And now, jist because the distiller of all this divilment got a small taste of his own midicin, they put it in the papers, and make sich a hellaballoo—'"

Dr. "Hold, Jimmy! I have no time to hear more of Mistress McGowan's lecture on strangulation; but, as you seem to be quite interested in the matter, suppose you put the facts in your patent rhyme-grinder, and turn us out something for the Journal."

Jim. "Faix! I'll do it."

(He brings out the machine and commences operations.)

I'll sing you a song that is rare and queer,
Of a nagar that fell in a vat of beer,
Which was rendered so fine as he slowly decayed,
   That the liquor was praised,
   Its price was much raised,
The business increased, and a fortune was made.

Dr. "Jim, you make strange work. You were going to grind out a song from facts that occurred in this western world, and your very first verse is about an old affair that happened twenty years ago, on the other side of the Atlantic."

Jim. "Niver mind, doctor, jewel. I'll come to it directly."

16*

(He turns again.)

>One Haman, the Scriptures relate,
> Got mad at the Jew, Mordecai,
>And built for him, outside the gate,
> A gallows some fifty feet high.
>"Ha! ha!" said his wife, "they will yet learn to fear us,—
> These stiff-necked, obstinate Jews;
>Now go to the party with Ahasuerus,
> Be cheerful and banish the blues
>   Come, hurry, my honey,
>   Drink wine and be funny."

>He went—and, bad luck to him! made such a bother,
>He got himself hanged jist, instead of the other!
>And he couldn't complain of the way it was done,
>For they let down the drap on a plan of his own.

Dr. "Worse and worse, Jimmy! you are farther from your proper subject than before. You have wandered in point of distance as far as Persia; and as to time, you have made a jump backward of more than two thousand years. What next?"

Jim. "Troth, yere mighty pertickular! If you don't be azy stoppin me, I won't grind at all, at all, and ye may turn ye'rself."

Dr. "Well, let go the crank, and I'll give you a specimen of my work off-hand."

(The Dr. now turns, while Jimmy looks on in amazement.)

>The fire glowed bright beneath the still,
> And fiercely boiled the foaming flood,
>Destined the drunkard's veins to fill,
> To scorch his brain and fire his blood.
>The workmen cheerly plied their tasks,

When in the great distiller came
T' inspect the work; and now he asks,
  "How boils the flood? How burns the flame?"
Vexed that the hell-broth cooks so slow,
  He mounts a vat with careless tread,
To stir the mixtures vile below,
  But slips, and plunges over head!
Panting and gasping hard for breath,
  He would have yielded there to death;
But helping hands were now applied,
  Which dragged him up the slippery side,
And forth from that fermenting vat,
  Resembling much a drowned wharf-rat.

Bedaubed with yeasty slime and foam,
  Fragrant and dripping as he passed,
This great distiller sought his home—
  By sad experience taught at last
This truth contained in Holy Writ:—
Who for his neighbor digs a pit,
Will sometime tumble into it!

CHAPTER XIII.

BOUND, AND HOW.

The Widow's Son—In the "Slough of Despond"—A fight for Life—Victorious—The Moral—A Speculation—Still moralizing—The Longevity of Reformers.

While a resident of Providence, R. I., during the year 1839, I had made the acquaintance, in the office where our temperance paper was printed, of two young men, practical printers, who, like three-fourths of that craft, were pretty free drinkers of intoxicating liquors. They were both, however, excellent compositors, and in common parlance clever fellows, in the American sense of the word clever, i. e., well disposed. One of them, the older, James Cary, had been a soldier in the regular army for years and had of course seen rough times. I used frequently to caution them against the habits they indulged in, but like millions of others they were ignorant of the real relation of alcoholic liquors to the physical constitution of man, and were under that *spell* or delusion with which narcotics blind and bind their victims. I could see from month to month, yes, even from week to week, that the power of the habit was increasing, and earnestly urged them to abstain; but it was in vain. "I can drink or let it alone, as I choose." "Don't worry about this child." "I can take care of No. 1," and "A man is a fool that can't govern himself and stop when he chooses," &c. All this I had heard hundreds of times before. It was the old story over again. At length the younger of the two, George W. Warner, (we called him Jerry,) called at my house one evening, in incipient delirium. He talked strangely, and seemed very much alarmed. I tried to persuade him to go over to the Dexter Asylum, and suffer confinement or restraint for a few days, until he should recover from his present attack and regain his power of self-control. He hesitated, and said he would go home to his mother's residence, (she was a widow,) and think it over, and would come in and see me again in the morning. That night he cut his throat. Not fatally, however; for our excellent surgeon, Miller, dressed his wounds, and he seemed in a fair way to recover. Before the wounds were healed, however, he got out to a drinking saloon, and although its proprietor knew what had happened to him while in delirium tremens, yet he handed down the decanter of liquor to him again. The poor deluded, ruined man took another draught; his delirium returned, and he made another attempt at self-destruction, and this time with success. Thus the Demon of the Still and the Cup could again exult as in the language of the song:

"The widow mourns for her ruined son.
What matter! what matter! *our work* is done!!"

His companion, Cary, was alarmed and drank less for a while, but soon filled his glass as before and hurried on his way to ruin. The typos of Providence, three-fourths of whom drank daily, but not quite so deeply or frequently as Cary, regarded him as a disgrace to the craft, and raised a purse for him, on condition that he would at once leave the city and not return. He left, and went to Boston. Among the results of long intemperance, ulcers had formed on his legs, and they were so offensive that he could no longer be tolerated in a printing office. The workmen would at once rebel, and insist that he must leave the office or they would. He was now pretty much at the end of his chain. He could get no work, was out of money, and for some days begged his food about the city and slept, when night came, in an old building near the wharf, among old barrels and boxes, as he afterwards told me. He had heard that I was in the city, and learning my whereabouts, came into my office on Cornhill late one afternoon and begged for money to buy food and a cheap lodging. He had suffered so much from the cold the night previous, that he dared not lodge among the barrels again. I gave him some money, extorting from him a promise that he would expend none of it for liquor and would come to my office the next morning. But what could be done with this ragged, bloated, diseased, weak, shambling, degraded, offensive creature? There was then no inebriate asylum to which I could send him. He was just on the very verge of death and a drunkard's doom. I remembered him as he *was* when I first met him, and thought of his companion and the manner of his death. But what could be done for him?—that was the *practical* question which pressed itself upon my mind; and I am telling this story, reader, because I wish that same practical question to press itself upon yours, concerning the wretched remnants of manhood all about you which the liquor traffic is sending to the grave. I went to my home in Newton, a few miles out of the city, stated the case to my wife, and after consultation we decided to make an effort for his salvation from the threatened doom. We had then six children of our own, and this was not a promising child to adopt into one's family; could not bring a certificate of good character; did not look very well, and withal, other senses revolted at his presence. I took him home, however, on the following day, furnished him a room, made such improvements in his *personale* as soap, water, and clean clothing could do, and he was "*one of us.*" It was a bitter pill to swallow, *that*. Those compounded of aloes and assafoetida are sugar-plums in comparison. But what else could we do but to make the trial? The widow's son, his former companion, had come to me in Providence, and I had given him—advice. That was all; and the rum-seller and the razor had given him—death. Who would make an effort now to save Cary, if we did not? That was *the* question. James Cary was saved; but it cost us five months board at—how much per week? His clothes did not cost much, for he wore those I had cast off, but they were clean, although here and there ornamented with a patch. You would have laughed, reader, to have seen the *set* of them, for my weight is about a hundred and eighty and he was as thin as Oliver Twist, who fared sumptuously on gruel, as you remember. But what a struggle the poor fellow had for a few days! The presiding genius of that home, (I had told him to call her mother,) had to make him a good many cups of strong coffee, and to bake for him a good many custards, and speak to him a good many encouraging words, during the first week. "Do not leave us, James, however badly you may feel; stay with us come what may, and we will do all we can for you." "I will, ma'am. I'll stick by, live or die. If I die with the tremens, I'll die here." "That is right, James; but you will not die. You may feel sometimes as if you would die, but you will not; you will live to retrieve the past; you have had a terrible education, but never mind, you'll be a man yet."

Such used to be the talk. In a few weeks, the ulcers upon his limbs healed without other medicine than pure water applied externally and internally, with clean dressings or bandages for his limbs, which he was able personally to manage. His appetite for food increased, and he gained flesh and strength daily. His shambling gait gave place to a regular and firm step, and at the end of five months he concluded that he was sufficiently strong in body, mind, and will-power, to be able to face the temptations of the city and to keep his pledge. I got him a situation in a printing office in the city, gave the journeymen printers an opportunity to assist me in getting him an entire new suit of clothes, and with the first money he earned he got a nice gilt frame for his temperance pledge, and hung it up in the sitting-room at his boarding-house that all might see what were the views and purposes of James Cary, the reformed man, in relation to the use of intoxicating liquors. Through the remainder of his life, which continued for many years, and which was honored and blessed by the gift of a good wife and a lovely daughter, he kept his pledge. I visited him occasionally in company with his "mother," as he called a lady friend of mine. The last time I dined with him, he still resided in Boston on a certain street upon which, directly opposite, was a distillery. As I stood beside him looking out of the front window, I pointed to the distillery and remarked: "Well, James, you have your old enemy pretty close at hand." "Yes," he replied, "but I thank God, I am his master now."

Reader, the *lessons* to be learned from this story, for there are a number of them, are, first, The *tendencies* of the drinking system, and of the practice of abstinence are quite opposite. Secondly, Drunkards who have gone down to a certain level cannot be saved without great sacrifices on the part of *somebody*. Thirdly, It will cost us, as a people, too much to rescue thus all the drunkards, or one-fourth of them, which the liquor system, if continued, will turn off. *Therefore*, and finally, that system should come to an *end*. Father, mother, one of a coming crop of drunkards may be that bright-eyed boy of yours. Look to it.

Although genuine reforms are aggressive and progressive, and from time to time present to the worker in them, new problems to solve, and to the public, new and interesting phases to contemplate, yet with the toilers, those called in the Providence of God to devote themselves especially to the work of demolishing the old and constructing the new, it is much as with laborers in other callings and professions; i.e., the labor of to-day is very like the labor of yesterday. There is a sameness which would become very tiresome to one who was simply laboring for the money paid him; but to the laborer whose heart is in the work, who accepts partial failure here and there as evidence only of imperfection in the use of means, which it is his business, and that of his co-workers to rectify; whose faith and hope are constantly stretching forward to the glorious *end* sought, there are peculiarities attaching to reformatory labor which render it very pleasant.

It conduces to health, not only by giving constant exercise to the muscles and mind, but because it gives exercise to the emotional nature of man.

The feelings and affections of men, their emotional natures, call for exercise as well as the muscles and the mind. So far as health is concerned, I believe it is far better that a man should shout for joy at the contemplation of the grand, the glorious, the happy, at one hour of the day, scowl with righteous indignation in view of wrong and injustice, at another, and weep with the suffering, and sorrowing, still another, than simply to read in his easy chair the morning news, take his usual business rounds during the day, digest his meals, and go off impassively to his bed without his emotional nature having been once stirred during the day.

We were made to *feel* as well as to think and act; and the non-use of any of our powers and faculties tends to dwarf them, and render impossible that symmetrical growth of our whole nature in which alone is the highest health and happiness. Excessive grief, anger, or joy may endanger our health or life, but their frequent alternation, and moderate indulgence, I believe, are not only helpful to men's moral and spiritual natures, but also to their bodily health.

Some men would be far better Christians if they would occasionally visit the abodes of the unfortunate, and witness suffering which would moisten their eyes; aye, more, they would be better Christians if they would get angry every day. Of course, the passion of anger should only be excited by the contemplation of wrong, injustice, cruelty to man, or beast.

Certainly there is enough of these all around us to excite indignation, if we were good enough Christians to get angry. These reflections are preliminary, reader, to an important item of information, and some hints at the philosophy of the facts stated. First, more than three-fourths of the early earnest workers in the temperance cause, whose labor in it was sufficiently earnest and protracted to make them extensively known as reformers, lived to pass their seventy-fifth year. No such longevity can be shown in connection with any other profession, or class of men of this age. Unless we conclude that health and long life were miraculously bestowed upon them as rewards of well doing, we must conclude that the facts stated admit of some philosophical explanation.

The latter conclusion is the more rational, I think, but what is the explanation?

That their abstinence from the use of alcoholic liquors conduced to health is unquestionable, and there is as little reason to doubt that the constant and healthful activity of brain and muscle, which attention to their ordinary duties, and their reformatory labors together secured, contributed to the same end; and for myself, I believe that the constant excitement of their emotional nature, which was inseparably connected with their labors as reformers, added another element of health and longevity.

If I am right in my philosophy, here is an argument for engaging in reformatory movements which, I hope, may have weight with my readers who desire health and long life.*

---

* See note A in Appendix.

CHAPTER XIV.

OUR LEADERS AND CHAMPIONS.

Rev. Dr. Justin Edwards—The First New England Regiments—Personal Peculiarities—Rev. John Pierpont—The Freedom of the Pulpit assailed—A Masterly Defence—Logic—Logic Versified—The License System—Sarcasm—Legitimate employment of it—Awful Exposures—Shall we give it wings? Yes—"Lament in Rhyme, Lament in Prose"—Square hits—Summing Up.

THE sad facts which render reform necessary, the specific ends aimed at by the reformers, the great truths, or principles upon which they base their movement, and the instrumentalities by which they propose to attain the desired end, *these* are the objects which most interest the public mind in connection with any enterprise of a reformatory character; but next to these, they are interested with the personnel of its leaders. Presuming that my readers who have followed me thus far in this narrative, are quite familiar with the interesting points above referred to, I will endeavor to gratify a natural curiosity which they may be supposed to possess, to know more of the men who stood forth as the prominent champions of the new movement at that period of the reform, and on that part of our great field of operations now under consideration.

In respect to the character and abilities of those who by common consent were granted the first place among the reformers of New England, from 1835 to 1845, we

JUSTIN EDWARDS, D. D.

had but one thing to desire, that was organizing talent. Neither Rev. Dr. Edwards, John Pierpont, or L. M. Sargent, were organizers. Every other faculty needed, they possessed in large measure. It would be difficult to find three men more unlike each other than the three named, and yet they were in perfect accord on this great question, and there was this striking similarity in their history, as connected with the temperance reform. *Neither of the trio ever struck a blow at the wicked system assaulted, or any guilty supporter of it, which was successfully parried.* The first, because he struck so carefully, and apparently with a heaven-directed aim. The the two last, because their blows were given with such consummate skill, and with a human power, which broke down by sheer force the guard of their opponent, however skillful he might be of fence. For the skull of the fencer, it was fortunate if that too were not cleft in the encounter.

Dr. Edwards was one of the earliest advocates of abstinence. In 1823 he made a communication to a clerical body, of which he was a member, on the evils of using intoxicating liquors at funerals. His views were extensively published, and that absurd and mischievous custom began to decline from the date of their publication. In 1825 he wrote the tract entitled the "Well Conducted Farm," a most valuable article, which had also an immense circulation. It was through his agency also that a meeting of a few friends took place in Boston preliminary to the formation of "The American Society for the Promotion of Temperance," which was formed February 13th, 1826. He drafted the Constitution of that society. The Address which they sent forth to the public expressive of their views and purposes was written by him. As the corresponding secretary of the society and their authorized agent, he raised in Boston, Salem, Newburyport, Andover, and Northampton, $7,400 as a financial basis of their operations. During the month of September, 1826, he set on foot a movement in Andover, Mass., which resulted in the formation there of a local temperance society, consisting of more than fifty heads of families and an hundred and fifty young men, a large proportion of them students of the theological seminary there located. To his personal efforts more than to those of any other man, or score of men, was the reform indebted for the forms it took and the influence it exerted in New England, up to the year 1837. He was one of the wisest men in council I ever knew, and there was never any deduction to be made from his influence or labors on account of rashness, crudeness, or ill temper. In all his labor, as a reformer, I presume no man was ever prejudiced against the cause or its advocates, by any injudicious or unkind word of his. Although not an orator, in the popular sense of the term, the simplicity, sincerity, gentleness, and eminently Christian spirit of the man, won all hearts, and gave his words weight and power wherever he addressed the people. He was an active participant in the labor of those two great Conventions which I have already described, that of 1839 and that of 1840. With the entire absence of all self-seeking and vanity in this great and good man, there was no want of confidence in himself as a pioneer or leader in a great movement. It was once said of Samuel Adams, the old Boston Patriot, that he wished New

England to control the policy of the country, that Boston should govern New England, and he wished to shape the policy and government of Boston; and, said the speaker, if his wishes could be realized, no part of the country would be *intentionally* ill-governed. The same remark might have been made of Dr. Edwards in connection with the temperance reform. The confidence in his ability to guide in the enterprise, was not the offspring of vanity or self-conceit, but it originated in his knowledge of the fact, which no acquaintance of the Doctor ever doubted, that he had given more time and thought to the consideration of the subject, than any half dozen of his compeers.

While acting as the agent of the Massachusetts Temperance Union, Dr. Edwards was one of my most trusted advisers in times of trouble, or in reference to matters of doubt. He passed away from the scene of his earthly labors much earlier in life than most of his co-laborers. In any truthhful and general history of the reform, especially of its inception and earliest periods, the labors of Dr. Edwards must be conspicuous.

While yet a citizen and servant of Rhode Island, I had heard much of Rev. John Pierpont of Boston. In my attendance on the memorable convention of the years 1839 and '40, I had seen the gentleman, and noticed the high estimation in which he was held in Boston where he had long resided and labored, and had ventured a reference to him in the poem recited by me before the convention of 1840, which called forth a round of applause, more out of compliment to the subject than the style of the reference. Anticipating a possible, yea, a very probable failure to deal worthily with the giant curse of the world, the rum Devil, in the effort I was about to make, I counseled the thousands before me as to what should be done in that event, as follows:

> "Faint not, but bid your Pierpont take the quill,
> And point keen satire's dart with *half* his skill.
> Then shall the well directed weapon fly,
> Home to its mark, and bid the Demon die."

Soon after I became an agent of the Massachusetts Temperance Union, I sought his acquaintance, and enjoyed his friendship during his lengthy and most useful life.

Like Dr. Edwards, he was one of my counselors, and I ran to him at all times with freedom and confidence. Not as I did to Dr. Edwards, to ask his judgment as to *what* was to be done, but how best to do it. There were few better scholars in New England than John Pierpont. There were no better logicians. He would have responded heartily to the sentiment of Holmes in the last line of his poem on the Deacon's one-horse shay, that "lived one hundred years to a day,"

> Its history closed in this very odd way;
> "Logic is logic, that's what I say."

With Pierpont, logic was logic, and in the discussion with him of a mooted question, the opponent who did not look well to his logic, would suffer severely. He had the rare faculty of so grouping facts, that the logical sequence or conclusion was seen at a glance. In his controversy with the Distillers, Importers, and Wholesale liquor dealers of his congregation, in Hollis street, they learned that fact to their cost. As the reader may not be familiar with the facts, I will briefly state them. In his public discourses before his people, as well as with his pen, he had expressed opinions relative to the entire system of making, selling, and drinking intoxicants, in terms not flattering. Some members of his congregation, who were largely engaged in the business, possessed of immense wealth, and consequently accustomed to have things pretty much their own way, could not endure to be thus disturbed by the words of their minister, whom they supposed they could easily control, and determined to compel him to vacate the pulpit. They trumped up a series of charges against him, seriously affecting his character as a minister and a man, and on these charges, after much discussion, agreed to go with him before a mutual council. Some of the churches who were invited to be represented in that council by delegates, refused altogether on account of the grossness of those charges. Finding their plans thwarted in that direction, they dropped the gross charges, and then proposed to go before a council on certain minor ones, which they retained.

Mr. Pierpont's answer to the committee is perhaps as good a specimen of controversial writing as has been put in print on this side the Atlantic. I will give the reader a few extracts which will, I think, justify the assertions I have made concerning the ability of him whom I have ventured to call our temperance Ajax, though unlike him, he never became blind. That splendid eye of his was as clear and pleasant at the age of eighty as at fifty for aught I could see.

"But, gentlemen, passing by this commendable jealousy of yours for the welfare of the Christian cause at large, I cannot see—though you may—how you can justify yourselves, as an accusing, and a prosecuting committee of a particular society of Christians, whose sole "purpose" it is to extrude its pastor from his pulpit in thus giving his greater sins the go-by, and bringing him before a council for his less. *If you believe* that the charges brought against me last July are true—charges of impurity of mind, indecency of language, and frauds and falsehoods in business—it seems to me that you owe it to yourselves, to your own church, to all the churches, and to "the Christian cause" at large, to prosecute those charges to final judgment. To yourselves you owe it;—for you will thus prove yourselves true men, in that you have said of me only what you believe is true. To your object you owe it;—for, if those specific allegations are proved, not only am I cast out of my own pulpit, and every other pulpit, but I am branded with disgrace to your entire satisfaction; and thus your object is effected. You owe it to your own church, to all other churches, and to the Christian cause at large; for all these ought to be ministered to with clean hands. If, on the other hand, you do *not believe* that those atrocious charges are true, let me ask you, as men who have either "raised a false report," or taken up a reproach against your neighbor," and accused him falsely, whether you do not owe it to *me* to retract those accusations;—openly, frankly, manfully to retract them; retract them as solemnly as you have made them; retract them in a document signed by all of you who have put your names to *them*, that I may file it with the other papers in this case; and retract them, too, upon the records of your society, so far as you have placed them there;—placed them there before they were communicated to me, and before I ever saw them; placed them there, as I cannot but think, in an evil hour for yourselves."

"So of all the rest of those vile specifications affecting my integrity and veracity. Bring me where I can confront the witnesses by which you have *ever* hoped to prove them, and I will brand "FALSE" upon the forehead of every one of them, with a stamp that shall burn to the bone.

This I expected to be allowed to do when I accepted your call to go before a Council with you, upon those charges " as reasons for the dissolution of my connexion" with you. This I had a right to expect. I have long expected, and I expect it yet. I have waited patiently for that time to come. For fifteen weeks I waited for your " Grounds of Complaint" to be forthcoming. Was not that long enough? If not, time was your own,—why not have taken fifteen weeks more? But they appeared at last, leaning for support, upon those false and libelous specifications; and now, after thirteen weeks more of negotiation, during which your call was accepted on my part, a council agreed upon by both parties, and defeated—you shall say by which—I am asked to go before a council upon a list of complaints from which all those accusations of fraud and falsehood are left out, on the ground that their character prevented some of the churches invited upon the council from accepting the invitation! Gentlemen, we have just heard of an attempt upon the life of the French king. In the heartiness of his hate, the regicide had rammed his carbine so full of bullets and buck-shot that the barrel burst and tore his assassin hand. Have you, gentlemen, loaded your piece so deep, that neither will the churches come within *hearing* of it, nor even your council stand by you when you let it off? And do you now "call" upon me to wait awhile, that you may draw the heaviest of your balls, and then let you try the rest? Gentlemen, I commend your caution in this, but I cannot consult your convenience.

No, gentlemen; as individuals, and as a body, you have made an atrocious attack upon my character, not as a clergyman only, but as a man; and when you consider that in morals, as well as in physics, action and reaction are equal, you will see at once, that the blow, if not fatal to me, will be so to yourselves. To me it is fatal if your charges are true; to you, if they are false and malicious. *Either meet me upon them or retract them.* I demand it of you, that if you do not retract them as above suggested, you carry me before a council, convoked expressly—not to attend to something else first, and then to take *them* up, if perchance they are of a mind to but—for the trial of your case as presented in your "Grounds" of last July, and with the knowledge, on the part of the council, that it is to take cognizance of those charges, and in your own words, "to deliberate and decide thereupon;" a council before which I can confront both my accusers and their witnesses. Or, if you will not do this, I think you will have no good reason to complain, if, remembering that not only as a clergyman, but as a citizen, I am under the protection of the laws, I carry you where you will be compelled either to plead "guilty," in an action of libel, or to come yourselves, with your witnesses, where I *can* confront you both."

I have said that Pierpont was a fine logician. His logic was distinguished from that article as employed by most men. It was not the hard, dry logic of the metaphysician, but rather an animated, ornamented article, having as it were the freshness of the dew-damp lawn, and the fragrance of flowers about it. Strong as iron, but ever with a touch of poetry to set it off. So, too, much of his verse was didactic, rhymed argument, philosophy, and logic on fire, and measured in dactyls perhaps, or Spencerian stanzas. Some able men who possessed both the logical, and the poetic faculties, have, like John Milton, given us splendid arguments, and immortal verse, but rarely on the same page. Many articles from the pen of Pierpont could be quoted in which we have both in a delightful compound.

A few extracts from some of his writings will, I think, justify the statement, that unlike most writers, he could put logic, and the very soul of poetry into the same stanzas.

From a poem which first appeared, if I rightly recollect, in 1834, in which he gave the license system such a tremendous blow, I make the following extracts:

> " For so much gold we license thee,"
>   So say our laws, " a draught to sell,
> That bows the strong, enslaves the free,
>   And opens wide the gates of hell;
> For ' public good' requires that some
> Should live, since many die, by rum."
>
> " And will ye give to man a bill
>   Divorcing him from Heaven's high sway,
> And, while God says, ' thou shalt not kill'—
>   Say ye, ' for gold, ye may,—ye may?'
> Compare the body with the soul!
> Compare the bullet with the bowl!"

> "In which is felt the fiercer blast
>   Of the destroying angel's breath?
> Which binds its victim the more fast?
>   Which kills him with the deadlier death?
> Will ye the felon fox restrain
> And yet take off the tiger's chain?"

The following stanza from a later poem, will, I think, further contribute to justify the opinion I have expressed of the peculiar character of his writings.

> "The prisoner's cell, that all
>   Life's blessed light bedims,
> The lash that cuts, the links that gall
>   The poor slaves festering limbs,—
> What is this thraldom, to the chain
> That binds and burns the drunkard's brain?"

Beside the faculties I have referred to, he possessed others which fitted him in an eminent degree to render to a great reformatory work like that in which we are engaged, incalculable service. Every vile system and every debasing vice has about it certain points or phases which render it fair game for ridicule and expose it to the laugh even of good men. The poet Pollock, it may be remembered, in his "Course of Time," makes hypocrisy appear not only a sin against God, but so supremely ridiculous that the spirits even of good men cannot resist the inclination to laugh at it, even before the bar of final judgment.

> "The righteous smiled, and even Despair itself
>   Some signs of laughter gave."

No wicked system that curses this earth presents so many ridiculous aspects as that with which we are contending. Think of a human being outside an asylum for idiots, sucking a mint julep through a straw. Think for a moment of distinguished gentlemen around a public table, bobbing and bowing to each other across it, and drinking to the health of " Her Majesty," or " Our excellent President," or " Count von Bismark." Why not nod or grin, hem, cough, or sneeze to his health, instead of drinking to it? It would be a safer operation. A simultaneous nod or grin or hem could be given by the whole company without injury to stomach or brain, to intellect or morals. But all this will not do. We must *drink* to the health of something. No matter what, a Prince, a President, or a Donkey, so that men can make an occasion for another drink.

Reader, think of this—and think, too, of many other tom-fooleries enacted in connection with the drink system, and then tell me if a keen sense of the ludicrous, wit, and ability to deal in biting sarcasm would not be desirable faculties for one who should attack such a system. All these Pierpont possessed in an eminent degree. His poem, entitled " The Lament of the Albany Brewers," is all we care to adduce to prove him possessed of wit, not a whit behind that of Butler, as exemplified in " Hudibras."

Mr. Delevan had made a terrible expose of the character of Albany ale, or beer. The wealthy brewers brought an action against him for the injury he had inflicted upon their business, and laid their damages at $100,000. In the legal trial of the case they were beaten, as Mr. Delevan proved all he had stated. He proved that the pond from which they obtained water for their brewing purposes was a common receptacle for dead animals; that the drainage of a certain slaughter-house and glue factory was into that pond. For the purposes of the trial and to aid the jury in understanding the case, a map was made of the pond, and the particular points where this or that fact occurred, sworn to by the witnesses, was indicated by figures. At No. 6, a certain swine had gone to pieces just in the edge of the water, after, of course, his breathing had been stopped by disease. There, at No. —, dead dogs had been seen floating, and there, a horse had decomposed, &c., &c. A pamphlet containing a report of the trial, with the explanatory map, reached Mr. Pierpont, and as he read, that fine brain of his conceived the idea of helping the brewers express, in a style which they never could have equaled, their regrets over the prospective ruin of their business as the result of this exposé. That job was done *con amore*, and the man who can read that poem without sore sides, should never be expected to laugh again. I shall never lose the recollection of the pleasure I derived from hearing the poem read by its author from the manuscript copy, in his own study. It afforded a joy for memory.

Having concluded the reading, he remarked, with just a touch of sadness, "After all, I fear I have labored in vain, for I doubt if I shall be able to get the article before the public through any proper channel. I sent it to our mutual friend, Marsh, and he declines to publish it in the 'Temperance Journal,' fearing a legal attack from the brewers." "I think Damrell will venture to publish it," I replied. "Allow me to read it to him this eve, and I will soon let you know his conclusion." He put the manuscript in my hands, and I had another treat in reading it to that sterling friend of the cause, Wm. S. Damrell. He decided at once that he would share with me the responsibility of publishing it. We got that comical genius, D. C. Johnston, to illustrate the subject in a proper drawing, representing the pond, the slaughter-house, glue factory, the dead animals, &c., &c., *in situ*, with which, from a plain wood cut, we embellished our sheet. We give our readers a specimen verse or two, and shall, ere long, reprint the poem entire, illustrated, as our contribution for 1871 to the popularity of Albany ale. Whether it has improved in quality since the trial of Mr. Delevan, I am not informed.

I hope the reader is aware of the fact that the water used in the manufacture of the famous London porter, is taken from the river Thames, into which thousands of sewers empty; and it is urged, in general, that water rich in impurities makes the better beer.

Referring to the proved fact that a certain swine had decomposed just in the edge of the pond from which they obtained water for their vats, the poet makes them exclaim:—

> "Thou ponderous porker, who wert numbered six
> Upon the map in Delevan's report!
> Who didst sink into our Albanian styx,
> And rise again before the Circuit Court;
> Like sightless Sampson, there thou madest sport
> For temperance Philistines; but 'tis clear
> The very place for thee was in our wort.
> Why should not we, who have from year to year
> Our beer in hogsheads put—put hogsheads in our beer?"

Again, in the most touching manner, he makes the

brewers acknowledge their obligations to the dogs, which decomposing in the pond, had helped them to give "body" to their beer.

> "Ye murdered dogs, who, when ye had your day,
> Were wont by moonlight o'er yon graves to howl;
> Who from cash customers would walk away,
> But at the ragged ones would turn and growl;
> Though round our premises no more ye prowl,
> Against the loafer to keep watch and ward,
> Still do ye serve us, though reformers scowl;
> For since ye dangled in the strangling cord,
> Ye've helped make many a lout as tipsy as a lord."

The services rendered the brewers by the slaughter house is thus acknowledged:

> "Bullocks, who bellowed just before your blood
> Was, for our benefit, poured out like water,
> Dreamed ye, as erst ye lay and chewed the cud,
> That from yon house where ye were led to slaughter,
> There would drain down for many a blowzy daughter
> Of our good city, who sits guzzling ale,
> Such real stuff? Our trial now hath taught her,
> (Grew she not, as she read it, very pale?)
> That from your horns and hoofs there hangeth quite a tale."

It would occupy too many of our pages even to make a catalogue of the contributions of this master mind to the literature of our enterprise. Very many of the strongest arguments against the use of intoxicants and the liquor traffic now effectively employed by all advocates of the cause, were first mined and hammered into shape by that massive brain. He was a laborious student, and studied thoroughly every phase of a great question before he gave to the public his views thereon.

His forms of expression, which were very iron for strength, had also a *finish* which the most delicate taste and the most consumate skill in the use of language only could give. His public discourses, which, when studied, were always able and aptly illustrated, had one striking peculiarity which distinguished them from all other temperance discourses to which it has been my fortune to listen. They bristled with sharp points which could never be forgotten by the hearer. Those who never listened to him will best understand me from a few examples.

Contrasting, on a certain occasion, the liquor traffic with other offences against society, he said:

"The highwayman, from his lurking place, springs into your path, and, presenting a pistol to your head, demands your money. But mark his language: 'Your money *or* your life.' Here, now, is a chance for you to choose; and as men generally prefer to part with their money on the instant rather than their lives, you give up your purse, and the chances are that thus you save your life. But what is the language of the liquor-seller as he passes over the counter or bar his infernal poisons? 'Your money *and* your life.'"

Such utterances, accompanied by appropriate gestures, and that expression of intense earnestness with which he was wont to utter his thoughts, fastened his words in your memory as securely as bearded hooks may be fastened in the flesh. On one occasion, where the use of a commodious house of worship had been denied to the friends of temperance for the reason that, if used by them, the carpets, which were new, would be soiled, Mr. Pierpont, in his speech on the occasion, said: "Perhaps it may be best, though I beg leave to doubt it, to keep the *carpets clean* and let *the souls go dirty*."

No man better understood the importance of emphasizing just the right word.

On one occasion the writer had commented, in his hearing, on the prohibition of wine to the priesthood of that age—Aaron and his sons—and recited the passage which indicates the penalty of disobedience — "Lest ye die."

At the close of the service, Mr. Pierpont grasped my hand, and with an expression of earnestness which burned his words into my memory, said, "Doctor, bear hard on that *Ye*. Strong emphasis on that one word, only can bring out the full force of that passage."

Let the reader study carefully and critically the tenth chapter of Leviticus, and he will rightly estimate the value of that suggestion.

I cannot close this imperfect sketch of this great man and earnest reformer, without expressing the hope that some one competent to the task, will collect the most important, if not all his writings and reported speeches in reference to the temperance question, and give them to the public in a fitting form, with such explanations of the circumstances under which they were written or uttered, as will greatly enhance their interest, not only to earnest friends of temperance, but to the general reader.

That our departed friend held opinions on religious and other subjects which many good men regarded as unsound, is undoubtedly true. His opinions in relation to the sale and use of intoxicants were by many thought false and quite revolutionary, but that fact did not prove them false. He was an independent thinker, and was governed by his own convictions, and not those of other people. Those personally acquainted with him could not doubt that his expressed opinions, on every subject, were honestly entertained and conscientiously advocated.

If, for any cause, that glorious spirit is denied, in the world to which it has gone, the companionship of the good and the pure, of those who love righteousness and hate iniquity, injustice, and wrong, in every form and shape and degree, it must be to him indeed an infinite misfortune, for he ever sought such companionship on earth, and was never happy in any other. Beside, such a catastrophe would involve him in eternal war, for if doomed to the society of the vile, the profoundly selfish, extortioners, unjust, unmerciful, impure, and brutal, he will make trouble among them, unless his spirit has greatly changed since it left the earth, for such had never any peace or quiet *here*, in his neighborhood.

CHAPTER XV.

"THERE WERE GIANTS IN THOSE DAYS."

L. M. Sargent—Personal peculiarities—The Temperance Tales—A Damascus blade well employed—"Deacon Giles' Distillery"—Providential and grand results—Father Taylor—Word painting—Eloquence.

Another of our champions, whose influence was even more extended than that of John Pierpont, was Lucius M. Sargent, Esq., author of the "Temperance Tales." The history of the reform in New England, could scarcely be rendered intelligible to an individual in a distant section of the country, without some knowledge of our three great champions. Subtract from the history of the enterprise from the year 1833 to 1843, all notice of the labors of *either* of those men, and you would leave a sad blank. In the retrospect I see not how either could have been spared.

Mr. Sargent inherited wealth, received a collegiate education, and studied for the legal profession, which, however, he never practised, partly because he did not need the avails of it, and partly because his literary tastes drew his thoughts and diverted his labors into other channels.

Before visiting Boston, in 1838, I had read a number of the "Temperance Tales," had dropped tears on the

L. M. SARGENT.

pages of "John Hodges, the Blacksmith," and "Fritz Hazel," and had laughed my sides sore over "Groggery Harbor," and I exulted in the prospective influence of those splendid contributions to the literature of the infant enterprise. During the year 1838 I saw the author for the first time in the Odeon at Boston, in the convention where was formed the "Massachusetts Temperance Union." His physique was one of the finest I ever saw. More than six feet in height by an inch or two, straight as an arrow, broad-shouldered, and very muscular. A glance at that peculiar form would readily enable one to believe the story of his tossing a fellow who insulted him over the high iron fence which surrounds Boston Common. Temperance men who made themselves at all prominent, had to bear very many insults from rum-pickled crowds in those days. Most of us bore them in silence, and passed on, but L. M. Sargent was about the last man on earth to do so. Conscious of his great physical power, and exceedingly sensitive, he allowed no man to elbow him off the sidewalk, or insult him with impunity. A stalwart drayman, with whiskers like the mane of a buffalo, interfered at one time, when Mr. S. was having some sharp words with a gentleman on the street.

Mr. Sargent grasped him by his whiskers, and turning his face up the street, remarked in a very decided tone, but in courteous phrase, "Sir, you were walking in *that* direction when you stopped; please to walk on." The drayman needed no further admonition, but as he moved off cast a glance back at the man who had dared to grasp, thus rudely, his magnificent whiskers, but a view of those mighty shoulders impressed him with the truth of Falstaff's conclusion, that "the better part of valor is discretion." Though a man of great kindness of heart, and like every *true* gentlemen *most* kind and courteous to the poorest and humblest of men, he was dignified and punctilious in his intercourse with his peers. There was a hauteur about him which repelled rudeness. No man ever slapped him upon the shoulders, and called him a good fellow, or inquired "how are you my hearty?" Although I enjoyed his personal friendship for many years, and esteemed and loved him much, I should as soon have thought of taking liberties with a locomotive when whirling the "Lightning Express" along at the rate of forty miles an hour. Yet his heart was as tender as a woman's. His eye moistened instantly at the sight of real misery, and I doubt if any man could have retained for an hour any hold on his personal esteem, after treating with cruelty, in his presence, the smallest creature which serves or is dependent on man.

At what precise date he wrote "My Mother's Gold Ring," the first of the series of "Temperance Tales," I know not, nor is it material. In the Mass. Temperance Journal, for Aug. 1837, I find a notice that that excellent tract had been translated into the German, and published by the Hamburg Tract Society. In another copy of the Journal for the same year, in advertising a new number of the series, the editor or publisher speaks of it as the fourteenth number. The series was finally extended to nineteen. So it seems the most of them were written prior to the close of the year 1837.

In the way of tales or stories, those of Mr. Sargent had a popularity and a circulation more extensive than anything of the kind which the reform had yet produced. Thousands of men before the year 1840 had been converted to the doctrine and practice of abstinence by their perusal—many of them by the perusal of a single number of the series. Although the stories, as such, are of absorbing interest, drawing the reader along from page to page, with a charm almost irresistible, yet the fact, stated I believe in the preface to one of them, should be known by all readers, that they are *genuine histories*, embellished.

Knowing the deep interest of Mr. S. in the cause, gentlemen visiting Boston from different sections of the country would call upon him, and in conversation, relate to him the histories of individuals or families, which had greatly interested them. These histories constituted the frame work of those admirable productions. As he was one of the most profound scholars in the country, and one of its most vigorous writers, with an inexhaustible fund of humor, and a power of pathos which could melt any really human heart, and considering too, the fruitfulness of his theme, and that he was quite at leisure, and able, therefore, to bestow on their production any amount of labor he desired, we ought to have expected great excellence in the work, and indeed we have it.

The prefaces of the series, being as it were, so many essays on different phases of the temperance question, would of themselves constitute one of the most instructive little volumes which could be placed in the hands of an individual who had become already somewhat interested in the subject, and desired more light and knowledge in relation to it.

If by a blow from some powerful fiend, visible or otherwise, all opposition to the liquor system could be annihilated, and with it all the temperance men and women now living, with all the publications and instrumentalities of whatever sort, with which we have ever assailed that system,—saving only from the general wreck " Lyman Beecher's Six Sermons on Intemperance," " Sargent's Temperance Tales," and the poem of Wm. H. Burleigh, entitled the " The Rum Fiend," they alone, ought, among any civilized people who can read, to originate another temperance reform, and to give it a glorious forward impetus.

The composition of the Temperance Tales, though a work of immense service to the cause, was, by no means, the only aid afforded it by Mr. Sargent. His pen was constantly employed for years, in exposing the vile and destructive character of the liquor traffic, and the folly and wickedness of licensing it; in arguing by tongue and pen the simplicity, economy, and efficiency of our system of warfare upon it, through our organizations pledged to abstinence, the education of the popular mind, and, when we should be prepared for it, the legal suppression of the traffic. Leaving to less able and less favored brethren the defense of the cause against ordinary assaults, he reserved his fire for its most dangerous and powerful assailants. When a distinguished divine ventured to assail the doctrine of total abstinence, as "fanatical, unscriptural, and absurd," it required but a few articles from the pen of Sargent to settle the question with him. When Bishop Hopkins of Vermont attacked our doctrines and measures, Sargent impaled him on his quill in a way that has saved us from any further attacks from so exalted a dignitary of the Church. No other Bishop has since ventured to repeat the absurdity, that "the triumph of the Temperance Cause would be the triumph of Infidelity." When the passage of the law of '38 called to the front the twelve great liquor dealers of Boston, with Daniel L. Gibbens at their head, with their address to the people, the pen of Sargent made short work with their address; and those gentlemen had the entire remnant of their useless lives in which to repent of their folly, which had for ten good rounds made them his target. The petition for the repeal of the law of 1838, headed by the Hon. Harrison Gray Otis, again summoned him to a work of demolition; for at the conclusion of his critical and masterly review of that plausible and dangerous document, the falsity of its statements and the unsoundness of its logic were made to appear so distinctly, that its author, whoever he may have been, must have been heartily ashamed of its production.

At a very advanced age—above eighty—this noble champion of our cause died, as he had lived, universally respected.

There was another early and able champion of our cause, the influence of whose labors I everywhere met in New England, but whose personal acquaintance I was not so fortunate as to make until very recently, the Rev. George B. Cheever. The masterly exposé of the character and influence of the liquor business, made by him in that famous production, "Deacon Giles' Distillery," though it subjected him to attacks both personal and legal, and called forth an immense amount of childish whining from timid friends and scores of apologies from the extra-wise and prudent, was notwithstanding one of the most masterly, timely, and effective blows ever inflicted on the liquor system up to the date of its publication, 1835. Mr. Cheever was prosecuted for a libel on one Deacon Stone, of Salem, who it was supposed sat for the portrait of "Deacon Giles," and as the result, spent some time in jail. His sufferings there, however, could not have been great, for he had the comfort of knowing that he had given a blow to a wicked system which was felt; and beside, the ladies of the city, who instinctively felt that he had been fighting a battle for them, their homes and most precious earthly interests, carpeted his room in jail, and sent day by day choice dinners to the royal prisoner, enough to have fed a considerable company. They stood by their champion through his trial and imprisonment with that devotion and untiring perseverance characteristic of true women where their intellects and hearts have both become enlisted in a good cause and in the defence of its supporters. This attempt to muzzle the press in relation to the liquor question came at a fortunate time, and the most fortunate circumstance about the whole affair, as we now see it in the light of subsequent events, was the partial success of the opposition in getting our champion into jail.

The fact was chronicled by the press throughout the country, that a learned and popular clergyman of Salem, Mass., was in jail for writing a very ingenious and sharp article, reflecting on the character and influence of the liquor business, especially of its production. Intense curiosity was at once excited in the public mind to see the production which had occasioned such an outburst of rum-wrath, and the demand was urgent on the conductors of public journals that they would give "Deacon Giles' Distillery" a place in their columns. Thus it got a very general publication, and the important truths embodied in that splendid production found their way to the minds of thousands who would never have seen the article but for the trial and imprisonment of its author. Thus it was in the days of Paul. The enemies of the new religion thought to hinder its progress by silencing, if possible, its most learned and eloquent advocate, and so violently did they pursue him that his life was in danger. Feeling assured that he could not have a fair trial among those who had crucified the faultless Master, he appealed unto Cæsar, and his exasperated enemies were compelled to send him to Rome. The authorities there, feeling little interest in mere questions of Jewish law, and profoundly impressed with the noble bearing and eloquence of that Christian hero, set him at liberty, and the first use he made of it was to preach Christ the Saviour of men to those around him, including the highest officers of the government. Hence the remark of a pious old divine, that the Devil and his special friends had, through the overruling Providence of God, been made the instruments of sending the first missionary to the heathen, and that too, at a time when the infant church was too weak in numbers and in wealth to have done so.

My readers who may be curious to see the admirable article which made so much stir in 1835, will find it at the Rooms of the National Temperance Society and Publication House, in New York.

Another gentleman of the clerical profession who ex-

erted considerable influence in favor of the cause during
the second decade in its history, reckoning from its origin
in 1826, was the Rev. E. T. Taylor, of Boston, the
very celebrated seaman's preacher. During the period
named, his voice was heard in nearly all the cities and
larger towns of New England, in favor of the reform.
A regard for strict truth, however, compels me to add,
that his views of the subject were greatly modified by
surrounding circumstances, and that the general knowledge
of that fact seriously impaired his influence. He
was a man of impulse, and the state of the weather—
of his health—the character and conduct of his audience
or any circumstance that impressed him strongly at the
time, determined the character of his utterances to a surprising
extent. I have heard at times bursts of eloquence
from him that produced with me, and I presume with
all present, an absolute forgetfulness, for the moment,
of all else on this planet or elsewhere, except the matter
he was just then presenting; and I have heard him at
other times, when I have been perfectly amazed at the
utter inconsistency of the views expressed, not only with
any standard of doctrine recognized as sound by other
men, but with his own public utterances of, perhaps, the
week previous. His imagination once fairly excited
could furnish in thirty minutes material for half a dozen
speeches of an hour's length each; and unfortunately,
it frequently happened that different parts of the same
speech could be used on opposite sides of the same question.
He was, however, a man of honest purposes and
strong and warm affections, as well as of varying moods.
He drew large audiences, whatever subject he proposed
to discuss, for all men loved to hear " Father Taylor."

Rev. EDWARD T. TAYLOR.

If he happened to be right, you rejoiced in the good he was doing; if wrong, you were still charmed by the originality of his style, and the vivid word pictures of men and things, which in one of his best efforts followed each other in as rapid succession as do the varying scenes thrown on the canvass by a magic lantern when manipulated by skillful hands.

I have a very distinct recollection of his speech at a temperance soiree, gotten up by the ladies of Charlestown, Massachusetts, in the year 1843, if I rightly remember. All matters connected with it had been happily arranged, and "Father Taylor" was in one of his best moods. After presenting to the assembled throng some startling views of the terrible system on which the ladies were then waging a pretty vigorous war, he closed by one of those bursts of eloquence which it would seem impossible to forget. Scores, perhaps hundreds now living in sight of the granite shaft will remember the occasion, and if they shall peruse these pages will bear witness to the accuracy of the report I am about to make of his words after the lapse of almost thirty years.

"And here it is yet, the accursed system to plague and torture us, although we have exposed its villainies until it would seem that Satan himself ought to be ashamed to have any connection with it—I am not sure but he is—but some of his servants have more brass and less shame than their master. Yes! here it is yet, and over there, too, in the great city—the Athens of America, where the church spires as they point upward, are almost as thick as the masts of the shipping along the wharves—all the machinery of the drunkard-making, soul-destroying business is in perfect running order from the low grog holes on the dock—kept open to ruin my poor sailor boys—to the great black establishments in Still House square, which are pouring out the elements of death, even on God's Holy Day, and sending up a smoke as from the pit forever and ever!

"And your wives and daughters, even as they walk to their churches on Sunday, brush the very skirts of their silk dresses against the mouths of open grog shops that gape by the way. And your poor-houses are full, and your courts and prisons are filled with the victims of this infernal rum traffic, and your homes are full of sorrow, and the hearts of your wives and mothers; and yet, the system is tolerated. Yes! and when we ask some men what is to be done about it, they tell you, you can't stop it! No, you *can't* stop it! and yet, (darting across the platform and pointing in the direction of the monument, he exclaimed in a voice that pierced one's ears like the blare of a trumpet,) there's Bunker Hill! and you say you can't stop it—and up yonder is Lexington, and Concord, where your fathers fought for the right, and bled, and died—and you look on those monuments and boast of the heroism of your fathers, and then tell us we must submit to be taxed and tortured by this rum business, and we can't stop it! No! and yet, (drawing himself up to his full height and expanding his naturally broad chest as though the words he would utter had blocked up the usual avenues of speech and were about to force their way out by an explosion, he exclaimed in a sort of whispered scream,) Your Fathers—your patriotic Fathers—could make a cup of tea for his Britannic Majesty out of a whole cargo—and you can't cork up a gin-jug! Ha!"

And such was "Father Taylor." His name and fame had reached distant states and cities, and distinguished scholars and statesmen would, when in Boston on the Sabbath, find their way to the Mariner's Chapel to listen to the man of the sea, who got his diploma before the mast; whose theology was about as variable as the winds and the weather, and yet whose earnestness and native eloquence had power to captivate and hold in rapt attention, often for a full hour, the most gifted and highly cultivated in the land, while bringing tears to the eyes of bronzed and hard men, as he cheered the desponding, startled the thoughtless and indifferent, and awakened in the breasts of many of the charmed circle before him, aspirations for a higher and better life.

Beside these prominent champions of the cause, there were many whose names are graven on my memory, not only for their steady devotion to the work of reform, but also for their great kindness to me personally, while I labored in Massachusetts. The brothers Tappan, John, and Charles, who lived but to serve God and man, a kind of service with which the labor of a life rendered both of them familiar. And there, too, was Huntington, of Salem, and Choat, of Essex; Bartlett, of Concord, and his brother in medicine, Boutell, of Fitchburg, and his neighbor the indomitable, indefatigable, irrepressible Trask, who not only warred on Rum, but his twin-brother, Tobacco. And there was our great surgeon, Warren, famous in his own profession and scarcely less so as an early and devoted friend of temperance; and our good Deacon Grant, of Boston, the friend of the poor, the friend of all men, even of *bad* men, although no friend to their pernicious practices and evil influence. Many pages would be required to make simply a catalogue of the names of the good men whose memories are still fresh and fragrant with me, who stood shoulder to shoulder in our ranks during the ten years I served the old Bay State.

It is one of the felicities of a life devoted to some grand reform movement, that it brings one in contact with the best spirits of the time and country, and secures, even to a plain man like me, ennobling friendships. Had I been worldly-wise, stuck to my profession, looked out for the "main chance," and turned all my energies in that direction, I might, perhaps, have acquired wealth; but I would not exchange the memories of the last forty years, devoted to the temperance reform, for a good many shares of bank or railroad stocks. Now, I can call around me by the aid of memory and a little imagination, a host of the good and true, with whom my work has made me acquainted. I see them even with closed eyes. They come trooping at my call, from all points of the compass. I am charmed with their shadowy presence, until possessed by the illusion, I am almost ready to rise and exclaim, "Mr. President, and Gentlemen of the Convention."

What could a large fortune do for me or mine, should my life be protracted to seventy or eighty years? It might fill a splendid home with elegant furniture. But a comfortable old-fashioned cushioned chair, with its stout legs and strong supporting arms, would minister more to the comfort of an old man, than costly furniture. Wealth could cover the walls of my library with elegant pictures, but it could not give me young eyes to gaze upon them. It could cover my table with luxuries, but simple, plain food is generally better suited to the wants of the aged, and with men who have lived as they ought, is better relished than costly viands and high-seasoned dishes. Wealth could procure me a splendid turn-out, like that of Bonner, or some other millionaire, but a particularly low-wheeled carriage, with a very gentle horse of moderate gate, would give an old man a more comfortable airing on a fine morning, than a dashing team of horses of two-forty pace, and the most costly carriage in the world. Had I desisted from reformatory efforts, and been guided by those senseless maxims, "Take the world as you find it"—i. e., don't trouble yourself about making it any better, but make it subserve your selfish purposes—and, "Look out for number one," or in plain phrase, bestow no time or thought on the welfare or happiness of others, &c., &c., I might have been rich; but that wealth might have spoiled my six boys, who, while their father was at work to promote temperance, grew up to industrious and frugal habits, and all together never cost me an hour's sorrow. Had I acquired wealth, I might have sent my two daughters to fashionable boarding-schools, to learn a little French and German, a little rhetoric and music, and a good deal that young ladies do not learn so often at home, ignorance of which is not only "bliss," but something better—purity. I have never spent a summer at Saratoga—could not afford it. I have been there on two or three occasions, to attend temperance conventions, and got away in the first train after their close. Was impressed while there with the notion that nine are injured in health and morals by the fashionable dissipation of Saratoga, where one is benefited in health by his sojourn there. To sum up in a word, had I sacrificed my "hobby," as my friends termed it, and devoted myself to my profession, and acquired wealth, that wealth could have added nothing to my personal happiness, or that of my family, and would now be a miserable possession, as compared with the memories of a life devoted to the reformation, education, and elevation of my fellow-men. My only regrets are that I have not done more, and done all, better, and that I have very often been unable to get my notions adopted by my fellow-laborers, who, though perhaps just as earnest friends of temperance as I am or ever was, and very likely better men otherwise, had never given a tenth-part of the time to the study of the subject that I have done. Hence, I have been grieved to witness disaster and defeat at times, when I know that I could have engineered, and led our forces to assured success and victory.

The sorest trials I have ever experienced in life, except the death of very near and dear friends, has been in witnessing a slow progress of a blessed enterprise which might by the use of proper means, entirely within our reach, have been sent forward with railroad speed; to witness partial defeats where we might have rejoiced over glorious victories, and to see the continued existence of a destructive system which could have been crushed in any one of our states where common schools have done their work, within the space of ten years, by the hearty, continuous, and well-directed efforts of those who have been, during that period, total abstainers from all intoxicants. The tax on their *time* should not have been greater than one evening per week, and two or three days a year for general meetings or conventions for consultation and discussion; not, however, for entertainment or steamboat excursions. The tax on their purses should not have exceeded twenty-five cents per month. If it were proper I would risk my head on the destruction of the liquor system within the period named, by a certain plan of operations, simple, peaceable, and not more expensive in time or money than what I have stated. My brethren will not adopt it, however, either because *they* have some plan of their own to which they may have devoted forty hours in all, it may be, instead of forty years; or because they will not sit down coolly, and in the light of history, of passing events, and right reason, consider the subject. They have not time, or think they have not, but must go ahead, on some ill-considered plan, until mortified, disheartened by successive failures, they are often discouraged, and quit the field.

We have no recognized Von Moltke in our enterprise, though wherever we have had any decided victories, it was because we had, on that particular field, a recognized leader. He may have been a modest man, who made no claims to leadership, but, nevertheless, he led.

Methodism lives through all mutations, and goes on conquering still. Why? Its communion is not a more intelligent or more holy body of Christians than some others. It works on a plan perfected in the mind of one man—John Wesley. The Suspension Bridge which spans that awful chasm at Niagara, over which heavy railroad trains pass and re-pass with safety, was not planned by a committee, but is the product of one mind. All successful campaigns in war, from Julius Cæsar to Moltke, and all great and successful undertakings in all human affairs are due, first of all, under the Providence of God, to a one man power. Disaster, of course, comes if the wrong man is trusted with leadership; but when the right one comes, things move on to a grand issue, if the proper tools are but furnished. When Boston capitalists would, for manufacturing purposes, throw a great dam across the Connecticut river, at Hadley Falls, they employed an able engineer. He perfected his plan for the work and submitted it to them. They thought they could improve it in certain particulars. His reply was, " Gentlemen, I, as your servant, will carry out any suggestion you may make, and agree upon; but if you thus modify *my* plan, you must not hold me at all responsible if the work does not stand." Wealth had ministered to their vanity and self-confidence, and they did modify it. The work was finished. It was an imposing and splendid structure; but the old Connecticut, vexed at this obstruction, got up, not her blood, but her waters, and swept it away, and with it the self-confidence of the committee. They then told the engineer to build a dam on his own plan. He did so; and although that skillful architect has since been conquered by the great enemy, strong drink, and went down to an early grave, much lamented, yet that splendid work of his still stands, a monument of his skill. He proved himself more than a match for Connecticut river, but strong drink was more than a match for him, as it has been for thousands of others as able and as useful men. No committee ever planned a successful campaign or led a host to victory.

CHAPTER XVI.

Joseph Breck—A glass of Gin—Compare them, Sir—Frightened—A laugh all round—A cup of tea—A home question—What do *you* say?—A new patron—Our best hold—Gough, Gough!—Discussion, its value—The tipsy Son—Afflicted—The old story—Converted at a blow—Temperance Conventions, how effected—Ruminating—Only to travelers—Travelers on short routes—Pretty much burned out—The poor old Doctor—Expelled—Why is it? The Major—" Take him off "—Threatened—Satisfaction—Recovered—Trying it again—" Ten cents"—The whole cost.

Joseph Breck, the author of a work on flowers, had an agricultural and horticultural warehouse and seed store but a few rods from old Faneuil Hall. He was a fine specimen of a Christian gentleman, with a hand for every good work, and so genial and pleasant, withal, that he won the hearts of all acquaintances. Even bad men, whose vices he reproved, loved him; they could not help it. He was, of course, a staunch friend of temperance; and when weary with labor and a little below par on the score of energy and resolution, I used to run in and see friend Breck. A free and easy chat for half an hour with an intelligent, genial, and good man like him, is a better stimulant for both body and mind, than any bought at the wine stores. So when I was below par, I took a dose of Breck, varying the prescription, sometimes, to a dose of Whittemore, at the "Trumpet" office.

One day I dropped in at friend Breck's, and observed a fine old gentleman, gray and venerable, sitting with him, and at the desk, in an undertone, I inquired of Mr. B. who it was. He replied that it was Mr. Samuel Stewart,* formerly a merchant of Boston, who had acquired a fortune, and was then residing at Dorchester. "He is a fine old gentleman," said Breck; "a great lover and patron of Horticulture, but I cannot convert him to our notions in reference to temperance. He will insist on his glass of gin occasionally. I wish you could have a little talk with him on the subject." "I will," said I, "if you can bring up the subject for conversation." But how was the thing to be done? Easy enough, as you will see.

"Come here, pup, come here," said the old gentleman to Breck's dog, slapping his knee gently the while, to show Pompey how delicately he would caress him if he would approach in a friendly way. But Pomp kept at a respectful distance. "He is afraid of you, friend Stewart," said Breck, "and I think I can tell you the reason why. Dogs have a keen scent, and he has discovered that you use gin, and, being a regular teetotaler himself, he dare not come near you."

"Ha, ha, ha!" roared the grand old man, who seemed heartily to enjoy the joke. "Do you think that is it, Breck?"

"Certainly, certainly!" was the reply.

Here I interposed, and reproved friend Breck for insulting a venerable gentleman by insinuating that he drank gin.

---

* That is not the real name of the gentleman referred to, which is suppressed for obvious reasons.

"Well, I do," said he, "think of it as you will."

The subject was now fairly up for discussion. My venerable opponent brought out in succession the common arguments for the use of stimulants, especially for old people. I replied to them as presented, treating him, meanwhile, with the utmost respect, and avoiding as far as possible every needless cause of irritation. At length the old gentleman discovered that he had a hard road to travel, and, losing his temper, began to assail the whole host of pledged men as a set of hypocrites, who, with all their professions, drank behind the door.

"Hold on, sir," said I. "You are an old man, and I comparatively a young one, and in this discussion I have endeavored to treat you with that respect which I consider ever due to age, and however sharp you may be on me, personally, I shall not reply in kind. But I cannot allow you to charge all our pledged host with hypocrisy, for we have many men in our ranks as aged and quite as respectable every way as yourself. I shall defend such from your charges, even at the expense of your feelings."

"Well, do as you like," said he, for his blood was up. "I have given you my opinion. You are all a set of hypocrites. You drink behind the door," &c., &c.

I, in turn, began to be quite in earnest, and replied: "Sir, I thank God I have no cause to be ashamed of my associates in the temperance cause, and I am quite willing to compare our several parties, as you seem to court such a comparison. Look on the two and compare them, sir. You will see on our side the great mass of the active Christian men and women of Massachusetts, all men engaged in good and benevolent enterprises of whatever kind, our clergy, our educators, from the college down to our district and our Sabbath schools, they are mainly with us. Now, what have you on the other side? True, you have some respectable men, like yourself, but go down into the liquor saloons, and into the gambling hells and houses of prostitution, where are the representatives of every rascally business in the city, and they are all with your party, sir. Blear eyed and bloated, ragged and reeling, hundreds of them hurrying along to their graves, they are all with you. Why, sir, Falstaff's ragged regiment, which he swore he would not march through Coventry with, were a set of well-dressed gentlemen compared with a portion of your rank and file."

He looked at me for a moment in silence, and then burst into a roar of laughter at the way I had rattled off the facts to him, when he exclaimed: "Well, well! I don't know who you are! You are an odd one. You talk too fast for me. Yes, yes—too fast for me!"

"You say you don't know this man," said Breck. "Why, you ought to know him. He is pretty generally known throughout the state, and I'll warrant you have heard of him often enough. This, sir, is Doctor Charles Jewett, the temperance agent."

"The devil it is!" said the old gentleman, with a look of astonishment and alarm; and with that he made for the door, and hurried into the street, as though escaping from a tiger. My friend Breck leaned forward on his desk and roared in a perfect paroxysm of laughter, and one of his clerks, unable to stand, and seeing nothing else near to sustain him, stretched out on a big plough until the convulsion had subsided. The old gentleman's notions of Dr. Jewett had been derived from prejudiced parties, and he had, doubtless, pictured him a perfect monster, a reckless, savage fellow, ready almost to devour an opponent; and now to learn, thus suddenly, that he had been for a full half-hour within reach of that terrible animal—it was overwhelming, and he got out of that jungle as soon as possible.

When next the good old man visited Breck, he was, of course, rallied on his causeless fright. He was assured by my friend that I was, on the whole, rather a clever fellow, and that on further acquaintance he would find me so. For weeks and months, as often as he visited the store, (which he seldom failed to do when he came to the city,) some allusion would be made to his encounter with that terrible temperance fanatic, and a good hearty laugh all round would contribute to the present cheer, as well as the health of the parties.

Some months after this occurrence, I had occasion to visit Dorchester. There were in that town, as there were in most of the fine suburban towns about Boston, certain wealthy gentlemen who annually contributed to the funds of the "Temperance Union." I went out to call on our patrons for their annual subscription. Among other names I found that of Samuel Stewart, and inquired of a man whom I met where that gentleman resided. "There are two persons of that name in town," said he; "father and son." Here was a source of embarrassment. The gentleman suggested that a knowledge of my business with Mr. Stewart, if I felt free to state it, might indicate which of the men I was in pursuit of. I informed him. "Ah," said he, "it is the young man. You would never get a subscription for the temperance cause from the old gentleman, for, though a very temperate and excellent man, he will have his glass of gin, and has strong prejudices against your movements." I called at the residence of S. Stewart, Jr. He had not returned from Boston, would be at home in about an hour. What was I to do in the meantime? I thought it possible that there might be some mistake about it, and it might be the older Stewart after all. At any rate, even should my information be correct, it would do no harm to have a little chat with a fine old gentleman, if he did drink gin. So I resolved to call upon him.

All this while I had not associated the name with the affair in Breck's store. I rang the door-bell of the old man's stately mansion, and he himself answered the call. The instant I saw his face I recognized him. "Is this Mr. Samuel Stewart?" I inquired. He answered in the affirmative. "This is Dr. Jewett, sir, agent of the 'Temperance Union.'" "Ah—yes—well—yes—I recollect you, doctor. I met you at my friend Breck's, in Boston. Walk in, sir, walk in, I am happy to see you." I stated the nature of my business. "Well, come, sir, I am about to sit down to my tea," said he; "I am quite alone, I like company. Throw off your coat, sir, and take a cup of tea with me."

Compliance with such an invitation at the hour of five or six, P. M., is the most natural thing in the world for me when circumstances will permit. So down we sat at the table. Reader, you will err greatly if you imagine me green enough to enter just then at once on the subject of temperance. I have studied men too much for that. So, by a reference to his fine fruit yards, I drew the conversation to the subject of fruit culture. He had paid much attention to it practically. So had I, and I had studied the science of the subject, as well, and we had a talk which I found was not altogether uninteresting or uninstructive to him.

But the time is passing, and we must draw the conversation somehow to the temperance enterprise, and how? That was the question for the moment. I soon fixed on a plan, which will develope itself in the subsequent dialogue.

"They tell me, sir, that your town is growing very rapidly, that it has nearly doubled its population within the last eight years." He confirmed the truth of the statement. "In connection with that fact I have heard a statement which, if it be a fact, also seems very remarkable."

"What is that?" he inquired.

"That while you have nearly doubled your population, there has been an actual falling off in the amount of your pauperism, that you have fewer paupers now than when your population was about half its present number."

"Well," said he, "as to that, I had learned that our pauperism had been reduced, but I did not know exactly to what extent."

I told him of whom I had my information.

"Oh, well, then it is so," said he. "He is a reliable man, and knows all about that matter."

"Well, now, Mr. Stewart, that is a remarkable fact. *What influence has been operating among your people to produce such a very desirable result?*"

There was but one truthful answer to be made to that

question. I well knew that, and it remained to be seen if he knew it. If he did know it, and would admit it, that admission would involve a pretty severe reflection on his own past indifference to the claims of the temperance cause.

He saw the trap, and sought to avoid it thus. "Well, I suppose *you* would say that it was the influence of the temperance cause in town to which we are indebted for this change."

I would not let him dodge it thus, but immediately added, "Never mind what *I* would say, I am not a citizen of the town, and am unacquainted with its history; my opinion would not be worth much in relation to the matter; but, Mr. Stewart, what do *you* say?

"Well," said he, with an honesty which was characteristic of the man, "if I must state my opinion, I believe *that* is it."

I have you now! thought I, and I was determined to push my advantage, kindly, but earnestly. "If the increasing temperance of your people, and the diminution of the liquor traffic in town has really reduced your pauperism, while you have doubled your population, it must, in the meantime, have done great good in other directions. It must have improved the condition of many families, who, though poor, have never asked aid of the town, and it must have contributed greatly to the domestic happiness of your people."

"Undoubtedly, undoubtedly!" said the good old man.

"And still further, sir, it must have contributed to the general improvement of the morals and intelligence of your people."

"Why yes, yes," said he, "it could hardly be otherwise."

"Well, Mr. Stewart," I inquired, "ought not an enterprise which produces such admitted and desirable results, to receive the countenance, good wishes, and patronage of all good citizens?"

"Yes," said he, promptly and decidedly; and with a thoughtful and rather sad expression of countenance, he added, "and now that the matter has thus come fairly before me, I am inclined to the opinion that I have not done quite right about that matter heretofore, and I think I must make a small donation to your society," and with that he drew his pocket-book, and made his first donation to the temperance cause. The amount I have forgotten. It was less material than the fact that he had now determined to make some amends for past neglect. I thanked the kind old man in the name of the association I served, and added to the list of our patrons the name of Samuel Stewart, *Sr.* Thanking him further for his hospitality, and receiving from him an earnest invitation to call on him again whenever I should visit the town, I bade him good-day.

Immediately, I called upon his son. He had just returned from the city. I gave him my name, and stated my business.

"Yes, yes," said he, "I acknowledge my obligations always to sustain the temperance enterprise. It is a cause I shall always support while I am able to aid any. Let me see, what was the amount of my contribution last year? I opened to the page, and showed him, and as he saw there next his own, the name of his father, he started back with a look of surprise, and asked,

" When did you get that subscription ? "

" Within the last hour," I replied.

He seemed utterly amazed, and added, "I would not have believed it possible for any man to have obtained a subscription from my father for that object. Though never an intemperate man, he defends the moderate use, and has entertained very strong prejudices against temperance societies."

I told him I was aware of all that, and I recited to him the foregoing history of our encounter at Breck's, in Boston, and the discussion at his own tea-table. When I had concluded the history, he added, " Well, that alone pays me for all my contributions to the temperance cause."

I received his annual contributions, marked " paid," against Samuel Stewart, *Jr.*, and was soon on my way to the city, for the day was spent.

The foregoing history teaches, I think, that in discussing the temperance question, even with very decided opponents, good policy would indicate that it be done with courtesy and kindness, and that in such discussion the practical working of the enterprise is, to use the wrestler's phrase, " our best hold."

I will record here another incident, which, though slight in itself, may interest the reader, from its relation to subsequent events, which have interested vast numbers of people on both sides of the Atlantic.

At the close of a public lecture in the city of Worcester, Massachusetts, during the autumn of 1842, I remarked that I had learned with great pleasure that recent efforts there to advance the cause I had been advocating, had been attended with very gratifying success—in the reformation of quite a number who had suffered much in years past from intemperate habits—and that I had further learned that they were not only exhibiting to those around them the benefits of the change, by sober and well-ordered lives, but had in public meetings borne interesting testimony in relation to their new and happy experience. I said it would gratify me if some of the new converts would permit me to listen to their testimony. The President expressed the hope that some of the recently reformed brethren would gratify Dr. Jewett and the audience by some remarks. Calls immediately came from various parts of the hall, for Gough, Gough, Gough!

It was a new name to me, but seemed to have become quite well known to the people of Worcester. The President remarked that, if Mr. Gough was in the hall it would undoubtedly gratify all present if he would come forward and address the meeting. He did so, and I shall never forget the first sentence he uttered on that occasion. I had stated in my lecture that it had then been more than ten years since I had swallowed a glass of distilled liquors—and in alluding to that remark he said,

"Mr. President, and Ladies and Gentlemen, I should really like to know *exactly* how a man feels who has not had a glass of liquor in his stomach for ten years," and with that he went on to describe his experiences of the new life he was living, in the practice of abstinence from the use of intoxicating liquors. I cannot, of course, report his address. It was brief, and admirably adapted to the time and surrounding circumstances, and delivered in a manner indicating perfect self-possession, and with a fluency and easy command of language, remarkable from one of his age, and who could have had but little experience in public speaking. At the conclusion of his remarks, I was introduced to him, and when, after a few words, he turned away to converse with some of the crowd who seemed anxious to speak with him, I said to the President and others of the group near me, " Look well to that young man, for, if I mistake not, you will be able to use him to some purpose, hereafter." Reader, was I mistaken in the opinion I then and there expressed?

It is no part of my plan or purpose, in the preparation of this volume, to express opinions of fellow-laborers, who are now active in the work of reform, except as they were connected with some special movement I may have occasion to describe. If my purpose were otherwise I might well make Mr. Gough an exception—as he is so universally known, and has, through an ample and interesting volume, told the story of his eventful life.

While in the prime of life, and with greater power of endurance than I now possess, I was accustomed to improve every favorable opportunity to discuss the subject of temperance and the liquor system, with individuals, as well as before public assemblies, when I found a man disposed to defend the use and sale of liquors, for thus, and thus only, could I learn how the subject was regarded by such men as made up a part of every congregation I addressed. I could not, in public, combat successfully the views and arguments of opposers, unless I knew exactly what they were. This, I could only learn, to my satisfaction, by discussing the matter with individuals *outside* the lecture room. It mattered not who the man was, or what his position in society, a learned judge, or a hod-carrier, a doctor of divinity, or a hostler. Men in different walks of life, and with different degrees of education, would take widely different views of the subject, and I wished to learn them *all* as far as practicable. I shall have occasion, as I proceed with the history of my labor, and that of my cotemporaries, to refer frequently to these individual encounters, for some of them furnished rich material for reflection.

I had lectured one evening in Westboro', a fine old town in Worcester County, and the following day a message reached me, through a professional brother, Dr. Rising, that an old gentleman living a short distance from the town, wished to see and have a talk with me. He sent me word that he had plenty of beef and pork on hand, a pretty good supply of rum, and an excellent well of water, and he would make me quite welcome to a share of his good things if I would call. I proposed to the Doctor at once to ride out and see him, and together we visited the old man. After a fitting introduction by Dr. R., he began at once to state his objections to our doctrines and measures, which I answered as well as I could. By the time we had got fairly underway, one of the old man's sons came into the room, and seemed quite desirous to take part in the discussion. The father requested him to be silent, but all to no purpose. He had, thus early in the morning, drank enough to give him great confidence in his argumentative powers. He was determined to be heard, and therefore went on with his senseless gibberish, which was perfectly disgusting. The old man was overwhelmed with confusion, and left the room. I followed him into the front yard, and renewed my talk with him, while my friend, the doctor, very kindly managed to keep the senseless young man occupied in an argument upon "liberty," "equal rights," &c.

As I joined the old man in the yard, he remarked with a good deal of feeling, "everybody, sir, must have their troubles. That boy, sir, that boy, has made me a great deal of trouble."

I inquired if the misconduct of his son had not been caused solely by his use of intoxicating drinks.

"Oh yes," said he, "I suppose it has."

"Well, then, sir," I asked, "will you not aid us in the great work of reform, and help, by your example and influence, to banish from the earth an accursed system which has dashed your own cup with such bitter dregs?"

It was, with the afflicted old man, a moment of hesitation, of irresolution, and he knew not what to answer. Finding that his desire for a discussion of the temperance question had very suddenly abated, I bade him good morning, and with my friend, returned to town.

One of the most common of all mistakes in relation to the public advocacy of temperance, is, the opinion that the value of such advocacy may be measured by the number of persons converted to the doctrine of abstinence, or induced then and there to drop all opposition to our doctrines and our measures, if indeed, they do not sign the pledge of abstinence on the spot. That opinion was most prevalent and most frequently uttered during the Washingtonian movement, but has prevailed with very many at all stages of the enterprise. Of course no thoughtful or reflecting person would entertain or express an opinion so utterly at variance with facts or common sense. But just here is found one of the most serious difficulties we have to contend with. Thousands who do a good deal of respectable thinking and reasoning on other subjects, will not take time to investigate or reason soundly on any matter connected with intemperance, or its opposite virtue, or on the movement intended to check the one and promote the other, but give utterance to crudities which are discreditable to their own intelligence, and mischievous in their influence. For more than forty years I have earnestly sought to mould others to my opinions in relation to this matter of the use of intoxicants, and having possessed rare opportunities for observation, I have carefully noted the various ways by which men are converted to our views and measures. Here and there one is converted by a single sound and able argument. Such individuals are generally fair-minded men, with good intellects, and a tolerable education on general subjects, but who had been led to entertain false notions on this question by the unfortunate concurrence of many misleading influences, or, they were able men who had been so immersed in other affairs that they had never before heard the subject fairly presented by an individual who had studied it thoroughly. Though wrong before in opinion, and it may be in practice, yet, being honorable men and lovers of the truth, they yield to legitimate influences, and from that moment may be relied upon. These however, are the few, as compared with the multitude who to-day are staunch friends of Temperance, and hearty haters of the destructive system we are seeking to overthrow.

By far the largest portion of these have been converted by their daily observation of the practical working of the liquor system, and their natural and just reflections thereon; and all sensible and decent people would be thus converted to the doctrine and practice of abstinence, were it not for counteracting and misleading influences, which I shall not *here* attempt to describe, or even enumerate, but shall make them the subject of remark in some other connection. Among the influences which contribute to the gradual, noiseless, but sound conversion of the millions of the class last named, should be reckoned also what they casually read in the daily and weekly journals of the results of the liquor traffic, in the records of brutality and crime, of mobs, street fights, &c., and of multitudes of casualities as clearly resulting from the imbecility or recklessness induced by drink.

These millions, scattered all over the land, come into our temperance meetings already converted to our views, and ready to join us in our efforts for the removal of the scourge, if they can do so without violence to their conviction of duty to other interests, or their acquired tastes, and if there were practical wisdom enough in our ranks to make satisfactory arrangements for their reception, their consolidation with our organized forces, and the proper employment of their energies, we might soon reckon our organized and working force by millions. Well——Perhaps——&c.

Of those converted to the faith by our operations, by far the largest portion, not less I think than nine-tenths, are brought to sound views, fixed purposes, and safe practices, by often repeated presentations of the truth to their minds. One of this class, we will suppose, hears to-day or this evening a lecture or discussion of the subject, and he goes home not converted, but favorably impressed. If he held false views, their falsity begins to be suspected, but is not fully conceded as yet. If he entertained ill-founded prejudices, they have been softened. His purpose, heretofore firm and controlling, to stand aloof from the temperance efforts of his time and neighborhood, has been shaken, but is not yet abandoned. Thus he returns to his home. To-morrow the subject will come up in his mind for review, while engaged in his vocation, unless, as is rarely the case, his calling be one which engrosses all his mental powers. He will reconsider the statements made, the argument presented, the conclusions arrived at, the practical duties urged, and if these were sound, as we should take care they always should be, the impression of last evening, instead of being effaced or lessened, is, in fact, deepened by his own mental operations. Next week, or next month it may be, he listens again to an argument, perhaps on another phase of the same great subject, and favorable impressions gain strength, and thus, in the course of a year, by a succession of appeals to his reason, his conscience, his interest, his affections, his patriotism, his sense of justice, his regard for general morality and good order, he is, at length, prepared heartily to join us in our warfare on the whole machinery of drunkenness—the forging as well as the finishing shops.

Such being the facts relative to the conversion of the masses to our views and practice, do they not afford us practical suggestions as to our modes of procedure?

Will not our brethren seriously inquire whether our present modes of operation are wisely fitted to produce the results we aim at? Is the weekly routine of the Division or Lodge-room, excellent as they may be, and are, for certain purposes, to be at all relied upon for the conversion of the masses to our doctrines? The masses in their homes, or in the street, are not *directly* moved by what we do up in the Hall yonder. Binding sheaves, and threshing the grain, is very necessary and very honorable labor, but we must look to other operations to cut the grain, and bring it to the threshing-floor. Steamboat excursions, oyster suppers, comic songs, or dramatic readings may contribute to present enjoyment and answer, therefore, useful ends; but woe—a thousand woes to our blessed enterprise, if these are to be mistaken for the means of converting the masses, or substituted for hard, self-denying, continuous, educational efforts.

In my public condemnation of the liquor traffic, of all the means and appliances of drunkenness, I have been accustomed to comment on recent occurrences in the immediate vicinity, where they had been of such a character as to intensify the hatred of the system condemned, unless, indeed, such comment would be likely to wound severely the feelings of parties interested. Sometimes such references gave rise to interesting discussions, or were productive of results worthy of record.

On the occasion of my first visit to Paxton in Worcester County, Mass., I learned that the keeper of the village tavern, who sold intoxicating liquors to all comers, was a member of a church in a neighboring town. I learned also, that in applying sometime previous for license, he assured the authorities that he did not wish to sell to residents of the town—only to travelers. Curious to see how a Christian gentleman would deport himself as a liquor seller, and to witness this nice discrimination between travelers and the thirsty of his own locality, I decided to spend a portion of the afternoon in his bar-room, which I could do without awakening his suspicions of my character or object, as I was an entire stranger. I assumed, therefore, the heedless, listless air of one quite at home there, and dropped in upon him. Picking up a paper from the table I seated myself in a comfortable armed chair, and gave myself to the reading of the landlord and his company, while apparently interested in the contents of the paper. A careless question or two, when a new customer came in, would readily determine whether he were a traveler or a resident. "How do you find the traveling to-day, sir?" "I have not been on the road, sir, I reside near by." "Ah! excuse me, sir, I did not know but I could learn of you the condition of the road, I shall have to travel it to-morrow." He takes his drink and is off. I mark him down in my memorandum, "Traveler on short routes,—to the liquor bar of our Christian landlord and home again; no reason to inquire the way; quite familiar with it." Here comes another. Drops into a chair to rest him a little before drinking. Suspect he may be a traveler *bona fide.* "Can you tell me what is the population of your town here, sir?" "I cannot, I am not a resident." "Ah! excuse me, sir, I did not know but you were a citizen of the town." Thus, by the answers obtained to my brief questions, I learned just how many of the parties were travelers, and not less than three-fourths of those who drank that afternoon at the bar, were resident tipplers of Paxton.

Late in the afternoon a grey-haired and venerable old gentleman, whose countenance and bearing, notwithstanding very marked appearances of dissipation, indicated intellect, education, and familiarity with the better class of society, walked in, made his way directly to the bar, and called for a drink. The landlord handed down a decanter of liquors of which the old man more than half filled his glass, and poured it down his throat without any mixture. What a draught to pour into the stomach of a living man! Familiar as I am with the varied exhibitions of the drink curse, there was something in this scene that excited unusual interest, and I determined to know more about it. Assuming, therefore, to avoid exciting his suspicions, that coarse and reckless style of expression common among heartless men *case-hardened by the constant observance of wrong which they do not care to lessen, and of sorrows and sufferings which they never seek to alleviate,* I inquired, as the old man left the bar-room, "Landlord, what old daddy was that?" "That!" he replied, "is doctor Harrison." "What! *he* a doctor? he don't look like one." "Well," said he, "notwithstanding his bad looks now, he has been one of the most celebrated physicians in this part of the country, and has in his time done a world of business." I remarked that from present appearances he was not likely to bless or trouble the world long. "No," said he—"*his copper is pretty much burned out.*"

These were the exact words of that obdurate man. Yet he had once had a heart in some measure susceptible to the influences of Divine truth. In other years he had listened with interest to the story of Calvary and the Cross. Those lips of his had once pronounced a christian vow and covenant, and now—this utterance— "His copper is pretty much burned out." It was now evident that he understood quite well what effect the alcoholic poisons he furnished were producing on the old Doctor's stomach, for in that coarse figure he had expressed the sad truth. As the continued action of the fire without, and the chemical action of the contents, burn out in time the copper of the still, so he knew that the fiery draughts which the old man daily swallowed, would soon burn out, or destroy, the vitality of the organs with which it came in contact. I practiced medicine ten years, and am acquainted with the trials, hardships, and overwhelming responsibilities incident to that calling, and here was one of my own profession who had, during a long life, served the community. Numberless nights had he passed without sleep, by the bed-sides of the sick and suffering. Often had he faced the driving snow and sleet, and the cutting winds of our northern winters, riding over the hills of Worcester County, at the call of the sick or their startled and anxious friends. He had grown old and grey in the service, and was now, in the decline of life, justly entitled to the enjoyment of ease and competence, and of whatever could minister to physical health and comfort. Nor is this all. When the infirmities of age come, and vitality is waning; when the step is feeble and the eye is dim; when the pleasant things of this material world yield less than their former pleasure to the enfeebled nerves; then an old man of education and feeling, if he has been a faithful servant of the public, has claims on that public for something quite as needful to his comfort as his books, staff, and easy chair, or the appropriate diet of age, his bread, milk, and fruit.—*The generous appreciation of his past services by the community which has profited by them.*

But this good old doctor, connected, as I afterwards learned, with some of the best families in that region—what had a grateful community for him, now in his second childhood? Fiery Rum by the half tumbler as often as a diseased and overmastering appetite impelled him to seek it. "His copper is pretty much burned out." Reader, I am not a bad tempered man, can bear personal abuse with more calmness than most people. Have had the ignorant and brutal shake their clenched fists quite too close to my face for convenience or comfort, while addressing to me language more emphatic than elegant—and I have felt for my wretched assailants at the time, only a yearning desire to be avenged on them, if possible, by doing them good—and yet, I must confess that just the remembrance of that heartless utterance concerning that feeble, wretched, despairing old man, makes my blood boil again along its channels almost as when I first heard it. In the lecture of that evening I informed my audience where I had spent the afternoon, and gave the facts above stated. The storm of wrath which was thus kindled around that liquor seller never abated until he abandoned the vile business. I reported the facts also to the church of which he was a member, and he was soon expelled.

Just here, reader, I wish you to consider a question I am about to propound to you, and especially do I wish you to consider it thoughtfully, profoundly, if you have hitherto had any doubts as to the propriety of licensing the sale of liquors, or preventing their sale where you may legally suppress it. Why is it that men once distinguished perhaps for their gentleness and kindliness of character, for their ready sympathy with the wronged or the suffering, before engaging in the liquor traffic, become such brutal and unfeeling wretches after following it for a few years? That is notoriously the fact. The State of New York, on whose territory I write these words, could furnish you with ten full regiments of men now engaged in the liquor traffic, who are among the most heartless and unfeeling wretches which the patience of God, and lax human laws permit to walk the earth unrestrained. Yet these men, hundreds of them, were once kind-hearted, sympathetic, and in early life could be counted on for the defence of the wronged, or the lifting up of the fallen, as confidently as their associates.

What has wrought the change? Not merely the pursuit of gain by traffic. Some of the best men now living have spent their lives in mercantile business. Buying and selling the products of the earth, or of human skill and labor, does not degrade men. A man may weigh out sugar, tea, coffee, and spices, butter, cheese, dried fruits, &c., for half a century, and be all the time growing a better man, and a more devoted christian. Why may he not advance in excellence while dealing in wines, ales, &c., if it be no wrong to sell them? Consider that question thoughtfully. The answer you frame to it, even in your own mind, may have an influence upon your future, and of those around you.

If the brutalizing process is due to the inherent wickedness of the traffic and the degrading associations with which it must inevitably be connected, then what follows? No man can sustain a system so accursed, even by so much patronage as the purchase of a single glass, without becoming responsible *just so far* for its results. No man can give his voice and vote for its toleration, without becoming, in part, responsible for the resulting crime, and the terrible evils inflicted by that traffic upon all the interests of society and man.

An illustration of the demoralizing tendency of the liquor traffic fell under my observation at the town of Holden. Major Adipose, I will call him, for he was a man immensely oleaginous, kept the village tavern. He was selling without license, and was, of course, exposed to the penalties of the law in case any body could be found courageous enough to complain of and prosecute him to conviction. He threatened all sorts of calamities to any one who should venture to do this. As an indication of what might happen, he used to ride through the town in his gig with any number of raw-hides conveniently arranged around him, and dedicated with diverse oaths, and great emphasis, to the special benefit of any cold water fanatic who might presume to complain against him. As he was a man of immense proportions he thought thus to frighten the fanatics and continue to violate the laws with impunity. He was however prosecuted, and now what was to be done? His prototype, Jack Falstaff, had declared long ago, that "the better part of valor is discretion."

The Major was discreet, and instead of inflicting the threatened chastisement on the offender himself, he engaged his hostler to do it; and when our small, but very energetic brother Damon was passing by one day, the said hostler assailed him. Damon did not fancy the

TAKE HIM OFF!—TAKE HIM OFF!!—Page 255.

titillation of the raw-hide, and grappled with his assailant, though a man of twice his size. He was, however, borne down to the earth by the superior weight and muscle of the huge fellow, but as he went down contrived to draw up his short legs, and plant his boots in the hostler's corporation. Poising him thus, as on a pivot above him, he clutched him by the throat with one hand, while with the other he snatched the whip dexterously from his grasp, and changing it in his hand, so as to strike with the butt rather than the small end, he belabored the face and head of the fellow with sharp and cutting blows, still holding him by the throat with the other hand. From all quarters men rushed to the aid of Damon, but found him really getting along nicely. The big hostler, however, was roaring for mercy, "Take him off, take him off," while in fact, Damon was flat upon his back directly under him. I was assured by parties who saw the encounter, that it was really one of the most comical, or tragi-comical they ever witnessed, to see that great lubber poised on the short, stumpy legs of little Damon, held by the throat, and receiving a shower of blows on what used to be his upper story, he all the while shouting "Take him off, take him off," while himself was in fact uppermost in the scuffle. The parties were separated, and Damon went directly to Worcester, made a complaint against his assailant, had him arrested and tried for the assault. He was fined smartly for this wanton attack upon a peaceful citizen. The magistrate, as I heard, remarked after the close of the trial, that with the evidence before him, he could do no less than fine the fellow, but that when he looked upon his bruised, blackened, and swollen face, he almost felt that he was inflicting extra judicial punishment.

This cowardly assault on Damon before described, instigated by the liquor dealer, Major Adipose, was but a specimen of that gentleman's performances. Another, indicating as little regard for decency, as he had before shown for law and personal rights, may help the reader to understand what I mean by the degrading influence of the liquor traffic.

At the close of an address on temperance in a public hall at Holden, by a blind lecturer, a Mr. Palmeter, it was proposed to take up a collection for his benefit, or that of the society by whom he was employed. The President of the Society requested that some gentlemen would pass through the congregation and receive the collection. Major Adipose, who was sitting in the back part of the hall and near the door, arose and passed his hat, into which many dropped their coin, supposing that out of pity to an unfortunate man, he was acting in good faith.

After having collected what he could, he left the hall for his bar-room, counted out the money, and furnished the loafers who had gathered there, with as much rum as the money collected would pay for. In my monthly report I gave these facts to the public, and as our "Temperance Journal" had there an immense circulation, the Major found himself famous, or infamous very suddenly. He vowed vengeance on Dr. Jewett. He would "pound him to a jelly if he could put an eye upon him." "Let him visit this region again at his peril," &c.

An opportunity to put his awful threats into execution soon arrived. I had an appointment at West Boylston, and the Major came over.

"Gathering his brows like gathering storm,
Nursing his wrath to keep it warm."

He came up to me as I came out of the church where I had just addressed the Sabbath School, and asked, "Is this Dr. Jewett?" I answered that it was. "I wish to see you in private, sir," he added. "Walk down to the house with me, sir," I replied, "and your request shall be granted." I suspected that it was the Major, though I had never seen him. As I passed into the house of my entertainer, I inquired if we could have the use of a private room. "Certainly, use this room," said the lady of the house, as we passed into the sitting-room, "you shall not be disturbed." So soon as we were alone I set a chair for this "huge hill of flesh" and bade him be seated. We talked the matter over. I declined distinctly to retract a single word of the statement, and without devouring me, or pounding me to a jelly, as he had threatened, he departed, muttering something about "satisfaction." "Well, Major," inquired his neighbors on his return, "did you horsewhip the Dr. as you promised?" "No, but I would, if he had not backed down on his statements;" and this shameless liar, and cowardly poltroon sought to make his townsmen believe that he had frightened me into an acknowledgment of my errors. I gave such an account of his visit in my next monthly report, as brought upon him the ridicule even of his own customers. I have occasionally found it necessary to make a thorough expose of such fellows to destroy their influence for mischief by making them the laughing stock even of the tippling crowds of whom they have long been the oracles and leaders.

Within the space of three years from the time the Washingtonian movement began to be influential, there was started in every city of Massachusetts, a weekly journal in the interest of that movement. In but few instances were their publishers able to prolong their existence more than a year or two at farthest, and in the case of some of them a longer lease of life would have been a calamity, for although they all advocated abstinence from the use of intoxicating liquors, yet so much false doctrine found place in their columns that their influence, on the whole, was injurious, and among intelligent and judicious friends of the cause the mourners were few when their existence terminated. A few of the number were well conducted, and rendered essential service to the cause. Among these was a paper published in Lowell, and edited by Daniel Kimball, Esq. He was the son of a much respected clergyman, and had enjoyed the advantages of a good education, but habits of intemperance blighted for years the hopes of his friends concerning him. The usual history of the intemperate was his, except that he never fell into other vices. He had been religiously educated, and the influence of that christian home and its inmates went with him whithersoever he wandered. For a time he followed the seas, but on distant oceans, in his lonely watch on deck, parental solicitude and love seemed still to whisper their warnings and entreaties in his ears, and like ten thousand other wayward boys estranged from home and its sweet and saving influences by the winecup and its usual concomitants, he repeatedly resolved on a thorough reformation. These good resolves were broken as oft as made, until, with the blessing of God, the influence of one lovely christian woman, judiciously exerted, was instrumental in saving him. . That influence is delicately alluded to in the following extract from a leading editorial of his paper on the occasion of its removal to Boston. "We beheld ' friend after friend depart.' We felt the curses of hate and the hisses of scorn which the unfeeling and heartless poured upon our head, and year after year we sunk deeper and deeper into the abyss of intemperance—without hope—without God—driven onward like a dismantled ship before the gale, in momentary expectation of being dashed upon the shores of an unknown world, and ushered into the presence of the Mighty God—a poor abandoned, lost inebriate. Just then, even while we heard the roar of the waters as they rolled upon that dark and stormy coast, an Angel's voice fell upon our ear, an Angel's hand was outstretched to save us. Allured by the sweetness of that voice and the gentle pressure of that hand, we retraced our steps and became from that hour, a *sober* man—a happy man, and consecrated our time, our talents—the powers of body and of soul—*all*—*all* that makes us man, to the promotion of the cause of total abstinence. From that to the present hour, we have labored in the cause according to our ability."

I have thus introduced Mr. Kimball to my readers, not only because his character and influence in connection with the cause entitle him to notice, but because the paper he conducted, which on its removal to Boston took the name of the " Temperance Standard," became the organ of the State Temperance Union, and the principal medium of my communications to the public, as the old and excellent " Temperance Journal " had been discontinued at the close of the year 1844. To aid me in recalling the dates and particular history of events which transpired during the years 1845, '46, and '47, in connection with the cause in New England, I have had frequent occasion to consult the bound file of the "Standard" for those years—and have often been hindered in my work by the great excellence of Kimball's editorials on the various phases of the enterprise which then presented themselves, which I found it impracticable to pass over without a reperusal. To some future historian of the reform, the bound volume of the "Standard" would be a treasure.

The year 1846 was signalized by an abortive attempt on the part of the opposition to establish and maintain in Massachusetts, a paper in the advocacy of their views. Two or three attempts had been made before to employ the press for the support of the waning liquor system, but they had been notable failures. It was resolved to try the experiment again, for by the election of temperance men as County Commissioners, the licensed traffic ceased to exist in all the counties of the state save two— Suffolk, in which was the capital, Boston, and Hampden, with its great grog-shop, Springfield, for its shire town. Thus in the counties where licenses were refused, the law was in fact practically prohibitory, and as it was enforced with considerable vigor, the pressure on the liquor traffic was quite severe. Something must be done, therefore, to turn the tide if possible, and Dr. Carlos Tewksbury started at Concord, in Middlesex County, a paper through which to advocate the views and sustain the interests of the liquor traders. What measure of encouragement he received from their head-quarters in Boston, if any, I know not. If considerable, their pledges were not made good, for only two numbers of the paper were issued.

To give the wretched concern a show of respectability it was christened "THE TEMPERANCE REVIEW." With the intent, I suppose, to stir the blood of the faithful and prompt them to heroic deeds in defence of their imperiled liberties, the publisher had placed directly under the head or title of the paper, the line of Burns:

"Scots wha ha' with Wallace bled."

In a brief review of the new paper which I sent to the "Temperance Standard," I ventured to suggest to the editor and publisher a few lines which I judged better suited to his purpose than any thing Burns ever wrote, although not quite so good poetry as his.

> Sots, wi noses fiery red,
> Sots, whose pockets long ha bled,
> Who can boast a rum swelled head
> Still contend for Rum!

> Steam it still by day and night,
> Yield not up that glorious right,
> And with temperance tyrants fight,
> Nerve yourselves wi Rum!

The leading article of the paper occupied six mortal columns, and its first sentence contained a very important piece of information, as follows:

"A quart of rum generally sells for ten cents."

Reader, please observe the care, the prudence, the scrupulous regard for truth manifested in the framing of that sentence. "A quart of rum sells for ten cents," would have been lame. It might have misled the readers of the "Review," but the "generally" qualifies all and renders it perfect. Dr. Tewksbury knew that a quart of rum sometimes sells for more than ten cents. Mixed in the shape of sling and sold by the glass, it would bring from respectable tipplers, ten times the sum. By the poor drunkard "a quart of rum" has often been purchased at a still higher price—his hat—his coat—the scanty wardrobe of his wife—or his children's shoes. The *first* sentence of the *first* article in the *first* number of the "Temperance Review," though very short, is very expressive—full of meaning. "A quart of rum generally sells for ten cents." Immediately after this sentence follows an interrogatory worthy of serious reflection and a sober answer. It has been repeatedly answered by the people of Massachusetts heretofore, and will receive an answer within a twelve month that will astonish the Doctor. "Now, if one person has a quart of rum and another has ten cents, whose business is it if they exchange property?" The beggared wife and children of the infatuated drunkard think it their business, and bitterly complain of such exchanges of property. The people of Massachusetts have thought it *their business* for three-fourths of a century, and have undertaken to regulate such exchanges of property. They have that "notion" in their head still, and will answer the Doctor's question, if I mistake not, by sending the selling party where thousands of the purchasers usually go. But a truce to this, I shall never get over the first page of the Review at this rate. With little comment I will add a few extracts from the same article. "Liquors have not an influence on the score of temptation, which they have not in common with all created things." It will be seen from the following that the Doctor can quote Scripture quite to his purpose :

"The proper rule which enables us to judge of our duty in relation to tempting articles, is this: 'my brethren count it all joy when ye fall into divers temptations.' James i., 2."

The following statement may surprise some, but we assure them it is seriously and unblushingly made:

"We have much direct testimony that the temptations that liquors possess is salutary discipline. Tavern-keepers' sons, or drunkards' sons are seldom drunkards, or even spree-drinkers. The constant exposure to liquor destroys its tempting influence, and disciplines effectually in the way which they should go." If "the way in which they should go" is to vice, disease, and infamy, no doubt "the constant exposure to liquors" disciplines effectually "in that way."

Again, we have the following items of truth and wisdom.

"Few fall by over-drinking, and few by each and every other sensual indulgence, yet it is clear that protection is not the thing needed; but a help to overcome the temptations which are everywhere very properly and serviceably strewn in our paths."

From these quotations the reader will be able to form a tolerable idea of the spirit and character of the "Temperance Review."

I had long desired that the defenders of the liquor traffic would put their views in good fair print, so that all interested could study them. I fancied there might be some advantage to us in having something tangible for us to strike at, for it strains a man's muscles severely to strike or kick at a shadow. I therefore welcomed the new publication, and calculated that I might at least get some amusement out of the concern. When the second number appeared, it was evident that the editor had poured the wealth of his mind into the first number, for No. 2 was filled with the most senseless drivel ever put in print. It was utterly unworthy of notice, and so I waited with patience for No. 3, but no number three ever appeared. That was the last attempt to establish an avowed organ of the liquor interests in New England, and I venture to predict that a long time will elapse before the folly will be repeated.

CHAPTER XVII.

Incompetent Advocates—Their influence—Our early Advocates—District Societies—On time—The Christian way—The Lunch—A Good Time—The lesson of it—Visit the Brethren—Rhymes—A new Field—How shall we fix it?—Plan of operations—Trouble in the Camp.

During the year 1845, I relinquished the agency of the Massachusetts Temperance Union. Through the operation of causes already described, it had lost its local auxiliaries and a large portion of its income. The full import of those facts were not appreciated at the time, even by the masses of our most devoted friends. Knowing that the society had once been powerful every way, they did not doubt but it had still ability to support one agent in the field, and hence friends in the localities where I lectured did not feel the necessity of efforts to reward my labor as they would were I not the agent of a once powerful society. I became convinced that I could better secure an adequate support by independent labor, and therefore resigned.

My judgment did not approve the change, so far as the interests of the cause were concerned, but the claims of my family made it necessary. My own observation has convinced me thoroughly that those who devote themselves to the public advocacy of temperance should go forth under the sanction of some well-known and reliable organization, and be able to show their credentials, if required. This may not be necessary in the case of individuals who have long labored in the cause, and whose relations to it have come to be well understood, but no harm can come to the enterprize or the public by having the labor of even such men performed under the sanction of some reliable National, State, or County organization. The cause has suffered immensely from the unworthy character of very many who have been engaged in its advocacy. Thousands and tens of thousands of influential men in every state north of the Ohio river, (I speak not of the South, for I am not acquainted with facts that will warrant it,) who are not as yet converts to the doctrine and practice of abstinence but who are kindly disposed to the temperance enterprize, have ceased to attend temperance gatherings altogether, as a consequence of having been so frequently and thoroughly disgusted with the character of the discourses they have listened to. This ought not so to be, but it cannot be otherwise, until our local societies of every form are more careful in relation to the character and qualifications of those whom they introduce to the public. I am fully aware of the difficulties in the case, of the pertinacity with which some mercenary characters press their services upon our local societies; of the deception practiced on them through the employment of circulars filled with complimentary notices, of the origin of which there is small occasion to doubt; and I am aware of the extensive demand for more competent lecturers. Still, it is far better that local societies, who for any cause are unable to command the services of a competent advocate, should be content with such services as they can extemporize or secure among their own people, than run the risk of introducing to a public meeting men whom they know nothing of, and whose senseless twaddle will, perhaps, cause the earnest friends of temperance to wish he had opened his mouth in China or the Fejee Islands, rather than in their hearing, and as an advocate of a great and holy cause. Men who are accustomed to listen to able public speakers, in the church, the lyceum-hall, the courts of justice, and at political gatherings, will not be converted to our views by a succession of mirth-provoking anecdotes—illustrating nothing but the speaker's folly and utter unfitness to grapple with a great question having intimate relations with all the interests and hopes of men. With the masses of men enterprises are judged by the character of their advocates. It is vain to argue that they ought not to be. They are; and in the conduct of a great reform movement, wisdom would dictate that its friends should adapt their measures, not to some imaginary state of things, but to the actual. There were no grounds of complaint in regard to the character and qualifications of those who went forth as temperance advocates in New England prior to the year 1840. Rev. Doctors Edwards and Hewett, Jonathan Kitteredge, Esq., Daniel Frost, Esq., Rev. Messrs. Hildreth, Coleman, and Cobb, all educated and able men, and they commanded the respect even of those whom they failed to convince of the soundness of their doctrine or the safety and policy of the practice they recommended. With those who acted as agents of the cause in the Middle, Western, and Southern States, I had no opportunity of becoming acquainted, with the exception of Rev. T. P. Hunt, of whom I have in a former chapter expressed a very decided opinion.

While serving the people of Massachusetts I became acquainted with a system of operations to advance the cause carried on at that time mainly, if not entirely, in Worcester County, which from its common-sense character and excellent results, deserves special attention. Since I resigned my agency in 1845, the system has been extended to other counties, mainly through the instrumentality of Rev. Edwin Thompson, an indefatigable and devoted servant of the cause, who through all changes and by all possible or conceivable modes of operation which commended themselves to his judgment, acquired tastes and habits of thought, has served the state and people of Massachusetts for a quarter of a century at least, and whose devotion to the cause was never questioned, even by those who differed with him widely as to modes of proceeding. I have never become acquainted with any system of county operations, or those embracing so large portions of territory, which I regard as equal in value and effectiveness as that I am about to describe; and if the account of it which I may here give shall lead to the formation of similar organizations in other sections of our country, my purpose will be accomplished and the cause of temperance surely advanced.

A pledge of abstinence from the manufacture, sale, and use of all intoxicating liquors and of mutual coöperation for the destruction of the entire liquor system, with a few simple and common-sense rules for the government of the society, comprises all its machinery. Its meetings are held quarterly, and no lover of temperance could attend one of them without being edified and comforted.

At each of these "District Temperance Meetings," (for so they are called,) the place for holding the next is fixed, and the future lecturer or essayist is announced. The hour of meeting is 10 A. M., and everybody is invited to attend and bring his family and neighbors. Go early that you may see the show to advantage. You will find on reaching the place a committee in waiting to receive and make you welcome. If you have ridden a long way, and purpose to return home after the close of the exercises and would have your horse fed, make known your wishes to the committee and the matter will be attended to. If you have reached the place some fifteen minutes before 10 o'clock, you will presently see lines of carriages approaching you on the several roads that centre at the village, and you will be likely to say, "How admirably they must have timed their starting." Why should they not? They are sensible, sober people, and can not only guess, but reckon. Every adult who will gather here to-day had in youth the benefit of our common schools—not select schools, or parochial schools —but the blessed common schools.

That line of carriages came from H——, a distance of ten miles. They knew that an easy drive of two hours would bring them here without injury to their horses, and so they started at 8 o'clock precisely. That was the hour. They all understood it and were on hand at the spot designated, at the time fixed, for it had been arranged that they should drive to the meeting in company. There is no feature about those District Meetings more noticeable than the nice regard of all parties to the rare virtue of punctuality.

Here they come! and as the carriages successively reach the door, and their occupants "jump out," you observe that some of them contained each a whole family. Yes, that is the true idea. Father and mother, sons and daughters, and if there was likely to be still a spare seat, word was sent, last evening, to the neighbor who owns no carriage, that "Susan can ride over to the meeting with our folks to-morrow just as well as not." That is the Christian way to do things. Would Paul have rode to meeting with an empty seat in his carriage if he had possessed one, while poorer neighbors wished to go, but could not for want of conveyance? I doubt it. I am sure I would not, and I reckon myself not half as good as Paul. The favor of a ride to meeting in a nice cushioned carriage would be, to many a poor boy or girl, a more promising means of grace with the gift of *one* tract, than a *dozen* tracts without the ride. Reader, will you think of that? But the carriages are empty and the church is full.

At these meetings I have often seen the church well filled during the first hour. The meeting is called to order, prayer is offered, and committees immediately appointed to fix the place for the next meeting, and to report during the session a speaker or essayist for the same. The next business in order is usually reports of the state of the cause in the several towns embraced in the society.

"Will some friend report the state of the cause in the town of H——," asks the President, and Mr. E. D. responds. Next we get a report from F——, and so on through the list. At precisely 12 the meeting is adjourned to half-past one—sometimes for even a shorter period. A dinner has been prepared by the ladies of the town, and is now ready in the vestry, town-hall, or other building conveniently near, and all are invited.

The bounty of the Heavenly Father is suitably acknowledged at table, and his blessing sought, after which all "fall to" with an appetite sharpened by the morning's ride. No ostentatious parade of regular courses, and dishes with unpronounceable names is here, but a substantial lunch, which, seasoned with cheerful conversation, and sometimes with mirth-provoking pleasantries, is heartily enjoyed by a happy company. Many of these friends have not met since the last quarterly, and may not meet again until the return of a similar occasion three months hence, for the people of Massachusetts are a very busy people. They rise earlier, work later, and move more rapidly, and in fact turn off more work than any other people I have ever met with; and that is equally true of operatives in the house, the work-shop, and the field. No easy, amiable laggard can keep step with those around him in the old Bay State, or be held, there, in high estimation.

But the lunch has been attended to, and a few strokes of the bell inform us that the moment for reassembling has come.

The committees appointed in the morning now report. The place for the next meeting is announced, and the name of the individual who is to deliver the address, or read an essay then and there, is announced, and now it is two o'clock.

The lecture for *this* occasion, which its author has had three full months in which to prepare, is next in order, and is listened to with profound and critical attention, and at its conclusion its doctrines and practical suggestions are made for a brief period, subjects of discussion. Any unfinished business is now attended to; an appropriate song, perhaps written for this special occasion, is now sung; a concluding prayer is offered, and the Christian doxology gives fitting close to the exercises. It has been a pleasant occasion. No needless formalities have occupied one moment's time.

The great question of the continuance or removal of the scourge, burden, and curse of intemperance has been brought fairly before the minds of all present, in its causes, influences, and results, and so have the needful measures for its extirpation. Friends from each town have learned the condition of things in every other town within the limits of the society, and when in the transaction of business the friends in town A shall visit town B, they will have a sharp look out for violations of the prohibitory law, and if reliable evidence of such violation is obtained, they will communicate the facts to their brethren in B, and the violater of law will be visited with its penalties. Another excellent feature of the meeting has been the attendance of many citizens of the town where it was held who have not heretofore taken that active part in the work of reform they should have done. They have been favorably impressed by the orderly and sensible character of the proceedings, and their own unfaithfulness has been rebuked in a quiet and inoffensive way while they have witnessed the zeal and devotion to a good cause of their neighbors and those excellent and influential citizens from adjacent towns. The social feature of this "quarterly" is by no means an unimportant one, though it has not at all hindered the business of the meeting. There have been pleasant greetings among old friends in the lunch-room, and the young men and maidens have had a favorable opportunity during the intermission for a little agreeable chat. New acquaintances have been formed which may ripen into lasting——friendships perhaps, and invitations exchanged for future meetings at periods less distant than the next quarterly. Best of all, the young of both sexes have been instructed in relation to their dangers and their duties. Reader, do you think that young persons who accompany their parents to such gatherings two or three times a year at least, from the age say of twelve or fourteen, until they attain their majority, will be as likely to become the future victims of intemperance, as those who are taken by their parents to the Lyceum hall, the opera, and the social party, but never to a temperance meeting? Those quarterly meetings have been regularly held in different sections of Worcester county for more than thirty years, and I learn from the temperance journals of the state that similar societies have been established in other counties. Whether they have elsewhere become as popular and influential as in Worcester county, I am not informed, but I see no reason why they should not. Suffolk county, on Long Island, has been blessed, I am told, for more than twenty years, with an organization of kindred character, though that, I believe, embraces the entire county.

I have been thus particular in the description of this mode of operation, that friends of the cause in other portions of the country may know *exactly* how to copy one of the most effective methods for advancing the cause and giving to it a desirable stability that I have ever become acquainted with. Where such a system is adopted, it does not of course obviate the necessity for local temperance societies holding their meetings more frequently, and taking measures for the recovery of intemperate individuals, the relief of suffering families, and the instruction and pledging of the young, which no organization, like the one described, could possibly attend to.

During the first half of the year 1846, I labored in Massachusetts. In the month of August, I attended the annual meeting of the Maine Temperance Union, at Augusta, the capital, and had the pleasure there of making the acquaintance of many of those excellent and sturdy reformers, whose persevering labors, during many years, have helped to place the state of Maine in the enviable position it now occupies in connection with the temperance reform.

While there, I was invited to read or recite at one of the public meetings held during the session of the State Union, a poem which I had written for a special occasion and read in Tremont Temple, and afterwards, on the invitation of members of the Massachusetts Legislature, in the State House, Boston. I complied with the request of my brethren at Augusta, and was made glad by the assurance of many friends that the exercise had added interest to the occasion.

On my return trip to Boston, by boat, and while steaming down the Kennebec, I was pressed to repeat the reading of the poem there for the gratification of my fellow passengers, and finding it always difficult to say no, when assured that I can in any legitimate way contribute to the enjoyment of those around me, I complied with the request.

The poem was of considerable length. Its proper recital before an audience requiring nearly if not quite half an hour. On the score of merit, its entire republication, in this connection, would hardly be warranted. The following extracts will give the reader a tolerable idea of its general character:

FUGITIVE PIECES IN VERSE.

* * * * *

An aged mother, in her fierce despair,
Scatters the tresses of her silver hair,
Frantic, rebels against the biting rod,
And spurns the comfort of the man of God.
Would you what caused the desolation know,
That wearies echo with its voice of woe?
'Tis not that yonder gibbet rears on high
Its black, grim outline sharp against the sky;
'Tis not that on that plank her first-born stands,
His brother's blood scarce dried upon his hands;
The cause lies farther—where that crime was brewed,
In a shop "licensed for the public good"!
Where murder, arson, rape, are brought to pass,
With hell-broth vended at three cents a glass.
And thus her hands that childless widow wrings,
And thus that fratricidal felon swings,
While the accessory before the fact
Goes free, in goods and character intact.

Look on yon alms-house, where from day to day
The grave seems cheated of its lawful prey;
Mark well those squalid paupers, and declare
What brought nineteen in twenty of them there.
Could but the truth upon the canvas glow,

The force of fancy could no farther go.
Ghast Atrophy should gather up his shroud,
And half-choked Asthma wheeze his wrongs aloud;
There pale Consumption by your side should stand,
And tottering Palsy point with trembling hand;
Fierce Frenzy's haggard eye with fury glare,
While Cholera should poison all the air.
All these, and more, with Babel-like acclaims,
Should cry to God and man their authors' names.
And thus this scourge holds on its noisome way,
To sicken, madden, poison, wound, and slay.
Ay, thus it ever has gone on, and still,
Till we apply the remedy, it will;
Till our New England be with graves o'erspread,
One vast, continuous city of the dead;
And we might build a pyramid of bones
As high as Cheops', instead of stones.

O for the potent rod in Moses' hand,
To bid this plague depart from out our land;
A plague more pitiless than Egypt knew,
It smites our first-born and our youngest too.
But why invoke the prophet's wand of power?
It lies within our reach this very hour.
Law, law's the rod we at this crisis need;
The courage, not the strength, we lack, indeed;
Our hands command the thong, but hardly dare
To lay it on. O, cowards that we are!
We pause and hesitate, when one more blow
Might end the contest with our common foe.

* * * * * *

Meanwhile rum-sellers, with exultant voice,
In their short respite from their doom rejoice;
Ply with increasing zeal the work of death,
Nor pause to let humanity take breath.
Shout, drunkard-makers, while ye may—your sport
Is nigh its close; root, swine! your time is short,

Though longer than we hoped, or ye had feared;
A few brief months shall bring you your reward;
And that ye may not chide us for delay,
We'll count you interest to the reckoning day.
Your dues shall yet be paid, all at a dash,
In fines, and costs, and *iron* window sash.

How will they sputter, scold, blaspheme, and swear,
To find themselves accounted what they are!
When justice, long outraged, shall ply her thong
On shoulders which have been unwhipped too long.
Methinks I hear their voice of wail and woe,
Falling on my prophetic ear-drum now.

" Alack! alas! and well-a-day! in vain did lawyers plead;
Our last appeal has surely failed! there is a God indeed;
I've doubted it this many a day, but now, perforce, I see
There is a Judge who can't be reached with any kind of fee.

" So many channels stopped, it is a sorry sight to see,
Through which my rum flowed constant out, and gain flowed in to me;
Where are the rights our fathers fought for? and pray tell me where
Our liberties are fled! O, this is more than I can bear.

" Ye sympathizing sextons, and ye undertakers too,
The ruin that descends on me is most as hard on you;
Ye doctors, and ye constables, come join with me and weep;
'Othello's occupation's gone,' and we may go to —— sleep.

" Behind the bar shall I, alas! no longer cut a swell,
The ragged drunkard's patron saint, the loafer's oracle?
And must I, ere my fortune's made, in my vocation stop?
And must I take to honesty? and must I shut up shop?

" Ah, woe is me! my customers will learn to drop their coin
And pawn their coats in other shops, in other tills than mine,

For bread, or such like useless stuff, but never more will see
One drop of comfort, such as they were wont to get from me.

"And must I go, indeed, to work? I cannot, cannot do it;
I doubt if stern necessity can ever bring me to it.
Does Satan, whom I've served so long, now leave me in the lurch?
At least, I'll be revenged on him—I'll go and join the church.

"When troubles thronged on every side, we, as a last resort,
Had turned our eyes, with grief inflamed, up to the Supreme Court.
But gone, alas! are all our hopes; *that* sun went down at noon;
Curse on those judges' judgment, they have blown us to the moon.

"Well, turn about, since Adam's time, was ever held fair play,
And 'tis a proverb, old and true, each dog must have his day;
And there's one comfort left for us, as law and gospel true,
That we've had ours, each dog of us—a pretty long one too.

"And if hard work should prove too hard for unaccustomed paws,
And should the law break us, who long were used to break the laws,
We still can steal; the sin, and shame, and risk cannot be more,
In secret theft, than in the work done openly before.

"My curse, a hot and blasting curse, on every temperance man,
On Beecher, Edwards, Hawkins, Grant, and all the accursed clan.
A special curse is richly due that rhyming, ranting Jewett;
Powerless himself to work us harm, he urged the rest to do it."

        But rising high above this cry and hue,
        Hark to the shout that rends the concave blue!
        The shout exulting multitudes employ!
        The shout of millions in triumphant joy!
        Hear the poor drunkard, ragged, sick, and sore,
        Thanking his God that grog-shops are no more.
        And hear that wife express her joy of soul
        That none shall dare henceforth to fill the bowl
        For her poor, thoughtless husband. Far away
        Her night of sorrow flies; she greets the day.

"Thank God," she cries, "my husband turns from sin;
He cannot, if he would, offend again.
My husband's safe; and now let *him* beware,
Who for his feebler neighbor spreads the snare.
At last the rod for which stern justice calls,
Not on the tempted, but the tempter falls.
Too oft, alas! a sense of grievous wrong
Drew forth the murmur, "Lord! how long, how long?"
I dreamed not then this day of days to see,
But thought myself forgotten, Lord, of thee.
I bow me now, repentant, in the dust;
Again I give thee back my boundless trust.
Join with me, mothers all, throughout the land
Join with me, little children, hand in hand!
Rejoice! your sufferings at length are o'er;
Your grovelling fathers can be brutes no more.
Our prayers are heard, at our extremest need,
For Massachusetts now is free indeed."

Men of the Bay State—yea, and women, too—
This triumph still remains in store for you;
On you humanity and duty call;
Up and about it, brethren, one and all.
Say, shall your own old Massachusetts be
Now backward in the cause of liberty?
Who struck the first resolved, decisive blow
Against the bondage of a foreign foe?
Who ever foremost stands in war and peace?
And shall the strife for independence cease
Now, when the need is greater than of yore;
Now, when a tyrant knocks at every door;
Now, when awakened Massachusetts stands,
And holds the remedy in her own hands!
Think of your children! all that's dear in life,
Combine to urge you onward to the strife.
Strike! for you owe it to your buried great;
Strike! for you owe it to your native state,

To rid her soil of this supreme disgrace;
You owe it to yourselves, your country, and your race.

I have always found my visits to Maine enjoyable. Even that during which, at a later period, I had the honor of contributing personally to the enforcement of that glorious statute of Maine, for which I have never ceased to thank God and those who framed it, from the moment I first read its stern but righteous and equitable provisions. Of that I shall have more to write when I reach, in this sketch of my labors, those of the year 1851. During the autumn I labored for some weeks in New Hampshire, and during the month of December made another visit to Maine, and delivered public discourses in all the cities and many of the principal towns of the state.

Early in the year 1847, I received a call from the Executive Board of the New Hampshire State Temperance Society to become its Agent.

The practical working of the plan of operations adopted by the Massachusetts State Temperance Union in 1840, I have described in a former chapter. Until crippled by the Washingtonian movement, its practical results had exceeded my anticipations; but it had been crushed by a blunder of its friends in consenting to the substitution for its sensible and reliable measures others which, from their very nature, could not be enduring under any conceivable combination of circumstances. This reformatory whirlwind had pretty much spent its force before the year 1847, and the order of the Sons of Temperance had been introduced. Sixty divisions had been organized, with an aggregate membership of 3,757 members. Friends especially and zealously interested to increase the membership and add to the influence of that order, were greatly encouraged by what they regarded as the rapid growth of this novel organization. To me it seemed a very unpromising measure of progress to add but 1,378 pledged members per year during two years, from 1845, and taking into consideration the very strong and pretty general prejudice against close organizations existing among that class of our population hitherto most active and zealous in the good work, I came to the conclusion that we could never organize but a portion of our real strength in that order. As we proposed a continued war upon a wicked and destructive system, sustained for various reasons by vast numbers of men and immense wealth, it seemed to me the dictate of wisdom to adopt forms less repugnant to so large a portion of our friends. But the movement had started, and many excellent and zealous friends of the cause were in it; and although it did not in many of its features approve itself to my judgment or accord with my notions of fitness, as did the simple forms under which we had formerly worked so effectively, yet I was then, as I have ever since been, reluctant to engage in controversy about forms where we were in agreement in reference to doctrines, principles, and the great ends to be sought.

The observation of a life extended somewhat beyond threescore, has taught me, however, that there is an immense power for good or evil in *forms*, and if it were possible, as it is not, for me to fight over again the battles of a life, I should be a more earnest advocate than I have been for simplicity and fitness in forms and modes of procedure. Cumberous machinery in a work of reform is as much out of place as was Saul's armor on the person of David. When grappling in right earnest with a giant enemy, oh! it is distressing to be hindered and embarrassed by needless harness, trappings, and tinsel, and to have precious time wasted in needless ceremonies.

Possessed, even more strongly in 1847 than I had been in 1840, with a belief that we could not carry the stout works before us either by surprise or storm, but only by systematic warfare and regular approaches; and finding our forces divided in Massachusetts by movements already described, I had been for some time anxiously looking for some unoccupied field where, with the coöperation of good men, I could apply and successfully prosecute the plan of operations broken down in Massachusetts, in the success of which, if faithfully carried out, I then had, and still have, unlimited confidence.

When, therefore, this call came to labor in New Hampshire, I accepted it with alacrity; there were no extensive and systematic temperance operations in the state at that time. The multitude of societies existing prior to 1840, had either died of financial starvation or had given place to Washingtonian societies, and these latter had in turn mostly gone to wreck; and as to the order of "Sons of Temperance," it had, to be sure, a Grand Division there, grand in principles and aims, but not very grand in numbers. It had but six subordinate divisions, with an aggregate membership of 227. In Portsmouth, 81; Nashua, 47; Dover, 33; New Market, 21; Concord, 45; Manchester, numbers not stated. These figures are from official records, kindly furnished me by that excellent friend of the cause and faithful officer, S. W. Hodges, of Boston.

The order, it will be observed, was confined, as yet, to the cities. The rural districts were without any forms of association which would be likely to conflict with any general plan of operation the state might adopt. All the essential features of the plan adopted in Massachusetts in 1840, were adopted by the New Hampshire State Society. For a detailed description of it, see chap. IX, from pages 124 to 130.

The "Temperance Banner," a monthly paper, was started at Concord as the organ of the society, and attained a circulation, in eight months, of over ten thousand subscribers. A list of state members had been secured, paying to its treasury one dollar each annually, sufficient in number to sustain handsomely two agents in the field, Thomas D. Bonner, a zealous and effective laborer, and myself, and our publications.

I had hoped by the close of the first year to have reached a paying membership of at least three thousand, with a circulation of our paper of not less than fifteen thousand. I think we should have reached that had our measures been carried forward without serious interruption.

Once more I was happy in my work. I saw a *systematic* movement in which all could engage gaining strength and numbers day by day, and destined, as I hoped, to accumulate a power that would, at no distant date, crush the hated system upon which we were warring, to the joy of many thousands of suffering ones, and to the certain advantage of all the substantial interests of society.

But again our plans were thwarted through the malign influence of one member of the Executive Board. He had a passion for managing all affairs with which he was allowed to have any connection, and it is doubtful if any movement or enterprise has ever yet been discovered having sufficient vitality about it to endure his management for six months.

He was a man of ability, a ready and forcible writer, a tolerable speaker—plausible, even while arguing in favor of the wildest projects, and often ingenious in his efforts to secure the adoption of his measures. He was, no doubt, an earnest friend of temperance, but beyond personal efforts in favor of the unfortunate victims of intemperance, which he has often put forth, with a zeal which ought to have shamed many of those around him more fortunately constituted, his friendship has never been useful to the cause.

Anticipating only disaster to the State Society and the cause from the adoption of measures which he was constantly planning with an industry very remarkable, I opposed the adoption of his plans by the Executive Board, for the most part successfully. Naturally enough, I became an object of aversion to him. He deliberately attempted to destroy my reputation for integrity and fidelity to the cause, by a system of measures which I shall not attempt to characterize or describe. His attacks upon me were of such a nature as, if not fatal to me, would surely be so to himself. But few words are needed to record the result.

At the next annual meeting, which was held in Manchester, a resolution was passed after a full discussion of the subject, expressing unabated confidence in the individual he had assailed, and in the list of officers for the year 1848 his name did not appear. His hostility and the measures he had planned to destroy my influence, had fully developed themselves by the month of August, and as there was no provision in the constitution by which a member of the Executive Board could be removed until the annual meeting in January following, I resigned my agency in September, as I felt that I could not without a sacrifice of self-respect continue to labor under the direction of a Board of which my assailant was a member, and for other reasons which will become apparent as I proceed in the narration of the facts.

The resignation of my agency was a serious error, which I have ever since regretted. I should have remained at my post and kept right on with my work, but I was disheartened by these blows from a professed friend, and though conscious of entire rectitude in the discharge of my official duties, I was impressed with the belief that the attacks upon me had been so persistent, and withal made with so much cunning, that they must have impaired my influence in the state, and I thought it might be better for the society for some other laborer to take my place. I was convinced of my mistake at the annual meeting, but it was then too late to repair the mischief already done by the too hasty resignation of my agency. I could not properly record the events of this year without reference to this unfortunate affair, but have purposely made the narrative as brief as possible. I have also withheld the name of my assailant out of regard to the feelings of his family, and the added fact that with all his errors, and they were many and grievous, I believe him to be at heart a real friend to the cause of temperance. God forgive the man for the wrong he purposed and sought to inflict upon me, and the greater wrong in hindering the progress of a blessed enterprise, on the success of which hang the hopes of suffering thousands.

A pleasant incident may relieve somewhat the somber character of the narrative just given.

The attacks made on the agent, and the character and animus of the attacking party, as well as the manner in which both had discharged their official duties, were subjects of animated discussion at the annual meeting. As the result, the resolution already referred to was passed, affirming the unabated confidence of the society in the integrity and official faithfulness of their former agent, who, though no longer agent, had felt it a duty to himself and all concerned, to be present where all these matters would be discussed and passed upon by the representatives of the cause from all parts of the state.

The dropping of the name of my assailant from the Executive Board and the passage of the resolution referred to, though a severe condemnation of his past course, did not seem to me to be discharging fully the duty of the society to itself. I urged a resolution of expulsion. Just at this juncture a very queer speech from a very eccentric man produced a universal roar of laughter, and terminated the discussion of the subject.

The speaker referred to was one Col. Miller, a long, lank, loose jointed, and awkward individual, so comical in all his movements that when he rose to speak, the facial and intercostal muscles of the hearers at once put themselves in condition for a laugh before the man could open his huge mouth, the largest, I am sure, I have ever seen upon man. When it was fairly opened one could not help speculating a little as to how slight an addition to the opening on either side would be needful to render the upper portion of the head and face an island. He rose to address the assembly, and was requested to come forward to the platform. He did so, and turning his face for some cause toward the left he began to speak, when some one on his right exclaimed, "Will the gentleman allow those on this side the house to hear some portion of his remarks?" Instantly he gave a comical twist to his huge frame, and with an expression on his countenance of blank astonishment, remarked as follows: "Why, Mr. President, *that* is a most extra-or-dinary request. I had supposed that, let me turn my face whichever way I might, my mouth would open to any part of the house." When the roar which that remark excited had ceased, he proceeded thus: "Mr. President, I hope that Doctor Jewett will not press his resolution for the expulsion of the offending member. I think, sir, that this body has sufficiently expressed its opinion of that gentleman and his course by action already taken. Any thing further would seem to me quite superfluous. Why, Doctor," turning his face toward me, "do you suppose that those lying critters, Annanias and Saphira, who fell down dead at the feet of the Apostles, would have felt any worse after their fall if thunder and lightning had struck 'em?"

When the laugh which that sally occasioned had subsided, I rose and withdrew the resolution, the matter was dropped, and the attention of the great assembly was directed to other matters.

CHAPTER XVIII.

Moving—Guerrilla Warfare—Almost discouraged—Retreating—Arrested and sent to the front—One thousand dollars—Getting into type—Front to Front—We rout them—Comfortable—Visiting the Prisoners—Sham Democracy—Republicans unsound and timid—A glorious opportunity—Political action—They beg off—A venal press.

After leaving New Hampshire, I labored in Connecticut for a few months, with but indifferent success. Systematic effort seemed quite out of the question, and I came finally to despair of it, and contented myself, as most of our lecturers did, at the time, with independent labor at the call of local societies, receiving sometimes a stipulated reward, and sometimes just the amount of a collection at the close of public services, whether much or little. The income from such labor, at that time, was, of course, unreliable, and the labor unsatisfactory; for if a good impression had been made by the lecture, there was seldom a gathering up of the results by the circulation of the pledge, for in many places, the Washington Temperance Societies had been abandoned, and in others, the order of the Sons of Temperance had been established, and it was not their usual custom to pledge the people to abstinence, except so far as they were ready to join the order; and I, for one, have never felt the same degree of freedom to urge membership in one of the orders, as I did the joining of open societies, because, in urging the pledge, which all needed, I should be urging many of my audience to do what their consciences did not altogether approve, and a compliance with new conditions, aside from the pledge, which, to many of the best people in my audiences, I knew were distasteful.

In urging the simple pledge of total abstinence, I had no such embarrassments. It was, under God, the anchor of our hopes, applicable and needful to the venerable statesman or divine, as well as to the children around our hearths, or in the school-room, to the occasional drinker, and the poor besotted drunkard.

It was a grand and potent preventive of intemperance, and it was, while kept, a perfect curative, which never has failed and never will. All other appliances without the pledge and practice of abstinence, cannot be relied upon to prevent or arrest drunkenness. The pledge and practice of abstinence alone will prevent drunkenness, whatever other good it may fail to do.

Despairing of any general system of efforts or operations, until years of comparatively unproductive labor and a succession of disappointments and partial failures should have educated my fellow-laborers to sounder views, and heartily sick of guerrilla warfare, and, withal, suffering from ill health, caused more by heartache in view of the existing state of things than by long and laborious service, I addressed to the editor of a temperance paper published in Worcester the following letter:

HARTFORD, CT., Nov. 21st, 1848.

Friend Goodrich:—

I have made up my mind fully to retire from the field of labor in which I have been employed for the last nine years, and return to the practice of my profession. A variety of causes have contributed to confirm me in the determination I have expressed.

I have received a pressing invitation to locate in a very pleasant town in New Haven county, from which a physician, advanced in years, is about to remove, and I think I shall accept the invitation. Before, however, I lay down the *teetotal trumpet*, and take up the *lancet* and the *pill box*, I propose to visit Massachusetts and spend a few days on my old battle ground that I may meet once more old friends with whom I have so long labored.

If in any of your good temperance towns, there are those who would desire to hear a farewell discourse from " Dr. Jewett," they will please direct a line to the editor of the Cataract, Worcester, Mass., and therein express their wishes. Yours fraternally,

CHARLES JEWETT.

Very many invitations came in answer to the above, and everywhere the friends urged me to reconsider my purpose of retiring from public labor.

While thus engaged, an event occurred which will be understood from the following brief editorial. It appeared in the " Cataract" of Feb. 15th, 1849.

THEY TOOK HIM AT HIS WORD.

At the conclusion of a discourse, recently delivered by Dr. Jewett, at Clintonville, and after the mass of the audience had retired from the Hall, a number of gentlemen took occasion to express to the doctor their regret that he was about to leave the field as a public lecturer. Dr. Jewett replied, that no one could regret it more sincerely than himself, but that a necessity seemed laid upon him to do so, as the experience of the last two years had convinced him that his health would not endure the labor of continued public speaking through the summer months, and that he could not secure subsistence for his family by the rewards he received for public services during a part of the year. He added, that, if he had been able to purchase a small farm in the country, from the cultivation of which he could, during the summer months, have secured the means of subsistence for his family, while he might have been recruiting his energies for a winter's campaign, he would not have left the field. "*Then you shall not leave it*," was the prompt reply of he gentlemen present. After Dr. Jewett had left the place, a consultation was held among the friends of the cause, and they are putting forth efforts to place $1,000 in the hands of Dr. Jewett, which, with his present property, will secure him "*the little farm*," and secure his continued services in the cause during the winter months, which constitute the most valuable portion of the year for the purpose of public instruction. We are happy to hear that the movement is meeting a hearty response from various quarters. We hope it may be successful. Friends of the cause, who feel any interest in keeping Dr. Jewett still at work in the temperance vineyard, will have now an opportunity to manifest it, as the gentlemen above referred to have sent circulars to our strong temperance towns soliciting aid in behalf of the object they seek to accomplish. A dollar each from a thousand teetotalers, sent to H. N. Bigelow and S. Harris of Clintonville, will do the business.

The immediate movers in this matter, it will be seen, were Messrs. H. N. Bigelow and Sidney Harris, both of Clintonville, Massachusetts. As they were both gentlemen of wealth and influence, and of established reputation as practical and successful business men, all who became acquainted with the project had confidence from the start that it would be a success. The prompt and liberal manner in which the friends of temperance responded to this call, gave me gratifying evidence of their kind regard for me personally, for which I have ever been grateful.

The thousand dollars thus placed in my hands, with the little property I had saved during ten years of labor as a public lecturer, enabled me to purchase a small farm in Millbury, Massachusetts, where I continued to reside until 1854, lecturing about eight months each year, and devoting the remainder of the time to the cultivation of my farm and to writing for the press. During these years my labor as an advocate of temperance was not confined to Massachusetts, nor even the New England states. I visited not only all the Western states east of the Mississippi, but the British Provinces. Some incidents of these itinerant labors start up in my memory as I take a retrospective glance over those years, and seem to claim a brief mention in this history of my life work.

Soon after my location in Millbury, I published a volume of two hundred pages, with the following title: "Speeches, Poems, and Miscellaneous Writings on Subjects connected with Temperance and the Liquor Traffic." It contained reports of six lectures, on as many different phases of the general subject of temperance as I had been accustomed to deliver them; three as reported phonographically by H. E. Rockwell, Esq., and the others from memory. The titles of those lectures only, I shall here record. If my life shall be prolonged, and the interest manifested in my views of the subject may seem to warrant, I may republish them, together with other lectures of later years, embodying more matured views of the subject, especially in its scientific aspects. The lectures which found place in the volume referred to, were on the following special topics:

"THE LAW AND TENDENCIES OF ARTIFICIAL APPETITES."

"THE WARFARE OF THE LIQUOR TRAFFIC ON ALL USEFUL TRADES AND OCCUPATIONS."

"CHARACTERISTICS OF INTEMPERANCE, AS SEEN IN ITS EFFECTS ON COMMUNITIES, STATES, AND NATIONS."

"INTEMPERANCE AS A VICE OF INDIVIDUAL MAN."

"Prospective Results of the Traffic in Intoxicating Liquors."

"Means or Instrumentalities for Removing the Curse of Intemperance."

These discourses filled more than half the pages of the volume, the remaining ones being occupied by extracts from poems delivered on public occasions, and short articles in prose and verse, by which I had sought to give interest to the various temperance periodicals with which I had been connected during the previous ten years.

The volume was kindly received by my fellow-laborers throughout the country, and I have often been comforted by the assurance of friends that it had been of essential service to them in their studies of the subject, and their labors to advance the enterprise.

During the first year of my residence in Millbury, and at the special request of that devoted friend of the cause, Deacon Moses Grant, of Boston, I performed a month's service in the county of Hampden. It was the only county in Massachusetts in which the license system had not been condemned by the vote of the people, and an effort was to be made to secure there the election of Temperance County Commissioners. Three good men were nominated for the office in whose integrity and devotion to the cause all could confide, and the host of bad or deluded men in the county were active in efforts to defeat their election, and thus to continue in office the old board, who had dotted the county all over with licensed grog-shops, which they themselves liberally patronized, unless rumor belied them. Both parties put forth all their strength in the struggle. I never worked harder in my life, than during that month, and I closed my labors there with an address to the people of Springfield, the county town, on the evening previous to the election. It was the eve of the Sabbath, and there were no vacant seats in the City Hall. I drew the attention of those before me to the extraordinary spectacle which the county was exhibiting to the world just then, in licensing a traffic which it had been proved produced four-fifths of the crimes in the country, multiplying criminals to such an extent that it had become necessary to enlarge the county prison, and while the street in front of the prison was obstructed with huge blocks of granite to be wrought into its extending walls,—a large portion of the people of the county were using all possible efforts to continue that destructive traffic in their midst. I expressd my approval of the enlargement of their prison, if licenses must still be granted, for the same reason that I would commend the forethought of the farmer, who, while planting additional acres, put an addition to his corn-crib. I judged from the manner in which that suggestion was received, that the people saw the point.

The following morning I returned to my home by the first train, as I was worn and weary, and could render no assistance at the polls, having my residence in another county. Tuesday morning I rode to Worcester, which was but five miles from my home, to get the news from Hampden County when the western train should arrive. As soon as it reached the Worcester Depot, I stepped into the cars and inquired if some gentleman could give me a glance for a moment at a Springfield morning paper. No one seemed to possess a copy, but one generous, though deluded man, divining my wishes, addressed me thus: "I suppose, Doctor, you want news from the election yesterday?" "You are right, sir," I replied, "that is exactly what I want just now." "Well," said he, "I am not one of your cold-water folks, and I did all I could to defeat them, but they elected their ticket by about one thousand majority in the county." "I thank you, sir," said I, "for the information, and I thank God for the result."

My ride home from Worcester that morning, was unusually pleasant. The last county in Massachusetts had condemned the wicked and destructive license system; the cause was onward, and I rejoiced. Reader, do you know by happy personal experience, the joy that fills the soul when some signal success is attained in some grand work, in which one can have no personal and selfish interest, but which will, if perfected, certainly and greatly promote the public good, and the happiness of all around you? I hope you have felt it, but if not, I hope you will attain to it while yet in the flesh, for you will never know that particular joy, even in Heaven, unless you experience it here.

Another season of personal happiness, related somewhat to that already described, and growing out of the events just narrated, as the harvest results from the seed sown, was of a character impossible to forget. The event afforded "a joy for memory."

Some months after the triumph already recorded, it may have been a year, I was advertised to speak again in Springfield on a certain Sabbath evening. Reaching the city Saturday eve, I spent the night and the Sabbath day with a valued friend, a Mr. Ingersoll, who was deeply interested in all good work, temperance of course included. On Sabbath morning, my kind entertainer, who was at that time Paymaster of the United States Armory, invited me to spend an hour or two in the Sabbath School connected with the county jail. He was its superintendent, and would, he said, omit the usual lessons of the day, if I would occupy the time with an address to the prisoners. I consented to do so, and walked with him to the prison. Taking our seats in the desk of the Chapel, we awaited the coming of the prisoners. Presently the doors at the rear of the Hall were opened, and preceded by one of the officers, and accompanied by others, the long line of prisoners, two by two, filed into the room, in an order quite military. When the congregation was seated and the preliminary exercises were being concluded by the singing of a hymn, and while my brain was unusually active in arranging a train of thought which should be suitable to the occasion, my friend, the Superintendent, turned to me, and in an undertone remarked, that I had probably never addressed such an audience before. "Oh, yes I have," I replied. "I have repeatedly addressed the inmates not only of county, but of State Prisons, where five times the number of prisoners here, were before me." Still he insisted, and with a very peculiar expression of countenance, as he spoke, that I had never addressed *such* a congregation before. "Well, what is there so very peculiar about this congregation?" I asked. Placing his mouth close to my ear he replied, in a very emphatic and happy whisper, thus: "A large portion of the congregation before you are liquor-sellers, sent here for violation of the law."

I wanted to shout "Hosanna!" but I did not.

"Well," thought I, "liquor-sellers are always in favor of moral suasion, and now, all good spirits helping me, I will give you a good dose of it." Of course I would not take advantage of my position to abuse the men, or needlessly to wound their feelings, but without doing either, I think I managed, in my address to them, to make tolerably clear the cause of a large portion of the needless suffering which all benevolent people are seeking to alleviate, and of the crime which society is compelled to punish, or submit to disintegration, bankruptcy, and ruin.

It should be stated, that under the laws of Massachusetts, and at that time, the penalty of a third offence for selling liquors without license, was imprisonment in the county jail. It struck me as a more just and politic arrangement altogether, to put, say, fifty liquor-sellers in jail, and thus stop their destructive business, than to allow them to go on with it, and sooner or later, be compelled to send to jail, or otherwise confine, some hundreds, or even thousands of their customers—rendered insane and criminal by their maddening liquors.

Such a decided condemnation of the liquor traffic by the legal voters of Massachusetts, coupled with the fact that nineteen-twentieths of the mothers, wives, and daughters of the state, denounced it as an unmitigated curse wherever it became a subject of remark, ought to have been followed at once by its entire suppression, and the question will naturally arise in the mind of the thoughtful reader, why it is still permitted to exist, especially as no other branch of business, institution, or custom of its people, has been able to resist an adverse public sentiment and the force of law. A variety of influences have contributed to this extraordinary and disgraceful result, some of which it may be well to mention: and,

First. An entire political party, the Democratic, has, through the influence of its leaders, been held for thirty years in an attitude of determined hostility to all effective legislation against the liquor traffic. Very many of its adherents have practiced total abstinence meanwhile, and in the communities where they resided, have been counted among the friends of temperance, often members of our organizations. They have, however, at least a large majority of them, been careful to have it understood that temperance, with them, meant only a war of words against the dram-shops, but no friendship to restrictive laws. The few of that party who have in their own localities favored the enforcement of restrictive or prohibitory laws, have never, in the annual conventions of their party or elsewhere, uttered any decided protest against the square and outspoken commitment of it to the defence of the liquor traffic and an attitude of hostility to all effective efforts for its suppression.

All that has been done by the enforcement of the state's laws against the liquor system has, therefore, been done in the face of all the opposition possible from the leaders and organs of one of those great parties, into which the people of this country have ever been politically divided.

When laws, enacted by the dominant party of the state, have been rigidly enforced in any particular locality, so as to render it difficult for the lovers of drink to secure their supplies—the astute leaders of democracy there, have at once referred the affliction to anti-democratic legislation, and have assured the complainers, if connected with the opposite party, that if they would but act sensibly, and give their votes and influence to the democracy, and thus put the party in power, these sumptuary laws, as they have chosen to call them, would be at once repealed.

This attitude of the democracy, and the occasional loss of political ascendency in certain localities where the law has been rigidly enforced, has made the party responsible for its preservation exceedingly timid, because its leaders well knew what in fact is quite evident to all observers, that the Republican party, even in the most favored of the New England States, numbers among its adherents many men bitterly hostile to the laws, aye, even supporters and patrons of the liquor shops.

This state of things has greatly complicated the work of suppressing the liquor traffic, even where there is a strong public sentiment against it.

Still, in Massachusetts, the Republican party may justly be held responsible for the continued violation of the law in many of the large cities of the state, and for that temporizing policy which has postponed the triumph of right and justice, as connected with the liquor traffic, because its majority was so overwhelming, that any disaffection in its ranks, which might be created by a faithful discharge of its duty in relation to the matter, could not have thrown it out of power. It has happened that, in the Providence of God, the states of Maine, Massachusetts, and Vermont, have afforded the most favored fields on which to exhibit to the world the assured prosperity and blessedness which would result from the complete suppression of the liquor traffic. Such an exhibition of freedom from pauperism and crime, by entire states, and the inevitable advance of the people, in intelligence, moral purity, and social happiness, would commend abstinence and prohibition to a gazing world, as all our arguments cannot, and would render the annihilation of the liquor system in all christian countries, only a question of time. If such an example, and the fruits of it, are lost to the world through the cowardice and faithlessness of the people of those states, they will surely incur the wrath of God, and the condemnation of all good men.

In states where, as in Connecticut, the political parties are nearly equal in numbers, and one of them shall fully commit itself against the legal suppression of the liquor traffic, the opposing party, embracing, as in that case it must, all our real available temperance strength, cannot, if they would, crush the trade, *until it attains to a unity of sentiment on the subject.*

If they attempt it, and are likely to be successful, many in their ranks who love whisky better than the principles of their party, will bolt, go over to the party opposed to the law, put it in power, and thus we should be thrown back on the infamous license system.

Suppose, now, the party embracing the mass of our friends, seeing the state of things, refuse to move forward to a position where political death is certain. What shall we gain by waging a war upon them, and attempting to cripple them by drawing off votes to a third party? We do not thereby multiply temperance voters. We may, however, do another work less desirable. We may offend and disgust many of our own brethren by our ingratitude and folly—so that for the future we may not be able to count on their support, when, by a further education of the people, and under more fortunate circumstances, an opportunity for a triumph of our cause is before us, could we but consolidate our strength.

A party which, in answer to our petition, has retained the law on the statute book for years, in spite of all opposition, which has already suffered at some points the loss of voters on account of its course, but which finds it impracticable to move further at present in the desired direction, without cutting its own throat, and imperiling all that has been gained, wounding us as deeply at the same time as it wounds itself, is not a proper subject for our maledictions. Our curses and attempts to cripple it, would be but a poor return for its support of our measures, up to the entire limit of its ability.

Doubtless some will still urge that the party holding the power at present, in Connecticut, should exert it to the fullest extent to promote the ends of right and justice, without stopping to calculate the possible consequences in loss of votes or influence. It is an easier task to commend the glories of martyrdom to others, than to secure them as a personal possession.

The world sadly needs instruction on this great question of the use or disuse of intoxicating liquors. To enlighten it is a blessed work. If now, my zealous and impatient brother will sell his farm, his bank shares, or

R. R. and Government stocks, and will, with the avails, scatter among the people millions of pages rich with glorious truths in reference to the matter, can he doubt that great good would result therefrom? He certainly cannot. But will he do it? Probably not, lest he should thereby reduce himself and family to want. Here, now, personal interests are permitted to come in and limit the amount of good he will undertake to do. Will our brother now demand of a great party greater devotion to the temperance cause than his own example is calculated to inspire?

The friends of abstinence and prohibition throughout the land may as well understand *now* as after a long series of struggles and disappointments, that where we have not overwhelming majorities educated to a hearty hatred of the liquor traffic, it is utterly in vain to make an immediate move for general prohibition. Could such a law be placed at once upon the statute book, and were all our magistrates thoroughly with us in sentiment, and the best men we have in our ranks appointed as executive officers to see to its proper enforcement, still we should fail to secure the end desired, where the public sentiment of the majority is against us. The question relative to the punishment of men for the illegal sale of liquors, must, if the violator of law chooses to appeal from our inferior courts, be ultimately submitted to a jury, and where the public sentiment strongly favors liquor-selling and liquor-drinking, juries will not convict.

We may pour our condemnation into their ears for their wanton disregard of duties they have sworn to perform, but they will care little for it. Our voices of censure will be drowned by the plaudits of the crowd, and recreant jurors will be thus sustained. It is vain for us to work ourselves into an impotent rage over the matter, afflicting ourselves and those around us. The work before us, under such circumstances, is not a quarrel with parties, legislators, or juries, but a steady, patient, kind, and persevering presentation of the truth to the minds of the people. It is thus we have prepared three states at least for thorough prohibition, and *there* I will join my brethren in sternly demanding it.

Beside the championship of the rum interests by the democratic party, other influences contributed to prevent the immediate and general suppression of the liquor traffic in Massachusetts, as demanded by the voice of an overwhelming majority of its people, prior to the passage of the present prohibitory law. The penalties of former laws were for first and second offences only fines and costs; and mere money penalties will never deter bad men from violations of law by which large gains are secured. Though liquor-sellers notoriously dislike to accompany the poor deluded victims of their traffic to the jail, they would still venture to violate law where imprisonment was the penalty only of a third and subsequent offences, for they would have two warnings in the shape of convictions, and if they chanced to be convicted of three offences at the same session of the court, and thoughts of bolts and grated windows happen to trouble them, they could generally appeal with success to the mercy of the good-natured temperance prosecutors, and in answer to their application the good-natured judge would postpone the passage of sentence until the next session of the court, the offender solemnly promising meanwhile to obey the laws. The true method of dealing with these public poisoners, I shall indicate when I come to consider that new era in the cause created by the passage of the Maine Law.

A number of the influential public journals of Massachusetts have largely contributed to prevent the thorough enforcement of its laws intended to cripple the liquor traffic. That they have been enabled to exert so extensive an influence for evil, is the fault of the friends of temperance of course; for had they generally withdrawn their patronage from such papers, and left them, as they should, to the patronage of the liquor party, whose views and claims they advocated, a diminished circulation and a failing income would soon have converted their proprietors and conductors to a more honorable course. As it was, a double motive prompted the conductors of such journals to the course they have for many years pursued—the gratification of their own depraved appetites, and a desire for a liberal portion of the ill-gotten gains of liquor-sellers, notoriously liberal in their support of those who will oppose the passage or enforcement of prohibitory laws. There are no more dangerous enemies of the civil government, good morals, and all the substantial interests of society, than able, ingenious, but venal and corrupt, conductors of influential public journals. I hardly dare think, after midday, of the course pursued by some of the daily papers of Massachusetts during the last twenty-five years, lest the sun should go down on my wrath.

CHAPTER XIX.

The Maine Law—Reaction, how created—False Witnesses—Working up a "reaction"—A Prophecy—Its fulfillment—How it grew—Search and Seizure—Cleaned out—A Viper without fangs—Trying it on—Terrible threats—Nobody hurt—We roll them out—Legs—Three cheers for the Law—Cargoes or Pint Bottles? Either!—Property—Pour it out.

The year 1851 constituted a new era in the temperance reform, for it gave us the Maine Law. Its enactment was the first attempt to crush *entirely*, by statute law, the *springs* and *sources* of drunkenness, or *all* traffic in intoxicating liquors to be used as a drink. Its enforcement, during the first years after its passage, demonstrated its ability to cope fully with the gigantic evil which before had broken through all legal restraints, as some strong animal would break through a spider's web. Former laws had been able to suppress dram-shops in communities where the public sentiment strongly favored such suppression, but the distiller and wholesale dealer, the proprietor of the great wine-store, with its elegant array of bottles of various hues, and the beer-bloated brewer, they had laughed at all restrictive legislation, and with their enormous profits had stood behind and encouraged retailers to violate the laws, had given bail for them at the courts when in trouble, apparently deeming it impossible for law to reach gentlemen of such vast possessions and high social position. But a rod was in pickle for those gentlemen of which they had not even dreamed.

A careful study of the law of 1838, given in a former chapter, and which was a great advance on all previous legislation of the present century, will impress the reader with the extreme mildness of its character as compared with the Maine Law, and the narrow limits within which its powers could be employed against the gigantic system of injustice and cruelty from which we were suffering. It aimed only at the traffic in " Spirituous liquors and mixed liquors a part of which were spirituous," " in quantities less than fifteen gallons." The Maine Law strikes at the whole tribe of liquid intoxicants in *all* their varieties and in *all* quantities; and while forbidding the traffic therein, forbids also the manufacture, and arrests the destructive agent *in transitu*. Its most effective feature and that which exhibits most the thorough knowledge and sagacity of its author, is just the one which our mere theorist and would-be Solons find most fault with, the " Search and Seizure clause." No one can properly estimate the value of that provision of the law, who has not seen and compared its practical working with that of other statutes which *lack it*.

Very much is said of the *reaction* which the stern and impartial enforcement of prohibitory statutes occasions in communities where the experiment is tried, and thousands who are profoundly impressed with the injustice and wickedness of the traffic, and who clearly see the necessity of legal measures to restrain or arrest it, are deterred from active participation therein, through fear that the wrath of the sellers or the drinking fraternity will be visited upon them in the destruction of their property. But let us consider how that much-dreaded "reaction" is worked up, and how the destruction of property results therefrom. Every liquor-bar, grog-shop, or saloon, from which intoxicating liquors have been retailed for a few weeks or months, has about it a regular list of customers, in the various stages of the process of descent from moderate but regular tippling to the consumption, perhaps, of a quart per day. Among these will often be found one or more daring fellows, not abusive or criminally disposed when sober, but ready for any kind of mischief when in the second, or criminal stage of intoxication.

Now let us suppose such a liquor-seller prosecuted for selling without license, and taken before a court of justice. His customers are summoned as witnesses. The chances are more than two to one, that the prosecution will fail for want of evidence, although no one doubts that some if not all the witnesses have drank and paid for liquors in that establishment repeatedly within the last twenty-four hours. Their memories are very treacherous. They "drank something there, but did not know what it was." It is quite evident to all present that the witness does not intend to tell the truth, lest the result should be that his friend, as he regards him who furnishes him his much-loved drink, shall thereby come to grief. But let us suppose that some of the witnesses tell the truth, and the grog-seller is convicted. He pays his fine and costs it may be, or appeals to a higher court and gives bonds for his appearance there, and then what follows?

It is worth our while to consider carefully the answer

to that question. He returns to his place of business, well stocked with maddening poisons, which will attract there the most dangerous and reckless men of that community, and fit them for any work of mischief he may suggest.

Ambitious to display their zeal for the persecuted saint who is profiting by their ruin, each vies with the other in expressing his hatred of the law, and of those who have been concerned in its enforcement. For such a manifestation of sympathy for him, and indignation against his enemies, as all agree to regard them, what return can he make so fitting as a treat all round? Stronger expressions of their wrath against the prosecutors follow, and another free drink, and thus the miserable satellites of the liquor-seller are wrought up to a perfect frenzy of rage which the crafty dealer will employ for the punishment of complainants, or parties engaged in his prosecution.

If the sufferer from legal penalties be sober enough to be cautious, he will not *directly* express his wish for the destruction of their property, but will do it by hints and prophetic suggestions. From reports of reformed men who, before the blessed change in their habits, were perfectly familiar with grog-shop operations and influences, we are quite well instructed in relation to the modes of procedure in cases like that under consideration. "I should not wonder," says Sir Toddy-Stick, " if some of those fellows should meet with some accident before long, that will set them to thinking. Awful judgments come on men that don't know enough to mind their own business, and keep meddling with the affairs of their neighbors. I should not wonder at all, if there should come a big thunder-storm one of these nights, and lightning should strike that Sam Jones's haystacks, or grain-barn, and he should have a bonfire that will shed considerable light on matters and things."

"Nor I, either," responds Bill Guzzle, "and I shouldn't wonder if lightnin' should strike 'em when there aint any storm."

This very ingenious suggestion of Mr. Guzzle calls forth a round of applause, and is rewarded by another drink. Bill leaves the company, and in half an hour the village is startled by the cry of Fire! Fire!! and it is soon learned that Mr. Samuel Jones is the sufferer therefrom. The results of a summer's labor perhaps, melt away in smoke and flame, as his reward for having performed his duty as a citizen in causing the laws of the State to be respected in his neighborhood.

Here now is the "reaction" so much talked of and so justly feared from the enforcement of laws against the sellers of intoxicating liquors. Is it not apparent now to the dullest intellect, that the producing cause of all this was the liquor? *That* was the attraction that drew the thirsty group to the grog-shop. *That* was the agent with which the liquor-seller testified his appreciation of the sympathy and devotion of his friends. *That* was the article that muddled the brain, excited the base passions, and paralyzed the moral sense of Bill Guzzle, and fitted him for the work of the incendiary.

A law to be effective, and safely enforced, therefore, should strike first of all *at the stock of liquors on hand*. Thus reasoned the author of the Maine Law, the Hon. Neal Dow, who is not the Utopian dreamer and fanatic that many have been taught to believe, but a man of large, and eminently practical intellect.

No statute can ever crush the liquor system, or be enforced with safety, that does not, like the Maine Law, strike first of all at the destructive agent. Having repeatedly aided public officers in the search for, and seizure of liquors in Maine, I can speak from actual observation, and strong terms would be required to express fully my admiration of that excellent statute.

It did not grow up like a mushroom in a night, but is an accretion of provisions suggested by the failures of earlier statutes. For many years its author had carefully observed the practical working of former laws. Whenever, through the aid of ingenious counsel, a notorious violator escaped justice through some defect therein, a note was made of the fact, and thrust into a certain pigeon hole in the secretary of Neal Dow, for future use. These suggestions accumulated, and when that gentleman sat down to draft that world-renowned statute, these practical points were all considered and provided for. Hence the perfection of the law, and its wonderful efficiency where a public sentiment has been formed which demands the extinction of the traffic.

Many honest, but ill informed men who were yet in favor of prohibition, have told me that they were heartily in favor of the Maine Law except that "search and seizure" clause. They had, by the clamor of interested parties, been led to believe that that provision authorized an unwarrantable encroachment upon the rights of the citizen, just as though the domicil had not for centuries been subject to search, and unlawful possessions to seizure, wherever the demands of justice imperatively required it. Good-natured friends of good causes are quite too apt to be influenced by mere clamor, and to pause in their work at a critical moment, thus giving our opponents a decided advantage, when duty to all concerned requires them to move steadily forward and " let the music play."

It ought to suffice for all to know that every provision of the Maine Law has undergone the searching scrutiny of some of the best legal minds of our country, of many of our most renowned judges, and received their unqualified sanction.

But to return to its practical working and the safety of its enforcement as compared with other forms of law intended to restrain or suppress the traffic. The " search and seizure" clause should be employed, in my judgment, in all cases to which it is adapted, and there are few cases to which it is not. As we have already seen, an unlicensed seller of liquors, convicted and punished by fine and costs, leaves the court-room, and returns to his place of business well stocked with liquors, very dangerous articles in the hands of a bad man; for by their use he can prepare his pliant and obsequious tools for any service, however perilous to them, or destructive to the interests of society.

But suppose we obtain a legal warrant for the search of the premises of Mr. Heartless, and the seizure of liquors " held with intent to sell." The officer executes the warrant, finds a stock of liquors of various kinds, seizes the same, and directs the truckman or teamster to convey them to a place for safe keeping until the final adjudication of the case. The *next* move is to arrest the seller or owner of the liquors. He is put on trial, and the possession of such a stock of villainous compounds, of the usual measures, with the decanters, glasses, toddy-stick, &c., are so many evidences against him. You have not now to depend on the uncertain testimony of his demoralized customers, but on inanimate materials which will not *lie* whatever other mischief they may do. There has been no gathering together of his customers as witnesses. They were not wanted.

We will suppose the individual convicted and fined. He pays his fine and costs, or appeals his case and gives bonds, and is then at liberty to return to his home, or place of business. How altered now is the state of things. His liquors, glasses, toddy-sticks, &c., gone, the place empty, and if not "swept and garnished," desolate enough. He paces the room to and fro, looks up and down the street, and wonders where, in this his time of trouble, are those devoted friends who have so often sworn to stand by him in every emergency. The facts are, that while he has deceived his poor customers, he has been himself deceived in supposing that they cared even so much as the price of a dram of poor whisky for him, in any relation other than that of a dispenser of liquors. Now he has no liquors to dispose of, and they know it. They have heard probably that his entire stock has been seized and taken away. Why should they trouble themselves to visit a place where there is nothing to drink? They know no reason why, and it would be difficult to frame one. Hitherto when he so warmly welcomed them to his shop, it was because he expected to profit by their folly, and when *they* talked of their devotion to him, they meant his *liquors* rather. Whence now is to come the dreaded reaction from the enforcement of the law? A liquor seller without liquors is one of the most harmless of all bad animals. A viper without fangs, a vicious but toothless mastiff, are his fitting representatives.

The enforcement of the Maine Law proper in the way described, has rarely been followed by the destruction of the property of complainants. The enforcement of former laws, or those which dealt simply with the dealer, but did not interfere with his liquors, has been followed by the destruction not only of vast amounts of property, but in some instances by the loss of valuable lives; two at least, in the smallest state in the Union, Rhode Island.

Soon after the passage of the law, in June, 1851, a copy was sent me by its author, and my opinion of the statute solicited. I replied promptly that the traffic would certainly be crushed under its proper enforcement, but expressed some anxiety lest it should be found in advance of the public sentiment of the state, and I urged that the friends should at once redouble their exertions to enlighten the public mind on all points at issue, and urged the immediate and stern enforcement of the law. Although I had intended to devote the summer months to rest and recuperation, I tendered my services in aid of the work which I felt to be needful in the emergency which the passage of the law had created, and a series of appointments were made for me, commencing on the Kennebec, and ending with Calais, on the eastern border of the state. Never did I engage in work with higher hopes or greater alacrity, and my experience and observation during that tour forever settled my opinion as to the true method of dealing with the liquor traffic in localities where the public mind has been properly enlightened.

On my way to this interesting field of labor, I tarried a day or two at Portland, with my friend Neal Dow, then Mayor of that city. The morning after my arrival an incident occurred which I thought worthy of record. After witnessing it, and enjoying a pleasant stroll through one of the most beautiful cities on this continent, I returned to the residence of my friend Dow, and wrote the following article, in which facts and fancies somehow got strangely mingled. The reader will find no serious difficulty, I imagine, in making the proper discrimination between them.

A VISIT TO THE SPIRITS IN PRISON.

While walking down the streets of Portland, this morning, in company with the very efficient mayor of that beautiful city, I was invited to step with him across the street and take a look at the imprisoned "spirits" shut up in durance vile beneath the City Hall. I accepted the invitation, and in a moment found myself in a large basement room, surrounded on all sides by the imprisoned fiends, which, under the recently enacted and most righteous law of the state, had been arrested in their march from the mouth of the still to the mouths of the wretched men who had become already so far demonized as to desire the further acquaintance and companionship of those liquid devils. Three or four extensive seizures of the spirits had been made, and here they were all gathered in one group; and a sorry-looking group it was. Their sad plight, piled on each other's backs around the apartment, recalled the language of Hamlet to the skull of poor Yorick:—

> "Where be your gibes now? your
> Gambols? your songs? your flashes of merriment
> That were wont to set the table in a roar? . . .
> . . . Quite chapfallen."

I looked upon the strong oak casks, some of them iron bound, and thought how fortunate it was that the hands of government had arrested them before their fiery and demonizing contents had got spilled into the stomachs of some of its poor deluded subjects. Long and ardently I had desired to see the government, in true paternal regard for its suffering poor, and for the thousands who are being hurried by the liquor traffic to ruin, exert its power promptly and effectually to stay the work of death. And here, at length, I am permitted to see the master spirit of mischief, the giant curse of the civilized world, chained. A feeling of exultation was kindled within me, which I have no words adequately to express. Aha! thought I; you who, with your kindred spirits, have sent thousands to the watch-house, to the jail, and to the prison; who have bolted the doors upon thousands of my brethren, and shut them out from the society of their families and the world, have gotten into limboes yourself! The angel of justice has at length come down, "with a great chain in his hand," and bound you. Here you await your trial, and if condemned, as you probably will be, you shall be led forth to execution, amid the rejoicings of an injured people, and your blood shall flow, not, as ye hoped, down the parched throats of men, but down the gutters and through the city sewers. Well, you are in a good way. Mother earth and the waters of the bay can swallow you and not reel, and that is more than men could do.

How long have you trampled on laws human and divine, taken your own wild, wicked way, and gloried in your might! Ye laughed at "restriction" and "regulation;" but stronger words have been whispered in your ears by the legislature of Maine—"suppression," "annihilation;" and lo, ye pause here to consider the import of the new vocabulary. Well, ye will learn it, no doubt, for ye are apt scholars. But how will your friends and adherents, not only in the city, but among the hills, regard your capture and detention? They have hitherto gloried in your strength, and have asked exultingly, "Who is like unto the beast? Who is able to make war against him?" Maine hath answered in stern and decided tone, and—ye are here! "The merchants of those things, which were made rich by thee, shall stand afar off, for the fear of thy torment, weeping, and wailing, and crying, Alas! . . . For in one hour so great riches have come to nought."

What varied forms have ye taken, as I see ye here in your prison, and how varied your destination! Here ye swell out in great bulk, like a corpulent, turtle-fed alderman, and there ye shrink almost to the dimensions of a water bucket. Let me look at your names, and learn whither ye were bound. "American Gin, Parsonfield." And what business had you at Parsonfield? Did the parson invite you to visit his field? Nay, verily. He would sooner have sent you to the Potter's field. But to Parsonfield you were going; and for what? Ah, I remember. There is a poor widow in that neighborhood, whose husband ye slew, and whose eldest son ye have poisoned, until the poor lad totters as he walks. His brain is on fire. He talks incoherently, and strange fancies possess him. Sometimes he curses the mother who bore him; and those hands which, when a child, she pressed in hers while she prayed, have been lifted in violence against her. She is almost distracted with her troubles, and knoweth not whither to turn for relief. Despair has sometimes almost taken possession of her soul. She hateth thee, and lifteth her eyes, swollen with weeping, and her feeble hands, to Heaven against thee. And thou wouldst afflict her still more! Heartless, obdurate devil! Yes, you were journeying to Parsonfield for that purpose; but the angel of justice met thee, and—thou art here. How will that widow rejoice and sing when she shall hear the glad tidings of thy fall!

But let me look at thy brother fiend. "N. E. Rum, W. A., Bethel." And what was thy errand to Bethel? Jacob went up to Bethel, and built there an altar, because *there* the Lord met him in the time of his troubles. And you, too, have built an altar at Bethel, whereon thou dost sacrifice to strange gods. But goats and bullocks will not serve thee for sacrifices. The blood of our sons, "the expectancy and rose of the fair state," is smoking upon thine altar at Bethel. But thou art not there. Iron bands confine, and bolts and bars detain thee. Thine altar at Bethel will grow cold, and the sweet waters of the rejoicing heavens shall wash away its stains. "Old Madeira, 10 gallons, Wm. Baker, Brunswick." And you, old gentleman, were bound for Brunswick. There is a college at Brunswick; and did ye covet an education? "No, ye were going to teach, and not to be taught." So I supposed. A professor of infernal mathematics and languages, en route for Brunswick, to teach the young men big oaths, subtraction from the pocket, multiplication of miseries, and reduction descending; ay, and to add thereto important instruction in *your* rule of three direct, to the poorhouse, the prison, and the drunkard's grave. Verily, a rule of *three*, and as *direct* as one could desire. And "you give instructions in navigation." Ay, I have seen your pupils making trial of their skill; and it was, indeed, an interesting exhibition!

But let us make the acquaintance of your next neighbor, Mr. St. Croix. And you, sir, were bound to *Freeport*, but—did not get there. It was not a "*port of entry*" for you, it seems, with all its freedom. And what do you purpose to do now? "Wait here the arrival of your friends from Boston." Very well; we pledge you the word of the mayor and city marshal, that your friends shall visit you here, immediately on their arrival. Farewell to your devilships; keep cool, and learn "the uses of affliction."

At Hallowell, no efforts had been made to enforce the new law when I reached the city. In conference with the leading friends of the cause, I urged an immediate advance upon the enemies' works. There was a man by the name of Gilman, who it was rumored had recently received a supply of liquors which he had determined to sell in defiance of law. He was reputed to be a man of violent temper, exceedingly belligerent, and, withal, a man of great physical power, and it was thought he would show fight if an attempt should be made to search his premises and seize his stock. He had sworn that if any man should enter his store to interfere with his business, he would cleave his head to the shoulders if there were any virtue in muscles and a good axe. I assured the friends that he would never strike a blow, if sober, when the officers of the law, with proper aids, should visit him. They thought otherwise.

I volunteered my services to accompany the officer, and aid in the execution of a search warrant, if they could find three citizens who would make complaint according to law. They were soon found, and officer

Smith declared his readiness to execute the warrant. An energetic man by the name of Allen, if I rightly remember, small of stature but of good grit, also tendered his services to aid the officer. All needful steps were taken, teams provided to take the liquors away in case any should be found, and early on the following morning we paid the gentleman a visit. No sooner were we seen to enter the building, than the rowdies of the vicinity at once divined our object, and in less than thirty minutes a group numbering probably an hundred, had gathered in front of the store, to resist the enforcement of the law, and make short work with the fanatics. To prevent egress from the store by the way we had entered, they backed a horse cart closely against the open door-way, filled it with loafers, and as many of the rabble as possible crowded the passage.

Matters began to look a little squally. Fourteen barrels of rum had been found in the store, but how were they to be taken thence, when the only passage therefrom was blocked with an enraged group of loafers? In a very threatening attitude Gilman demanded of me what business I had upon his premises. I informed him that I was there at the request of a civil officer, to aid him in the execution of a legal warrant.

"You are, ha!"

"Yes, sir."

Well, get out of this store —— quick, or you will find yourself in trouble."

I assured him I should not leave the store until ordered by the officer.

He stepped backward a few paces to arm himself, and

advancing toward me with uplifted axe, said, "I understand you to say that you will not leave my store."

"Yes," I replied, "I will not leave your store until ordered by the officer."

The reader will desire to learn what awful event immediately happened. Well, just as I expected, he laid away his axe, and contented himself with less terrible measures than splitting heads. In an undertone I remarked to the officer, that when he should give orders for those barrels of liquor to go out the store, they would go, notwithstanding the cart at the door, and the loafers who blocked the passage way.

Approaching the group crowded in the door-way, he said, "Gentlemen, I request you to clear that passage. I have a legal warrant to execute, and you may be sure I shall discharge my duties."

He was told to go to a place not laid down on the maps.

Turning to Allen and myself, who were awaiting orders, the officer bade us roll the casks of liquor forward. They came forward.

"Now," said the officer, "I once more command you to clear that doorway."

He was again told to go to ——, a warm climate.

"Words are of no avail," said the officer, addressing his helpers, "we must act; put those barrels into the street."

We laid hold of the barrel nearest the door, Allen at one end of it and I at the other, and when we were ready to send it forward I quietly advised those in the passage to remove the legs which were in our way, or they might get hurt, when I was told to go to a place, which, from the character of the company about me I had reasons to believe might not be distant.

With that we sent that barrel with all the force we could command against the obstructions, and after a slight recoil of the casks legs were put in motion with alacrity, and the doorway was cleared of loafers. There, however, stood the horse-cart, its rear backed as near to the door as possible.

Seeing that his doughty champions had failed him, Gilman seated himself in the rear of the cart, and thrust his feet into the doorway. After assuring him that he was playing a losing, and very dangerous game, in resisting a civil officer, I advised him to take his legs out of the way, or the weight of a barrel of rum would test their strength. He did not remove them, and the barrel was rolled directly upon them. Fortunately they were strong legs, and stood the strain well, but the weight of the cask held him firmly in his place. I sprang over the barrel, and seizing it by one end tipped it off those rather novel skids, greatly to his relief, and he concluded to make no further resistance.

The horse and cart were removed, and the way being now cleared, the remaining casks soon followed the one which had encountered so many obstructions.

The entire stock, fourteen barrels, were loaded on wagons in waiting, and preceded by the officer and his aids, the precious stuff was deposited in a secure place, to await the final adjudication of the case by the proper authorities.

A knowledge of what was transpiring had spread rapidly through the city while we were making the seizure, and when the job was finished, and the teams, loaded with liquors, were passing up the streets, it was evident to all that the law had triumphed, notwithstanding the weakness of the legal party, and the mothers, wives, and daughters of Hallowell, waving their handkerchiefs as we passed, cheered us on our way. This was my first experience of the practical working of the Maine Law. *It had worked like a charm thus far.*

Some time elapsed before the session of the court and the trial of the case. After filling my appointments and returning to Boston, I met John Hawkins, who had also just returned from a tour in Maine, closing with labor at Hallowell. After the usual salutation, the faithful Washingtonian informed me, with great exultation, that he had happened to reach Hallowell just in time to see the fourteen barrels of condemned liquors poured into the gutter, and he informed me that after the emptying of the first cask, he turned it on end, and taking his stand upon it, he addressed the crowd who had gathered to see the show, while the remaining thirteen casks were being emptied.

"It was," said Hawkins, "one of the happiest hours of my life."

We can well believe it was a glad time for Hawkins, to see his old enemy, which had for so many years held him in a slavery worse than Egyptian, led out to execution, and amid the cheers of its enemies, mingled with the contents of the sewers.

The third day of my stay in Hallowell, officer Smith seized the cargo of a vessel just arrived from Boston, and with his former aids, and two or three other volunteers, was hoisting the liquor from the vessel's hold, and putting it upon the wharf, when our operations were arrested by a call for a compromise. A consultation was had by the interested parties, and the best terms the friends of the law would grant to the captain of the vessel, or rather the owners of the liquors, for whom the captain was authorized to act, was, that not a gallon of the cargo should be landed in the State of Maine, but that, putting on board what he had already landed on the wharf, the vessel should immediately make sail for Boston. This must be done, or the whole cargo would, after the proper legal condemnation, go to swell the waters of the Kennebec. The terms were accepted, and those who had shipped the liquors in Boston soon learned that the Maine Law could deal with *cargoes*, as well as the contents of a pint bottle.

Does the reader wonder at the great outcry against that law from the time it began to be enforced to this hour, and the unnumbered falsehoods which have been uttered to prove its inefficiency? Like a steam engine of an hundred horse-power, or a hydraulic press capable of pressing an inch pine board to one-eighth of that thickness, the Maine Law is inefficient *if not used;* but give to its enforcement a tolerably healthy public sentiment, an honest purpose, and faithful officers, and it is glorious to see how the liquor traffic will expire under its pressure.

As a further objection to the law, it has been urged that its successful enforcement involves to too great an extent the destruction of property. This was urged some years since, I remember, at the close of one of my public lectures in Worcester County, Massachusetts, wherein I had expressed my views of the law. An individual rose and urged the objection above stated, and added, very foolishly as I thought, that God's way of reforming human society or saving men was not to destroy that which was useful and valuable. "He, on the contrary," said the gentleman, "accomplished His beneficent purposes by the providential diffusion of knowledge and manifestations of His love." I replied that the gentleman had evidently read the history of God's dealings with men to very little purpose, or he would never have referred to them to prove the very high estimation in which the Deity regards what we choose to call property; for at the Deluge, as well as by the destruction of the corrupt cities of the plain, according to the scriptures, there must have been some heavy losses of property. The gentleman, I added, should remember too, that when God miraculously rescued his people from the terrible exactions and oppressions of the Egyptian King, that a very large number of horses and chariots were destroyed by a very summary process, and that recent excavations on the former sites of Herculaneum and Pompeii gave evidence that a large amount of property, the results of human labor and skill, had been destroyed *there*, and at very short notice.

There is no important question now agitated among men, about which so many lies and so much unmitigated nonsense have been uttered, as in defence of the liquor traffic and the use of intoxicants. It requires more of Christian patience than I possess to listen to and bear with it all without getting sometimes religiously angry. To what legitimate use can the contents of an ordinary liquor store or dram-shop be devoted? Some of it might be re-distilled and the alcohol might be employed for chemical or mechanical purposes; but if this service was committed to private individuals, even as agents of the state, the evil genii that seem ever associated with alcohol in its relations to man would be very likely to make heartless rogues and scoundrels of them. No; the very best disposition that can be made of them is to pour them into the gutters. The moral effects of such an exhibition upon those who witness it is excellent, as it testifies to the worthlessness of articles which many have been accustomed to value quite too highly. God be thanked for the Maine Law! and the grand inspiration, energy, and honest devotion to the public weal by which it was created! May no backward step ever be taken in that noble State, which now bears the flag of prohibition, in the advance of our temperance host.

CHAPTER XX.

Will you come? Yes—A Challenge—A four days Debate—The Whisky Champion—A Bill of Indictment—Plausible but baseless—Still Debating—Parallel Cases—Shad in Connecticut River! Ha, Ha—A good time—A capital arrangement—A Colloquy—A distiller at the front—Political Economy—Still-fed Pork—"Tender"—Hard Work but poor Pay.

During the summer of 1852, while lecturing in Oneida County, N. Y., I received from S. F. Cary, of Cincinnati, a pressing invitation to perform some service in Ohio, during a campaign in which they were just about to enter. A move had been made to fix in the Constitution of the State, by the vote of the people, a provision that the Legislature should not thereafter have power to license the traffic in intoxicating liquors. Some weeks would elapse before the time of voting on the question, and the friends of temperance in Ohio wished to make a pretty thorough canvass of the state and bring out the largest possible vote in favor of the proposed amendment to the constitution. Four public lecturers of New England had been engaged to aid in the canvass—Rev. B. E. Hale, of Massachusetts, and three others—and now they desired to add Dr. Jewett to their list of public speakers for the campaign. I was reluctant to leave a field of labor where my services were kindly appreciated and generously rewarded. Many years of steady labor at public speaking, except during the summer months, when audiences are gathered with difficulty, had overtasked my lungs and they had consequently become somewhat weakened, and I doubted whether it would be quite safe to engage in a campaign where I might be required to address large assemblies in the open air. My friend, Gen. Cary, however, would take no denial, and pressed the matter with so much urgency and zeal, that I at length consented. For reasons already stated, I made it a condition of the engagement, however, that I should not be required to speak often in the open air. As to pecuniary reward, I informed my friend Cary that I should not consent to receive, besides traveling expenses, more than I was receiving in the State of New York at the time I left it, which was the modest sum of ten dollars per lecture.

I reached Columbus, the capital of Ohio, at the date agreed upon, had an interview with some members of the Executive Committee, and went heartily to work, filling appointments previously made for me. While thus engaged, a matter was arranged at Columbus, which, it will be seen, seriously concerned me, but about which I was not consulted. The leaders of the party who, from pecuniary or other motives were laboring to prevent the adoption of the proposed amendment to the constitution, had imported an advocate of their views from the State of New York, and challenged the Executive Committee of the State Temperance Society to debate with him the points at issue, through any individual they might venture to pit against him. The Committee, as I subsequently learned, after consultation with the other lecturers from New England, accepted the challenge for a public debate, to be continued through four successive days, at Columbus, Lancaster, Circleville, and Chillicothe, and decided to rely upon me to sustain, in the debate, the views and measures of the temperance party. I was directed to come at once to the Capital, and not until reaching the city the night before the contemplated encounter, did I learn of the arrangement. Nowise reluctant to debate, at any time and with any party, the soundness of views I had long held and publicly advocated, I was not quite pleased with some of the arrangements. For example: no measures had been taken to secure a full report of the debate and its subsequent publication, that the citizens of Ohio, who could not be present might read, if they could not hear, the argument on both sides of the question. I urged the importance of such a measure upon the Committee, assuring them that, if it were not adopted, the friends of the liquor traffic, one of whom can generally make more noise than half-a-dozen temperance men, would proclaim a decided victory for their champion, no matter what the result might be in the estimation of candid men present. It was, however, too late to mend the programme, and the debate proceeded according to previous arrangement.

My opponent, though a man of little general information and still less knowledge of science, possessed a good deal of that tact and assurance so useful to a fourth-rate lawyer before a country justice of limited legal attainments and a crowd of honest but credulous people, not qualified or disposed to be critical. He was thoroughly versed in the art of defending the liquor system by scriptural arguments, and could quote Paul's advice to Timothy as accurately and aptly as any of our few wine-drinking doctors of divinity. Some of his views of scripture truth, however, were not far removed, in point of absurdity, from those of the poor fellow who, attempting to show that nearly all the good men mentioned in the Bible drank, insisted that " even Zadoc the Priest took a horn."

Ere the hour fixed upon for the commencement of the debate had arrived, a large crowd of citizens had assembled around the platform, which had been erected in the open air, and a glance over the upturned faces of the throng was not calculated to lessen one's hatred of the liquor traffic, or of habits which could so inflame, disfigure, and brutalize the human face Divine. Not often is the temperance advocate called to face such a crowd, for, alas! hard drinkers generally keep as far from the public teacher and reformatory influences as possible. Deluded by the "mocker" and the miserable sophistries by which its use is generally defended, and zealous in the support of the Diana they had so long and devoutly worshiped, they had gathered to listen to the defense, by their champion, of the system which, beside its other manifold mischievous results, was ruining themselves, body, soul, and estate. Reader, do you wonder that, seeing in the crowd before me many such poor deluded men, I silently but earnestly prayed that God would enable me to utter there some truths which might be blessed to their instruction and rescue from an impending and terrible doom.

The question to be debated, though I may not state it in the precise words employed in arranging for the discussion, was substantially this: "May the State of Ohio, in accordance with its own constitution, the constitution of the United States, and the eternal principles of right and justice, prohibit entirely the manufacture and traffic in intoxicating liquors?" In opening for the affirmative, I employed the time allotted me in presenting the grounds on which we claimed for the state the right disputed. I affirmed that the traffic had resulted, not only in the personal ruin of thousands of its citizens, deeply afflicting, meanwhile, their families and connections, but that it had, at the same time, been waging perpetual war on all public interests, sanitary, social, moral, educational, material, and governmental, and that, while doing all this mischief, it benefited permanently nobody; for there was, I asserted, abundant proof that a large percentage of those engaged in the manufacture and sale of liquors were personally ruined in health and morals by the evil influences of their own business, or suffered from the ruin, thereby, of some members of their families. Having thus presented, as well as I was able in a single hour, a bill of indictment against the liquor system generally, I rested the case, for the time, and yielded the floor to my opponent. It is but just to say, that from the crowd around the stand, made up, as it was in part, of dealers in and drinkers of whisky, I received no insults or interruption, but was listened to with that respectful attention with which true American citizens should ever listen to public addresses, even when they do not at all accept the doctrines or approve the sentiments of the speaker.

The reply of my opponent, though having but a feeble foundation, certainly possessed the charm of novelty, and was presented with considerable force and with evident sincerity. I doubt if a suspicion had ever entered his mind, that it was utterly fallacious.

He called attention to the fact, that in the creation of living beings, in almost endless varieties of form, size, and structure, to inhabit every zone from the equator to the arctic, and with habits and modes of life varying almost to infinity, God had established, in relation to their means of subsistence, one law, and that was that they choose, through the aid of an instinct which he had implanted, their own diet and drink.

Was it to be supposed, he asked, that man, the paragon of animals, the lord of all inferior races, and made but a little lower than the angels, was less capable of choosing his own diet and drink than the cattle of the hills, the winged races, the crawling reptiles, or even the tiny insect that sports its little day of life in the air around us? The supposition, he said, could not be indulged for one moment. He further urged that this right of choosing their own diet and drinks was so sacred that even the Creator and Eternal Law-Giver had never interfered with it, and "here we have," said he, "in these prohibitory laws, an attempt by our poor imperfect human law makers, to do what God himself has never done—to regulate the diet and drink of man." Of course, I cannot pretend that I give the exact words of the speaker. My language may be better or worse than his, but those were his leading ideas.

In reply, I admitted the truth of the gentleman's statement, so far as the lower orders of animals are concerned, but urged that the fact had no bearing on the matter under discussion; that in his treatment of man, the Creator had certainly made him an exception to the rule stated, if we were to believe the Bible, for, according to that, one of the earliest, if not the very first command given to man in Eden, was a restriction on his diet, forbidding him, on pain of death, to eat of the fruit of a certain tree of the garden. Furthermore, I called attention to the fact, that under the Mosaic economy very precise directions were given for the regulation of the diet. Of the flesh of certain animals the people were permitted to eat, of the flesh of others they were forbidden to eat. What, I then asked, became of the gentleman's assertion that the right of *man*, as well as of all other animals, to choose his own diet, was so sacred that the Creator had never interfered with it?

It is not my purpose to attempt even an abstract of the four days debate, especially after the lapse of eighteen years. So far as it was strictly relevant to the question at issue, there were no points presented on either side except the novel but baseless one already reported, with which my fellow-laborers are not familiar. They have often listened to the stereotyped objections of the liquor party to restrictive or prohibitory legislation, and many of them, doubtless, have often answered them quite as well as I did, as they were successively presented by my opponent on the occasion referred to.

To his assertion, that the legislature of Ohio had no constitutional right to prohibit the traffic, I replied by quoting the unanimous decision of the Supreme Court of the United States, rendered five years previous, and suggested, very respectfully of course, that the aggregate wisdom of our Supreme Court was probably quite equal to that of the gentleman from New York.

My opponent, though evidently a man of kindly disposition, and rarely resorting to offensive personalities, and never to the employment of the billingsgate in which advocates of the liquor traffic are wont to indulge, manifested, as might have been expected, an utter want of candor in refusing to admit an error when fairly convicted of one, or yielding a point when fairly turned against him. In such cases he would dodge the point where his position had proved untenable, seeming to forget that he had made it, and drive at some other point as remote from it as possible. As an illustration of his method in such cases, take the following. It occurred in our debate at Chillicothe.

He asserted distinctly and repeatedly that in the history of legislation on this continent, there was no parallel to that provision of the Maine law which protects a man in the possession of liquors as a valuable property, while in his own dwelling, but confiscates and destroys them if found in his store as articles of merchandise—condemning and destroying to-day what it protected as a valuable possession yesterday, because the location of the property had been changed or surrounding circumstances slightly altered. With a show of entire confidence in the truth of his statement, he challenged me to point to any specimen of legislation equally absurd, as he proclaimed it.

During the next half-hour the floor was mine, and I proceeded at once to answer his urgent call for cases parallel to the one he had chosen to condemn, as an anomaly in the history of legislation. I cited the laws then existing regulating the taking of fish from the Connecticut river, where the boats, seines, and other tackle of the fisherman, which might be lawfully used on certain days of the week, are forbidden to be used for the same purposes on other specified days—protected as a valuable possession up to the stroke of twelve on Tuesday night, say, but if found in use on the river an hour later by the officers of the law or others disposed to complain of the offence, confiscated and destroyed.

I cited the law concerning the possession of cards or other gaming apparatus, which a man might legally use in his own dwelling for the amusement of his children or friends, but found in his store, employed in gaming, are forfeited or destroyed. I referred, also, to the fact, that a gentleman might, if he chose, import from Europe or elsewhere a valuable horse, and that our laws would defend his right to the property, even on mid-ocean, or wherever the vessel might float under our flag, not only against the fraudulant claim of an individual, but against that of a nation if need be; and yet, by the laws of my native state, that very horse would, after reaching our shores, be confiscated and lost to its owner, if found on a race-course and running for a wager.

Who now would venture to say that the cases cited were not in point and did not fully meet the gentleman's demand? What could a candid man in his position do but to admit that he had been mistaken on that particular point, that he had not been aware of the existence of the laws referred to—or still to deny their existence and call for the proof. My opponent did neither. He rose with an expression of unabated confidence, I might almost say of exultation, which was instantly answered by a broad and sympathetic grin on every whisky-bloated face before him, and said,

"Mr. Chairman, and citizens of Ohio, the gentleman who has just taken his seat, has given us a full half-hour's instruction in relation to horse-racing, gambling, and —— shad in the Connecticut river!"

This called forth from the whisky element in the crowd a shout of derisive laughter, and after pausing a moment to enjoy this manifestation of sympathy, and joy at his assumed triumph, he proceeded, " but what has all that to do with the question, whether the people of Ohio are to be deprived of their inalienable rights by oppressive and infamous laws, dictated by a set of cold water fanatics." From this he went on, without another word of reference to the point from which he had been driven by incontrovertible facts, to multiply points equally untenable, with an assurance almost sublime.

What possible profit can come of a public debate conducted on one side in such a style ? As I had anticipated, and as a matter of course, the liquor party, who from long practice, have become expert in misrepresentation, telegraphed over the country that in the four days debate in Ohio on the liquor laws the temperance party had been terribly discomfited.

The excitement and fatigue incident to that debate which, as has already been stated, continued through four days, on three of which it was held in the open air, was a severe tax on my powers of endurance, considering the state of my health at the time, especially as it was preceded and followed by a public service at some point daily. My labor during the entire campaign, which occupied nearly eight weeks from my arrival at Columbus, was unintermitted, and contrary to the conditions of my engagement; not less than twelve or fifteen of my discourses were delivered in the open air. Notwithstanding the severity of the labor, the tour through the state, and the daily contact with earnest friends of the cause, afforded me much pleasure. At one point especially, I enjoyed my work so well, that I love to recall the particulars. Some varieties of food skillfully prepared, and delicious when first served, are still excellent when warmed up for a second repast.

It was at Cincinnati that the circumstances surrounding me, created in a large measure by the practical wisdom and tact of the local committee of arrangements, secured me a rare opportunity for pleading the cause of temperance with the people, such as I have seldom enjoyed during my thirty years of public service. They obtained leave of the city authorities, to erect, at the junction of Fifth street and Market square, if I rightly remember, a platform from which I might address the people for a number of successive evenings, which were then pleasant. The platform was raised about four feet from the ground or pavement, and its supporting posts at each corner extended some six or eight feet higher. Nailed to the sides of these posts, at a proper distance above the platform, were small cross-pieces extending therefrom each way two or three feet, and on these very many gentlemen suspended their lanterns which they must have brought from home for that special purpose, as the principal streets being lighted, lanterns would hardly be needed on a pleasant evening except in traversing some narrow and unlighted streets. Each of the four posts of the platform was thus rendered a grand chandelier, and the street was lighted far better than are some of our public halls when in use. Around that platform were gathered for a number of evenings a crowd consisting entirely of male citizens of all ages, from ten to eighty years, and a more orderly crowd of equal numbers I never saw. Except an occasional clapping of hands, or an approving exclamation when some point made by the speaker gave special pleasure to a portion of the audience, there were no noisy demonstrations, but a patient, respectful attention to the views advanced. Just here I would earnestly recommend to our friends of the cities a similar arrangement for the instruction of the people in reference to this great practical question. With the laboring men of our cities, and during the warm season of the year, the evening is generally a time of leisure, and if that season be chosen, when the evenings are usually pleasant, and the plan of our Cincinnati friends be adopted for lighting the locality of the meeting, it will leave those who would speak to the people little to desire in the way of opportunity. The thorough lighting of the space for a wide distance around the platform, is essential to success, because those inclined from any cause to disturb the meeting will not venture to do so when a glare of light reveals the offender to those around him.

After developing my views of the subject for several evenings, I decided to devote the concluding service to replies, from the platform, to questions from the crowd relative to any phase of the subject concerning which they might desire my opinions, and to answering, as far as I might be able, any objections to the doctrines advanced during the preceding evenings. I was so well pleased with the result of that experiment, that I have pursued a similar course very many times since at the conclusion of a series of lectures in churches, public halls, and wherever the people had gathered to hear. But we will, in thought, return to Cincinnati, and the throng around that platform. Fearing that there might be some hesitation at first, in presenting objections by those who honestly entertained them, I had arranged with some of our most devoted and influential brethren, to mingle with the crowd at points some distance from the stand, and when I should invite questions, to have in mind some popular objection of the liquor advocates, and with great earnestness launch it at me at once and thus set the ball in motion. The arrangement worked like a charm, and for an hour and a half at least, I was constantly and pleasantly employed in answering objections to the doctrines, plans, and measures of the temperance party. In doing this I was careful in all cases to treat the objector or questioner with all possible respect as an honest seeker after truth, as doubtless many were, avoiding whatever might give needless offense; for my aim was to convert men to correct views of a great practical question, rather than any momentary triumph over those who might seem, for the time, to be ranging themselves with our opposition. Invariably I would pause at the conclusion of every answer or explanation and ask, "Is my answer to that question satisfactory to my countrymen around me? If so, I will attend to the next objection, if others shall be presented." At length an individual, mighty in avoirdupois, who was standing in the doorway of a house across the street, bawled out in a very excited voice and manner, that I had uttered from the platform a statement absolutely untrue concerning a very important interest of Ohio. While he was speaking, a friend standing by my side, remarked to me in an undertone, that the person I had now to deal with was one of the great distillers of the city.

"Keep shady," said I, "I must seem not to know his vocation, and shall gain an immense advantage by so doing." I invited him to specify the false statement, when the following colloquy substantially occurred. I cannot of course be certain that I give the precise words but will report it as nearly as possible, after the lapse of eighteen years. A frequent reference to the affair since, in conversation with friends, has helped to keep the matter fresh in my memory, for the story was too good to spoil by close keeping.

Dist. "You stated that the manufacture and sale of intoxicating liquors, works great mischief to the State of Ohio, which no one will deny, but you also stated that no corresponding advantages result, which is not true, for many millions of gallons of whisky are annually exported from the state, adding *greatly* to its *wealth*."

Dr. J. "Sir, you are mistaken. Private individuals may add to their wealth by the liquor business, but the State does not."

Dist. "That is quite a new notion in political economy, that you can increase the wealth of the individual citizens of a state, without adding to the wealth of the state."

Dr. J. "New as it may be to you, sir, it is yet true. When Mr. A. picks the pocket of Mr. B. *he* is the richer by the contents of the pocket-book, but nothing is added thereby to the wealth of the state."

[Just here comes a loud shout from the listening throng, which for a moment somewhat disconcerted the distiller, but he soon rallied and proceeded thus:]

Dist. "We were not talking of theft or of other crimes, but of legitimate and honorable business."

Dr. J. "Well, sir, by the business of manufacturing and selling intoxicating liquors, men do accumulate wealth, and therefore pay heavier taxes for the support of the state government, but meanwhile thousands are made so poor by that same traffic, that they pay little or no tax at all, and thus the state is a loser rather than a gainer by the entire liquor business, even in a money point of view —not to speak just here of its immense loss in the health, happiness, and morals of its people.

"But I wish to call your attention, sir, and that of the crowd around us, to another point, which perhaps you have not considered. Pork is one of the great staples of Ohio, and the state exports an immense amount annually, five-sixths of which, I am informed, is corn-fed, produced by the farmers of the state, while one-sixth is still-fed pork, of an inferior quality. This gets so mixed with the farmer's pork, while passing to the great markets of the country, that it cannot be distinguished until it reaches the consumer. That fact being well known, depreciates the value of western pork in the aggregate, often three or four dollars on the barrel below the price of pork produced and packed in the eastern states. Thus the farmers of Ohio are losers to an immense amount, that the distillers may sell, *above its real value*, their miserable still-fed pork. That, sir, is one of the ways in which Ohio is enriched by the liquor business."

[Here came another shout from the listening throng, but the veteran distiller still stood his ground, and made another point thus.]

Dist. "That is but one-half the truth, the other half is, that the smoked meats produced by the distillers bring up the price of the entire aggregate exported, as they are a better article, and are preferred in the markets."

Dr. J. "*Why* are they preferred?"

Dist. "It is no use denying it, the fact is notorious."

Dr. J. "I have not disputed the fact. I only wish to know *why* they are preferred, that is all."

Dist. "It is no use to quibble about the matter. Meet the fact, and dispose of it if you can."

[He seemed to suspect that I might make some bad use of any explanation he might make of the fact stated, and sought to avoid it, but I still thrust the question upon him.]

Dr. J. "Why are the smoked meats of the still-fed swine considered more valuable," until at last he responded.

Dist. "Well, sir, if you must know, I believe it is because the meats are more tender."

Dr. J. "Aye! That is it! Please notice that fact, citizens of

Ohio. The smoked meats of the distillers are 'more tender' than those produced by the farmers. I will now explain to you why they are more tender. Causes which lessen the vitality of an animal during life, hasten its decomposition after death. Some diseases of a low type produce such changes in the solid structure of the human body, that parts here and there lose their vitality, run into a state of decomposition, and slough off, while the patient yet lives. Now, still-slops form an imperfect diet for animals, for although you can, by their use, load an animal with adipose or fat, as you may a man by the use of whisky, yet the tissues of the whole body have but a low degree of vitality, and are at the very verge of decomposition before the butcher ends the life of the animal. No wonder that the flesh of such animals even when cured for the market, is tender. Let those who fancy such tenderness enjoy it. For one I prefer hams from the corn-fed pork, though the fibres be a little less tender."

[The colloquy was here interrupted by a peal of laughter from the crowd, and our friend the distiller, lost for the moment his good nature, and declared, with a moderate explosive, my statement unfounded, or at best an exaggeration.]

Dr. J. "Hold on, sir," I replied. "You declare my statement false. Listen a moment to another, and deny it if you dare in the presence of this crowd, who are doubtless acquainted with the facts. A man accustomed to that business, is sent daily through those large enclosures where swine are fed in connection with the great distilleries around this city, to examine the swine in every pen, and when he finds one with a scratch or wound upon him, as often happens, he is at once withdrawn from the pen and sent to the butcher, and why? Because, sir, it is well known by all concerned, that wounds on still-fed hogs do not heal."

The Distiller here broke down and quit the field, and it would have done the reader good to have heard the shouts and roars of laughter that went up from that crowd as he withdrew from a contest which he had himself provoked.

While serving the cause in Ohio I occasionally called

on the Committee for funds needed to pay traveling expenses, and to transmit to my family. It was furnished me. Of course I could not present a bill for my services until my work was ended, and I felt no anxiety about the matter, supposing that I was dealing with honorable men, amply able to discharge any obligations they might incur. When, at the close of my labor, I did present my bill, giving credit, of course, for what had been already paid, I was informed that the treasury was just then exhausted, but that funds would be forthcoming, presently, from local organizations which had pledged certain amounts toward the fund for the campaign. As I was to return immediately to my family, it was arranged that the balance due, $160, should be sent me in a draft as soon as possible.

Not one cent of it has been received to this day!

Of course I had nothing to do with the local organizations of Ohio, and their pledges to support the movement. My engagement had been with a committee. They failed to discharge their obligations, and I suffered loss, my wife and a family of dependent children sharing it with me. I had this, however, to comfort me. The wrong attached to others, the lesser evil of suffering, only, was mine.

After that campaign in Ohio, I was unable for years to labor continuously in the way of public lecturing, for although otherwise in tolerable health, I could speak but for a few evenings in succession, before my lungs would fail me.

CHAPTER XXI.

Westward ho!—On the Prairies—A Thanksgiving extemporized—Whisky and the Indians—Life on the Farm.

The ordinary rewards of such limited service as I was able to render by public lecturing, being quite insufficient properly to support my family, consisting at the time, of five sons and two daughters, beside the parent pair, I resolved to remove to the west, where, on a new and fertile soil, my boys could aid me in securing for the family the necessaries of life, expecting, of course, to lack some of the comforts and social advantages which we had enjoyed in older communities. I sold my little farm in Millbury, settled up my affairs and found myself possessed of about eighteen hundred dollars with which to transport my family a thousand miles or more, and on some new field start anew in the journey of life. I spent one year in Batavia, Illinois, one of the most delightful villages in the northern portion of that state; and so long as memory remains to me I shall never forget, or cease to be grateful for the great kindness of its people. Of course while with them I did what I could as a private citizen to advance the interests of the temperance cause.

As I had often heard or read glowing accounts of the excellent soil and climate of Minnesota, where lands could be obtained at government prices, I visited the territory in the spring of 1855, and with my eldest son, who had attained his majority, stuck our "claim stakes" on the prairies a couple of miles from what is now the thriving town of Faribault. My wife, daughters, and youngest son I had left in Illinois.

As two of the family could, at that time, claim lands under the laws of our government, we secured a quarter section, an hundred and sixty acres each, of excellent prairie, and my second son coming of age in a few weeks after we reached Minnesota, took a claim in the timber near by as soon as he could legally do so, and erecting our tents and securing teams and the needful tools, we set to work with stout hearts, strong hopes, and Yankee self-reliance, to make us homes on the prairies, where Sioux Indians, and prairie-wolves had held undisputed possession since—when? I do not know.

We succeeded, and I succeeded in another direction,—in soon using up my limited stock of funds in the work of breaking up and fencing our lands and erecting a plain, but not very cheap dwelling, with needful granaries, cattle-sheds, and in getting pretty deeply in debt. Nevertheless, we looked for "the good time coming," and toiled on, paying a pretty stout interest on a few hundred dollars for years. How soon interest money becomes due! I doubt if time ever seems so short, except to lovers tete-a-tete, or to those sentenced to be hanged, shot, or decapitated, as it does to men having notes coming due at twenty per cent. interest. Weeks and months fly with the speed of wild pigeons. How heavily that debt bore upon us for years, none can know who have never been in debt, while so far west that of two bushels of grain the value of one is required to send the other to the great markets.

It is doubtful whether, even with the constant labor of the whole family, and the exercise of the most rigid economy, we should ever have been able, while paying such heavy interest, to have lifted the mortgage from my prairie farm, had it not been for the timely and efficient aid of two generous friends. Returning to my home one evening, some years after our settlement in Minnesota, and in fact after our removal from the state, though we still retained our property interests there, some member of my family, all of whom I noticed seemed remarkably cheerful, just then placed in my hands a very kind letter from Mr. John B. Gough, enclosing a check for five hundred dollars. Some of my readers will never be able *fully* to appreciate our feelings on the reception of that gift, for they were never poor, and in debt. Some others, with a different experience, can understand them.

We had scarcely had time for mutual congratulations all round, and for wiping a few stray tears, when one of my lads, just returned from the Post Office, handed me a letter from my son Richard, then in Boston, conveying to us intelligence of the gift of another five hundred, from an excellent friend of mine in Massachusetts; L. M. Sargent, Esq.

Reader, we did not wait for a "proclamation by the Governor," but got up a family Thanksgiving directly, which was none the less hearty because less formal.

To one of my generous benefactors I can no more, in the flesh, express my thanks; he has gone to his reward with the benediction of thousands whose homes and lives were made the happier for his sojourn on this earth, and his noble efforts for the improvement and elevation of men. To the other, who still lives and labors in the same grand enterprise, my thanks are hereby publicly renewed.

While residing in Minnesota, I had frequent opportunities to learn from actual observation how much whisky can do to improve the character and conduct of that amiable race of beings, the Sioux Indians. In view of all I have seen and heard of the consequences of furnishing intoxicating liquors to the untamed savages in their own wretched and forever shifting homes, or on the borders of civilization, I here give it as my deliberate opinion, that wherever a scoundrel is found engaged in that business, he should be hitched up by the neck to the nearest tree able to bear him, or, if more convenient, shot in his tracks.

The results of the liquor traffic are terrible, almost beyond the power of words to express, even in civilized communities, where the most helpless class of sufferers therefrom, the mothers, wives, and children of drunkards, are, to some extent, protected by law and Christian neighbors, from extreme violence; but think, dear reader, what must be the influence of that traffic upon the inmates of the "tepee," or frail tent of the Indian; to have a veritable *savage* come to his home drunk, with a loaded gun upon his shoulder, and a huge knife in his belt, to drive thence, if so his insane fury shall direct, wife and children, poorly clad, among the piled snows of a northern winter, when the thermometer ranges perhaps between twenty and thirty degrees below zero! And all this for the miserable profits on the sale of a quart of whisky! In view of injustice and wrong far less than is involved in such affairs, a man may "be angry and sin not."

As the incidents of my life on the prairies have no direct bearing on the progress of the temperance reform except as they contributed to strengthen my lungs for its further advocacy in after years, I shall not pause to narrate them. Lest, however, the reader should conclude that while engaged in agricultural pursuits, of which I am exceedingly fond, I forgot the temperance cause, I will say that as my worn lungs gained strength, I occasionally employed them in assailing the liquor system, and urging on the citizens of Faribault, and neighboring towns, the practice of total abstinence. Another fact I will simply allude to in passing, that I found time, even amid the hurry and worry of pioneer life, to read the temperance papers. Believing that my public labors as an advocate of temperance were ended, except perhaps in my immediate neighborhood, I could not be content to remain in ignorance of the state of the enterprise, and so the temperance papers found me there. Some of them find every man who is able to have two coats and three meals per day, and who has at the same time any tolerable appreciation of the importance of the temperance reform to all the great interests of human society.

While on a visit to the East, during my residence in Minnesota, I was describing to a listening group, the depth and fertility of the soil on my prairie farm, when one of the listeners, being of a speculative turn of mind, enquired if it would not be an excellent soil for the cultivation of tobacco. I told him I presumed it would, but that I would see every acre of my quarter section sunk so deep that a lake should occupy its place before one acre of that splendid soil should, with my consent, be used to supply with a filthy and poisonous weed, the depraved appetites of men, and to abet the nuisance of tobacco-smoke, cigar-stumps, and stale quids! He seemed quite astonished at my respect for a principle, to the neglect of—the profits.

CHAPTER XXII,

Return to New England—Organization and Finance—Instruction the Great Want—Sensation versus Education—What Might have been—Poverty and its results—Mistakes of Good Men—Why is it permitted?—A "New Departure" Suggested—Will you attend to it, Sir?

In the year 1858 I received from the Executive Committee of the Massachusetts Temperance Alliance an invitation to enter their service. I accepted the invitation, and not without reluctance left a home and a people endeared to me by many associations, for my former field of labor.

I wish I could truthfully say that I found the temperance cause in a better condition in Massachusetts, than when I left for the west, five years previous. Much had been done, and well done, by earnest friends of reform, but their efforts had failed to secure two important results,—the thorough organization of our forces, and the thorough or *progressive* education of the people in those important truths which the progress of the enterprise had developed. As to the first mentioned object, it is a sad fact that in more than half the towns of the state no local temperance organization existed in 1858. The Executive Committee of the Alliance were aware of the fact stated, and were troubled with some anxieties on account of it. One member of it, Mr. H. D. Cushing, in his correspondence with me inviting my return to the state, called my attention to the fact, and requested me to make it the subject of special thought while preparing to enter anew my old field of labor. I did so, and immediately after reaching Boston I prepared a form of constitution for local societies, embodying such provisions, and such only, as I had come to regard as essential to efficiency and continued existence. My form was printed, and pretty widely distributed, and for some months I urged the friends of temperance where no organization of any kind existed, or where existing ones embraced but a part of the total abstainers in its locality, to organize at once—either under the form I had prepared, or some better one, if such could be produced. It was in vain. I was grieved to find that even my fellow laborers in the lecture field did not sympathize with my views, and were disinclined to attempt so formidable a task. I reluctantly abandoned the effort, believing then, as I now do, that time and successive failures to carry the enemy's works with our present regiments, will convert my brethren pretty generally to the necessity of multiplying them, and embodying in them all our available force.

A serious objection often made to the form I had prepared for local societies, was, that it contained a provision for a paying membership! Just as sensible would be an objection to any tax on the citizen for the support of government, or the general education of the people—or to the plan of a campaign in time of war which embraced no commissary department. It is not creditable to the intelligence and forethought of the friends of temperance anywhere, if they fail to see the necessity of some sensible provision for obtaining from the rank and file of our own force, the means of its own financial support,—its enlightenment, enlargement, and perpetuity. Such a provision next to the pledge and practice of abstinence, constitutes the very life-blood of the Temperance Orders; without it they could not exist a twelvemonth. Thoroughly impressed as I was with the importance of the truths stated, the reader can judge of my feelings, when I have found my form of organization employed *with that essential feature stricken out.*

And yet, where such things have happened, I did not swear—nor call my brethren fools—nor commit suicide—nor do any other desperate thing; but I saw in such occurrences no foreshadowing of a temperance millenium. Until the power of speech fails me, and my palsied fingers can no longer guide a pen, I shall continue to ring in the ears, and place before the eyes of my fellow laborers a conviction long since formed, and which I have often pressed on their attention, that every attempt to crush the entire liquor system in any state, until the great mass of those who believe in and practice abstinence, are banded together, and accustomed to work together in local organizations, will prove like the labor of Sisyphus, toiling eternally to roll up-hill a huge stone, only to have it roll back upon him the instant his fatigued muscles were relaxed. Zeal and devotion are utterly vain in any cause, where the essential conditions of success are not complied with. Unorganized masses of men, however excellent they may be personally, are of small account in a battle. But one citizen, who did not belong to some military organization, fought with the Union forces at Gettysburg.

It was painfully apparent to me, on my return to Massachusetts, that the efforts of those interested and active in the temperance cause were sadly defective in another particular. No adequate means had been provided for *such* a presentation of reformatory truths to the people as would command the attention and respect of the educated and influential classes of society. I urged, therefore, that means must be had to put into the field additional agencies which would supply what was deficient. It was evident to me, that one of the agents of the society should be a first-class man of the clerical profession, who would be welcome to the most influential pulpits of the state—as were Dr. Justin Edwards, and the Rev. Dr. Hewitt, in their day. Such a servant of the Alliance could, in a town or village where were two or three churches, occupy the pulpit of one in the morning, of another in the afternoon, and of a third one in the evening, if a third existed. Thus, by his public labor and his intimate relation to his professional brethren, he would contribute to identify our work as closely as possible with the permanent religious institutions of the state—as is the work of the Bible and Tract Societies. After resting a day or two from the fatigue of his severe Sabbath labor, our clerical agent could fill other appointments during the remainder of the week. It seemed as clear that another of its agents should be of the legal profession, whose reputation for ability would draw full houses, and who could instruct the people in his discourses, on the legal phases of the question, and who could give the friends of the cause, in private conferences, safe counsel in relation to any legal measures in process or contemplated, for the restraint or suppression of the liquor traffic in the places he might visit. Still another, it was quite evident, should be of the medical profession, qualified to instruct the people in regard to those truths of natural science which lie at the basis of the enterprise.

In the absence of some one better qualified, I proposed to undertake that service myself.

I failed altogether to impress the officers of the Alliance with the importance of my suggestions in relation to the character of those they would send forth as public teachers, and beside myself and their former and faithful agent, Edwin Thompson, they put into the lecture field two recently reformed men, whose labors were more sensational than educational. Both of them have since been inmates of inebriate asylums. What was most needed at the time in that state, was, to call out to our meetings and identify with us in our work, the educated and strong men of the state,—those who give character and influence to every movement with which they are connected. Many thousands of such men were living in Massachusetts in the year 1858, who had been active in the cause formerly, but who for various reasons were so no longer, although they still retained the old hatred to the liquor traffic and all its supports. We needed greatly the aid and coöperation of such men. It could only be secured by measures which would commend themselves to their judgment and notions of propriety. Let it suffice to state, that they were not won to our support by the agencies employed.

If in the retrospect the friends of temperance in Massachusetts cannot detect a sufficient amount of blundering in our operations to account for the successful introduction of half a score of giant breweries among them, and the disgraceful vacillations of their

Legislature for a few years past, there is no hope for them.

Many earnest friends tell us that breweries have been introduced and our legislation is unsatisfactory because our friends have not carried their principles to the polls as they ought, and the suggestion is undoubtedly true; but *why* do they fail in reference to that particular *now* more than formerly? When the question of license or prohibition depended in each county on the character and action of three public officers, the County Commissioners, did our friends fail us then? I trow not. If, as happened in certain counties, the regular nominees of neither party could be trusted, they called temperance conventions, nominated true men, and elected them over the nominees of both parties. When, in those days, temperance called for votes, as well as talk, it got them. What influences have been operating to divide the councils, abate the zeal, and lessen the devotion of our rank and file below the old standard? The reader will find my answer in some of the preceding chapters.

The establishment and steady support in the state from 1858 to the present hour of a wise system of educational temperance efforts, with *such* a general organization of our forces as existed from 1835 to 1840, would, ere this, have rendered a public brewery, or such a shuffling, compromising Legislature as the state has been cursed with for a few years past, an impossibility. The labor of forming a Prohibitory Party could have been spared, for the Republican Party would never have taken a backward or even a doubtful step, and the Democratic Party, pledged as it is to the support of the liquor system, would have done no mischief, through lack of power and opportunity.

In justice to the officers of the Alliance it should be stated, that the financial resources of the society were limited; too limited, in their estimation, doubtless, to warrant them in putting into the lecture field such men as I had suggested. It was not for me to press my own views or attempt to dictate to those gentlemen, being myself but a paid servant of the society, with definite duties before me; but, with my views of the needs of the cause in the state at that time, it was to me a source of extreme regret, that I could not have the aid in the work before me, of such men as I could have selected at the time from among the citizens of the state.

There has been in my opinion no time since 1835, if we except the years of our great war, when the judicious expenditure of fifty thousand dollars annually, for six successive years, in the organization and proper temperance education of the people of Massachusetts, or any other New England state, by such advocates as money could have secured, and by the liberal distribution of reformatory publications of the right stamp, would not have prepared the people and their public servants for the complete and final overthrow of the whole liquor system. But that, in the estimation of its aggregate wisdom, was quite too much to pay for the redemption of the state from its greatest scourge and curse, and the subsequent *certain* and *rapid* progress therein, of every enterprise which can contribute to render a people great, good, and happy. And so the Christianity of Massachusetts employed its fifty thousand and more, annually, in fighting heathenism and false religions in distant lands—an excellent work undoubtedly—and permitted the home manufacture of heathen, by thousands, from its own sons, while they had ample power to prevent it.

If there be, in ancient or modern history, any record of folly more astounding, perpetrated by a Christian state in connection with its systematic benevolence, I should be glad if some one would point it out. Our ablest men, and money by hundreds of thousands, sent to distant regions, and a home enterprise, declared by the utterances of our great religious bodies, Conferences, Consociations, Synods, and General Assemblies, to be of primary importance, left to die of financial starvation, or so feebly supported that those conducting it have been compelled to employ cheap labor, and send into the field third rate or sixth rate men, to present to the people suffering in *all* their interests from a *present* and terrible scourge, the nature and claims of a remedial system. It should be borne in mind that the remedial measures awaiting general application are not of doubtful efficacy, but absolutely certain in their operation, and that *no instance of their failure to remove the scourge, where properly applied, has yet been reported.* Hundreds of localities can be found where even their imperfect but *steady* employment from 1830 to 1840 revolutionized public opinion and the social customs of the people, crushed the license system, and drove the traffic from the community, as thoroughly as any other crime or system of wrong has ever been driven out by public opinion and the will of the people embodied in law. As examples, I will refer to more than half the towns in Barnstable and Plymouth counties of Massachusetts; to more than one-third of the towns in Essex, Bristol, Norfolk, Worcester, and Hampshire counties, of that state; to many towns in the states of Connecticut, Maine, and Vermont, and to Suffolk county, Long Island. If, in some of these localities, the traffic has been again introduced, and a laxity of public sentiment now prevails in relation to the use of intoxicants, it is not because the remedial measures once so potent have lost their efficacy, but because they are altogether neglected, or are no longer employed *as they were when effective.*

With such a remedial system known to the Christian people of the land, why has this most terrible curse of modern times been permitted to remain and to gather from among the youth of our country its thousands of victims annually?

It is not from ignorance on the part of American Christians of the existence and terrible extent of the evil. From the day when the writings of Lyman Beecher, Justin Edwards, Rev. Dr. Hewitt, Jonathan Kittredge, Asahel Nettleton, Heman Humphrey, L. M. Sargent, Wilber Fisk, and Rev. Dr. Wayland, reached the clergy, were scattered among the churches and became a part of our Christian literature, there has been no hour when the traffic in and use of intoxicating liquors have not been regarded by the great mass of intelligent Christian people as the greatest evil in our country, with perhaps the exception of slavery, which has passed away. No, it is not ignorance of the existence, extent, nature, and causes of the evil.

Can it be, that the descendants of a heroic ancestry find more congenial employment in fighting with heathenism and false religions abroad, which cannot possibly strike back, so as to endanger the property and persons or the ease and comfort of American Christians, than to engage an enemy at home which erects its batteries in the sight of our churches, and openly defies all the armies of the Living God on this continent!. Must we entertain a supposition so derogatory to Protestant Christianity in this nineteenth century? Before we do so, let one more measure be adopted, one more experiment tried.

Let the great religious bodies already referred to take a "New Departure" in relation to this great question, and instead of contenting themselves, as heretofore, with passing resolutions approving the doctrine and practice of total abstinence, or declaring the immorality of the liquor traffic, or even the necessity for the legal prohibition of it,—let them declare to the churches and the individual Christians of the land the undoubted and important truth, that the unparalleled progress, if not the early and complete triumph of many other excellent, benevolent, and Christian enterprises of this age, *only awaits the removal of intemperance*, and that a result so desirable is entirely within our reach; and let them inaugurate some system of measures through which the aggregate Christianity of the land can unitedly assail it.

Now that Slavery is dead, and the worse than heathenish system of Polygamy is dying of railroad rot and the faithful execution of just laws, let them point the churches of the land to the liquor traffic and the drinking usages of society, as the next great line of satanic entrenchments to be carried, and sound the trumpet for the charge. Then, if the churches and individual Christians of the land who are now active in many other good works, do not move at their call on the enemy's works, we shall be compelled to choose between two most damaging conclusions—either that the love of artificial stimulants is stronger with American Christians than their love for God and man, or, that they are a set of arrant cowards, choosing to fight at *long range* unanswering batteries, rather than to engage at close quarters the defiant and deadly enemy of all public and sacred interests, entrenched in their own villages and in sight of their own homes.

Our great ecclesiastical assemblies are looked to by the churches of the land to point out to them the most promising fields for Christian enterprise, to suggest appropriate employment for our Christian activities. This they frequently do, and their suggestions have always been respected and responded to.

Perhaps appropriate action on their part is all that is needed to inaugurate some grand system of operations in which all Christian people could heartily unite, and to the support of which, financially, all sects and denominations will give as freely as they now do for educational purposes and Christian missions.

In behalf of a great, beneficent, but imperiled enterprise, I implore the clergy and Christian laymen connected with our various religious sects, who judge my complaints well founded and my suggestion wise, to see to it, that at the next general assemblage of your clergy and the representatives of your several churches, that this subject comes squarely before them, not for expressions of opinion merely, but for the forming and adoption of some grand system of measures commensurate

in extent and power with the enemy to be assailed; a
system which all good men can aid in carrying out.
Then the doom of our modern Moloch is sealed. It
cannot withstand the united assault of the American
churches, added to the organized forces now arrayed
against it.

CHAPTER XXIII.

The Million Fund—Massachusetts Alliance—Old Dr. Beecher—To the West again—Thurlow W. Brown.

To one who has watched the progress of the temperance enterprise from its origin, in 1826, it is interesting to recall the various expedients resorted to, at different periods, to supply needed funds—to meet a want which should have been provided for in the outset by the originators of the reform movement. In the conduct of no other enterprise of this age has the financial department been so unworthily managed, especially during the first fifteen years of its progress. All our local organizations, prior to the revolutions of 1840–41, had each a treasurer, but no sensible provision had been incorporated into their working plan to supply him with needed funds, and so the officers of the society had to pay current expenses or resort to the contribution box at the close of public meetings—a very unreliable resource. After the passage of the prohibitory law, in 1852, the need of funds became more pressing than at previous periods. To secure its successful enforcement, able legal counsel would be required and other auxiliary agencies which money only could command. In this emergency, a very earnest and energetic friend of the cause, B. Dunbar, from Bristol county, proposed, at a State Convention held in Tremont Temple, Boston, in May, 1853, to raise, by subscription, a fund of one million dollars, to be taxed annually at such rate as the exigencies of the times might require, the tax not to exceed, however, three per cent. during any year. The amount which might be thus obtained was to be expended under the direction of the State Temperance Committee, to aid in the proper enforcement of the law. The proposition was carried in the Convention, and a committee raised to secure subscriptions to the "Million Fund," as it was termed. Dunbar was appointed chairman, and a better one could not have been found in the state. He was a mechanic of limited education but of indomitable energy, of unquestioned integrity, imperturbable good nature, and a zeal which knew no bounds, and, withal, a man who never seemed to have learned the meaning of the word *failure*, whether in reference to a public or a private enterprise.

His movements in relation to any matter of interest would be likely to recall to any one who had ever read them, the lines of a humorous English poet in reference to the wonderful assurance of a genuine live Yankee, his penchant for pricing everything he sees, and other corresponding traits:

" He'd kiss the Queen 'till he raised a blister,
With his arm round her neck and his old felt hat on!
He'd address the King by the title of 'mister,'
And ask him *the price* of the throne he sat on."

Such a man makes a first rate chairman of a financial committee, and Dunbar secured, in Bristol county alone, as I have been informed, subscriptions for more than three-fourths of the whole amount. Whether the full million was obtained I am not informed, but the annual tax on the amount raised constituted for years the most reliable and considerable support of temperance efforts in Massachusetts. A remnant of that fund still remains, it seems, and is taxed as formerly. While on the subject of the financial support of temperance operations, the following exhibit of the receipts of the Massachusetts Temperance Alliance for the year 1871, may interest the reader. I clip it from the Annual Report of that society, kindly sent me by its secretary, Rev. Wm. Thayer.

FINANCIAL EXHIBIT
For the Year ending September 30, 1871.

1870,
Oct. 1.—Cash balance on hand, - - $130.48
        from Million Fund, - - 75.00
        from life members, - - 745.00
        from donations, - - 4,804.00
        from Alliance members, - 5,923.68
        from sales at office, - - 524.49
        from collections, - - 51.83
        from room letting, - - 91.77
        from borrowed money, - - 512.99
        ————$12,659.24

It flatters what the reader may call my vanity, if he chooses, to perceive that the most considerable amount in the foregoing exhibit comes from the dollar membership plan introduced at my suggestion in 1840, and which, though abandoned on the breaking down of the "Temperance Union," as described in Chap. IX, has been resuscitated by the Alliance, and is now its most reliable means of support.

During the years 1858 and '59, I met frequently in

the Committee Room of the Alliance, that old intellectual Giant and early champion of the reform, Dr. Lyman Beecher. I had never known him personally at the period of his greatest strength, but it was a rare privilege to meet and confer with him in his old age. Occasionally something would occur to excite the old veteran and rekindle for the moment the fires of an earlier period, and it was worth a journey to Boston from the Rocky Mountains to see and hear him then.

At one of the prayer meetings held at the Old South Church, he gave a terrible shock to the usual decorum which characterized those meetings, by a burst of enthusiasm over the Maine Law.

He had pictured, as he only could, the conflict which had been going on in the Universe for centuries, between the powers of light and darkness, of good and evil, and the anxiety and dismay which he, as well as millions of others, had felt at times, notwithstanding their trust in God and the promises of His word, in view of the fierceness of the struggle and the seeming advantage sometimes gained by the powers of evil. "But, brethren," said he, "let us rejoice and be glad, for the powers of hell are just now in dismay. That Glorious Maine Law was a square and grand blow right between the very horns of the Devil, and from the moment of its reception I seem to see him falling back—stubborn and terrible, but falling back! and the consecrated host of God's elect pressing close upon him!" While thus giving vent to emotions too strong for words alone to express, the grand old man was advancing on the floor, swinging his big cane with a powerful energy, which showed very clearly the spirit in which he would fight the biggest devil in existence had he been there. He wound up magnificently. "So it shall be brethren— I believe it—I *see* it—they will crowd him back, and crowd him back—(still advancing and swinging his cane)—until they shall push him over the battlements, and send him back to the Hell from which he came forth! and then shall come up from a redemed earth the shout: Glory to God in the Highest, and on earth peace and good will to men!"

The old man has left us in his family some grand representatives of his intellect, his brilliant imagination, courage, and zeal in good enterprises, but it is doubtful if any one, or all of them ever knew, or can know, until they have been two or three centuries in Heaven, that tempest of grand emotions which sometimes swelled the great soul of Lyman Beecher.

Having become convinced, after a trial of some months, that such a reorganization of our forces in Massachusetts as I had contemplated, was for the time impracticable, I resigned my agency and returned to the West. During the year 1860 I labored in Wisconsin under the direction of the Wisconsin State Temperance Society, visiting and lecturing in all the cities and large towns of the state. I was greatly aided in my labor by Mr. George E. Sickles, who has exerted a very decided influence in favor of the cause for more than thirty years, in various capacities and in different sections of the country. He was with us in the early campaigns in Massachusetts— and recently, as a financial agent of the National Temperance Society, has rendered to it essential service.

During the year, and while delivering a course of lectures in Milwaukee, Wis., I made the acquaintance of a number of earnest brethren who were warring upon the common enemy through an organization then quite new to me, the " Good Templars." I was earnestly invited to become a member of the Order, and was there initiated into its mysteries. It seemed to me at the time a work of supererogation, if not very like a joke, to put an old servant of the cause who had advocated temperance by tongue and pen before three-fourths of those in the Hall were born, through the ceremony of initiation into a temperance society, pledging to the practice of abstinence, in the most solemn manner, one who had practiced it for very many years, and devoted more hours to the advocacy of temperance than any man in the United States. No harm could come of it, however, and so I pledged anew to the cause under the forms of that Order, as I had done nearly twenty years before, when joining the Sons of Temperance.

While yet engaged in Milwaukee, the Good Templars of the city addressed a circular to the local Lodges throughout the State, informing them of my connection with the Order, and commending me to their confidence and fraternal regard; and urging them to secure me, as far as possible, an audience with the people. I have no doubt that my usefulness in the state was thereby promoted. Since that date, I have, at different periods, served the Grand Lodges of Ohio, Pennsylvania, and Vermont, and very many local lodges in other states, as well as very many Divisions of the Sons of Temperance; and I have always, with one single exception, received, not only from the officials of those organizations, but from their rank and file, the utmost kindness and consideration.

A man may, without any sacrifice of principle or self-respect, advocate a great cause without a specific endorsement or any special advocacy of all the forms or machinery employed to advance it in the locality where he may happen to be laboring. A Presbyterian or a Congregationalist may preach Christ acceptably and faithfully from a Methodist pulpit, without yielding his own peculiar views of Christian doctrine or church government, or assailing those of his Methodist brethren. To do the former, might show a want of fidelity to his convictions; to do the latter, would certainly prove him wanting in courtesy.

During my labor in Wisconsin I visited the home of that able champion of temperance, Thurlow W. Brown. Although his usefulness was marred by some eccentricities, which were undoubtedly due to the infirm state of his health, he was a most faithful and earnest advocate of our especial doctrines for many years. The grand truths connected with some phases of the enterprise, have never been more ably presented than in some of the leading articles of the "Wisconsin Chief," while under his control.

With faculties of observation unusually keen, a brilliant imagination, strong logical powers, a rare command of language, an iron will, and a hatred of the whole liquor system as intense as ever glowed in a human soul, he contributed largely to mould the public sentiment of his time. His influence was widely extended and beneficent.

During the year 1862, I labored in the state of Illinois, and notwithstanding our great war was then in progress, engrossing largely the thoughts and energies of the people, I generally addressed good audiences. As the population of our western states comprises a larger portion of young men, or those in the most active period of life, all movements and enterprises there are characterized by a greater measure of energy than in the older states. If sometimes that energy and the fiery zeal that prompts it, should, in the estimation of our eastern people, assume the appearance of rashness, it would be no matter for surprise. The cause is not sustained, financially, at the west, as in the New England States, for the people are not generally so wealthy. Close organizations are almost the only ones existing there, and although they break down from time to time in particular localities, as other temperance organizations are wont to do, yet the pressing need of organized opposition to the liquor system soon prompts to their renewal. They embrace in the rural districts a larger portion of the clergy and influential Christian laymen, than kindred societies in the older States. Only a portion of those, however, who practice abstinence from intoxicants, and hate the liquor traffic, are organized. They never can be while our organizations retain their present forms and features, and the triumph of our cause there, awaits the coming of that measure of practical wisdom which can organize and employ all our available force. A determined effort to secure the prohibition of the traffic by law, is now being made in Illinois, by separate or independent political action on the part of the friends of temperance. Whether they will succeed in obtaining a controlling majority, or in influencing the dominant political party to add prohibition as a plank in their political platform, time only can determine. From facts which have come to light and obtained publicity, it would seem that the elements of intoxication played no minor part in the great calamity which has so recently befallen Chicago. It would be very extraordinary if it did not, for it is an important agent in the production of at least three-fourths of the ordinary casualties which occur, and seven-eighths of the *great* calamities which afflict our country.

While laboring in Illinois, with my residence in Chicago, I had noticed from time to time in the religious papers, articles from the pens of earnest friends of temperance, who were troubled in view of its slow and unsatisfactory progress, and were laboring to solve the problem of its causation. A careful perusal of those articles convinced me that their authors had not studied the subject sufficiently to see clearly the sources of the mischief they deplored, and were seeking to remedy. I had the vanity to believe that I could help my brethren to see clearly what was wanted, and therefore published my views of the subject in a pamphlet (to which I have had occasion to refer in another chapter) entitled:— "The Temperance Cause, Past, Present, and Future; or—Why we are, Where we are," in reference to the enterprise. I sent about two hundred copies of it to leading men in different parts of the country who had distinguished themselves by great devotion to the cause, and through a note which I addressed to them individually, solicited their opinion of the truthfulness of my historical statements, of the doctrines I had advanced, and of the practical suggestions contained in the concluding chapter of the work. I received a pile of letters from distinguished men, scholars divines and philanthropists, including among them the Presidents of three colleges, and such men as Benjamin Silliman, Senior, of Yale College, L. M. Sargent, John Pierpont, Gerrit Smith, E. C. Delevan, James Black, Rev. Dr. Hawes of Hartford, Rev. Jacob Ide of Massachusetts, and many other distinguished men, and from ALL I got substantially but one answer;—you are right in the views expressed.

Notwithstanding such endorsement of my views by many of the wisest men of our times, the great mass of our active reformers have still gone forward, reënacting the blunders which have hindered our progress, just as though they had never been pointed out. It is, to say the least, very unfortunate that those engaged in a great and good work should ignore the teachings of experience, and persist in going ahead on ill-considered plans. Most of the points argued at length in the work referred to, are reconsidered in the foregoing chapters; some at considerable length, others very briefly. As to the practical suggestions contained in this volume, I hope my fellow laborers will heed them, or prove to the world by a courteous discussion of them through some fitting channel, that they are unwise. For one, I should be glad if we could have a convention of the leaders of the enterprise from all sections of the country, at some convenient and central point, to continue in session ten days or a fortnight, if need be, to consider the practical methods of securing an united movement of all good men, and all good influences, to stay the plague of intemperance in the land.

During all the weary years of our great war, no progress was made toward annihilating the drink scourge, but, on the contrary, that struggle manifested the power of intoxicants to work mischief, in ways and to an extent unknown to us before. On many a bloody field, thousands of brave men went quickly down to death through the blunders of intoxicated officers. It was to be expected that drunkenness would increase in time of war. Liquor sellers always calculate on increased sales and extra profits during seasons of great excitement, even though that excitement be caused by the results of their own nefarious business.

A sad case illustrative of that truth, occurred in Massachusetts during the year 1840. A citizen of Maine reached the great cattle market of Brighton, a few miles from Boston—sold his drove, and the proceeds soon found their way into the pockets of the liquor sellers and gamblers of the town. Shame, sorrow, and financial embarrassment were of course the results. Still deeper drinking was now resorted to, to benumb his faculties, render him insensible to the pangs of remorse, and to dissipate troublesome thoughts relative to the future consequences to his family and creditors, of his guilt and folly. He went to his room in the "Cattle Fair Hotel," it was directly over the bar-room, and in a paroxysm of drunken frenzy cut his throat. The smoking blood of the wretched man found its way through the imperfect floor of his room and through cracks in the plastering beneath, and trickled down upon the bar-room floor. Those present, startled at the sight, rushed up to the room above, burst open the door, which he had fastened, only to witness the speedy death of the wretched man who in his desperation had severed completely the great arteries of his neck.

Doctor Whittemore, a physician of the town, who had been hastily summoned as soon as the terrible event had become known, informed me, that as the news of the affair flew abroad an unusual crowd gathered at the hotel to learn the distressing particulars, and that *an extra hand was required at the bar to furnish liquors to the company.*

The doctor stated to me that he repeatedly saw men leave their seats in that bar-room, for another drink, when they had, in their short journey to the bar, to turn aside from a straight course to avoid the pool of blood on the floor—blood which they knew had just flowed from the gaping and ghastly wounds of a liquor-crazed suicide. Is there any other matter known to you, reader, in connection with which men become so strangely infatuated, as they do in the use of intoxicants?

Nothing worthy of special remark occurred in connection with my labor for the furtherance of the cause, during or after the close of the war, until the year 1867. Prior to that date, central Iowa had been the extreme limit of my journeyings *toward* the west—which I have not yet been able to reach.

At the date named, I received an invitation to spend a few months in Kansas. I think the temperance sentiment is stronger, and pervades society more generally in that State than in any of the States I have visited west of the great lakes, if we except Iowa, which has reached and maintained a very advanced position in connection with the cause.

While laboring in Kansas, an incident occurred which all friends of reform will regard as most fortunate, and which as strongly as almost any recorded fact of modern times, warrants a belief that God does *now* occasionally, as in former times, discomfit the enemies of truth and justice and encourage the faithful by special or exceptional arrangements of his Divine Providence. The Legislature of Kansas was in session at Topeka, and we were holding there a State Temperance Convention. The railroad by which a large portion of our temperance delegations reached the place, was on the west bank of the Kansas, while Topeka is on the east side of the river. The bridge which had formerly spanned the river had been swept away, and we had crossed the swollen stream in boats. During the session of the convention a bill had been introduced into the legislature for the control or regulation of the liquor traffic, with a novel but very just provision, that no license should be granted to any individual to sell intoxicating liquors within the state, until the party applying for license should present to the proper authorities a petition for the same, signed by a majority of the adult citizens, both male and female, of his district, or if in a city, the ward in which he proposed to engage in the business. It was argued, and with decided ability and force, that wherever tolerated, the results of the traffic would be sure to put in peril the safety and happiness of the mothers, wives, and daughters of that locality, and that therefore they ought certainly to have a voice in deciding whether it should there be allowed or not, and all the more so, as they could not, at the polls or otherwise, render their wishes or wills potential in the matter, except by such a provision. The bill was of course opposed at every stage of its progress, by the friends of the liquor system, but they were few and feeble in that legislature, and it seemed quite evident that it would become a law.

In this emergency a dispatch was sent over the wires to the liquor traders of Leavenworth, the great center of the liquor interest for Kansas, stating the condition of things at the capitol, and urging them to come on with all available speed and appliances, to check, if possible, the impending disaster. The liquor fraternity were thoroughly alarmed, and a full car-load of them reached the depot at Topeka, the morning after they received the notice, confident that by such influences as they might bring to bear on the members of the House or Senate, they could prevent the passage of the bill. But here they learned the truth of the Divine word, "The expectation of the wicked shall perish." Alas! It had happened that during the night the ice in a tributary of the Kansas, the Republican Fork, had broken up, and was being whirled along toward the Missouri at a rate which rendered it impossible to cross the river in a boat. Not all the blood-money in those liquor-sellers' pockets, and they were well lined undoubtedly, could tempt a boatman to risk his boat and life in an attempt to cross. They fumed, and raved, and swore worse than did a certain famous army in Flanders, but all in vain. They were compelled to remain in plain sight of the State House, while the bill passed through the several stages and was enacted by an overwhelming majority in both branches, and received the signature of the Governor. The temperance convention, in the mean time, had finished its business and adjourned, but as the river was impassable a large portion of the delegates were compelled to remain, and so it was concluded that we would have a grand glorification over the passage of the new law. It was held in the Representatives' Chamber, and a happier group than there assembled I have never met. It was one of those occasions on which a man with a tolerably keen nervous system, lives very fast, without artificial stimulants.

Learning, when the river became passable, that they could effect nothing by crossing, the liquor-sellers took the earliest train homeward, pondering, no doubt, on the probabilities of success in getting a future license, when the women of their district must be consulted in relation to the matter.

Thus, to the young state of Kansas belongs the honor of having first accorded to woman, the greatest sufferer from the liquor system, a potential voice in reference to its continuance or suppression.

The winter of 1868-9 I spent in Ohio, a part of the time in the employment of the Grand Lodge of Good Templars for that State, and the remainder in delivering courses of lectures, on private contract with the brethren, in some of the larger towns and villages in the State. While thus engaged, and during the month of February, my health began to suffer from too severe and protracted labor, and becoming somewhat alarmed by symptoms indicating approaching paralysis, I discontinued my labor and started for a visit to one of my sons, who resides on the Cumberland Plateau, in East Tennessee.

Finding the scenery quite novel and the climate healthful and delightful, I concluded to spend the summer there, and—don't laugh, dear reader—bought me a small farm, which I purpose to occupy and Yankeefy, when I get my thoughts on the temperance question fully before my countrymen,—provided always—Cincinnati shall build its projected railroad across Eastern Kentucky and over the Cumberland Plateau, direct to Chattanooga, the great railroad center of the South. I must, however, add one other proviso, viz: that the line of that road be run so near my farm as to render it quite convenient for me to get the "Cincinnati Gazette" and the "Commercial," by twelve o'clock at noon on the day they are printed,—and from the other direction, my basket of Georgia peaches, in the season of them, by express, the same day they are picked from the trees, as the peach crop of the Plateau, though fine, and generally abundant where trees have been grown, does occasionally fail.

East Tennessee has many attractions for northern men of limited means and industrious habits, who must buy cheap lands if any—who desire a mild and equable climate, are fond of good fruit, venison steaks, and a cheerful wood-fire on the hearths of their sitting room, and who would be entirely out of the way of ague-shakes and cholera-contagion, and whose habits and dispositions are such that they can find more pleasure in shaping aright a *new* community, than in the quiet enjoyment of the stereotyped institutions, and—if you please—the manifold advantages of an old one.

For the information of those who would become my neighbors on the Cumberland Plateau, I will here inform them, that real estate on the moutain is cheap—hence I bought *my* farm *there*.

Having recruited my energies by a summer's residence on the mountain aforesaid, I visited, in September,

Her Majesty's Province of Ontario—formerly "Canada West"—on the invitation of our brethren there, and spent a month delightfully in laboring with and for them. The temperance Orders, Sons of Temperance and Good Templars, are the only temperance organizations I found in Ontario, except here and there one for the youth and children. In the mother country, England, nineteen-twentieths of the temperance organizations are on the pattern I prefer—open to all the world. When men trained in those English societies visit the Provinces, our brethren there will do well to notice whether their temperance *education* be not in advance of those trained on this side of the Atlantic, in close organizations. From what I learned during this tour and on previous visits to the Provinces, I judge there is *there* less hostility to the peculiar and characteristic features of close organizations among the clergy and Christian people generally, than among the same class on this side of the line. Be that as it may, the Orders, there, are doing pretty much all that is done, in the way of organized efforts for the advancement of the cause.

Whether, while our brethren shall operate exclusively through those forms, they can sufficiently educate the masses in temperance doctrines, and thus prepare for the annihilation of the liquor traffic, remains to be seen.

While making the tour last mentioned, I received an invitation from the officers of the National Temperance Society to visit New York, and while making that the center of my lecturing operations, assist in the editorial management of the "National Temperance Advocate."

I have continued thus to serve the cause of temperance from the autumn of 1869 to the present date, and with my view of the importance of the "National Society and Publication House" to the temperance cause generally, and consequently to all the most precious interests of the American people, I only regret that I have not been able to render that important organization more essential service.

CHAPTER XX.

Charles Dickens—The Logic of Facts—Narcotism and Death—Slightly intoxicated—What we must teach—Starvation and consequent feebleness—Foundations and Connections—Temperance and the Doctors—New Years Calls—Our Colleges—Wine and Silence—Crowding matters too close—A muddle indeed—Tobacco.

The following are selected from my recent writings. Most of the articles have reference to practical points which are now everywhere under discussion among the friends of temperance. If many years of careful observation, investigation, and experience, in connection with reformatory labor, attach any value to my opinions relative to the matters I have had under consideration, the careful perusal of these selections may be useful to the reader.

The first of the series was occasioned by the death of one of the most voluminous and popular writers of our age, whose influence upon the minds and morals of his millions of readers was very earnestly discussed on the platform and through the press, for some months after his sudden decease. My contribution toward the settlement of a much vexed question, is respectfully submitted.

CHARLES DICKENS.

The death of this popular author has naturally given rise to much discussion relative to his peculiar merits and the influence he has exerted on the popular mind and heart, and the habits, lives, and destinies of men. All concede to him the first rank as a prose writer, and gratefully recognize the eminent service he has rendered mankind in giving us, in his voluminous writings, such vivid and startling portraitures of folly and wrong as have compelled thousands to laugh at the folly and hate the wrong which perhaps themselves had unwittingly practiced, and to turn from both with clearer views of truth and duty, a better mind, and an earnest purpose to live thenceforth a better and a nobler life.

The advent of his works has wrought in many a home the same result as did the visit of William Fern and the helpless Lilian to the home of Toby Veck, and sent its inmates forth to the duties of life with the same cheerful spirit that prompted Toby to serve so efficiently his humble friends, with his "Here we are, and here we go."

But it cannot be said, truthfully, that the perusal of his writings has contributed to advance the cause of temperance in this drinking and drunken world, or to put men more on their guard against the insidious assaults of the most potent enemy of human health, purity, and happiness. The drink-traffic and drinking customs and habits of the people of England are a more terrible enemy to the working classes, and particularly to the poor, in whose more especial interest he wrote, than all the other unfortunate circumstances and influences with which they are surrounded; whether directly emanating from unjust laws, oppressive customs, or the selfishness and wickedness of individual men. How happened it that he who dealt such unerring and stunning blows on almost every other folly and wrong of human society, had no blow for this gigantic system of wickedness, this destroyer of human industries, this panderer to every nameless vice, this relentless crusher of hearts and hopes, this parent of mobs and riots, of barbarities and butcheries, this filler of poor-houses, prisons, and untimely graves? Our complaint is *not* that the brandy-bottle, the punch-bowl, and the wine appear so frequently in the scenes described, but that they come forth with *eclàt*, with evident approval; and that the free use of intoxicating liquors, even to the production of insane babblings and maudlin intoxication, is nowhere reprehended. In his Christmas stories, ghosts and phantoms exhibit to different individuals, with startling effect, the legitimate and inevitable results of the false principles they entertain, and of the wrong courses they are pursuing, until they turn from the false and the wrong with loathing and resolve on thorough reformation. But where, by ghost or phantom or otherwise, in the works of Dickens, are the consumers of brandy and rum-punch shown the frequent and terrible results of their indulgences, and led to resolve on their abandonment? In his *Christmas Carol*, everybody drinks, man, woman, and child, from Scrooge to Tiny Tim; though, to the credit of the dear little fellow, it is said he cared nothing for it: "Tiny Tim drank it last of all, but he didn't care twopence for it."

Dickens's most estimable characters, whom he compels us to admire and love, drink, and drink freely. The kind-hearted, sympathetic, and philosophical Pickwick drinks always, when the article is at hand; and on one occasion he drank, we are told, until "his head was sunk upon his bosom, and perpetual snoring—with a partial choke occasionally—were the only audible indications of the great man's presence." This was a sad state *physically* for a good man, not to speak of the small matter of morals; but no thoughtful member of the Pickwick Club, nor ghost, nor phantom hints at a possible apoplexy by and by, or a visitation of the gout, as the probable outcome of such indulgences; so he continues to drink.

Nowhere, and in no way, so far as we recollect, are we taught by this great master of the noblest art—who holds, as it were, our very hearts in his hand, and moves them at his will—to class free drinking with habits and characteristics to be avoided. They are generally treated as matters of indifference, as in the case of the Drum, a private friend of Trotty's, in the *Chimes*: "The Drum was rather drunk, by the by; but never mind."

If our best writers, those who inculcate the purest morals and the loftiest sentiments, in relation to other matters, will treat this most destructive of all man's vices with such leniency, and thus instruct their admiring readers to do the same, what is to come of it? Reader, we put that question to you. Free drinkers, in the pages of Dickens, are not only companionable, excellent fellows, but they are sometimes pious withal; and, quite unlike what we have observed on this side the Atlantic, the piety seems none the worse for the liquor. As an instance, glorious Bob Cratchet drinks; and in the overflowing of his heart he does what even our few wine-drinking doctors of divinity with all their piety fail to do, so far as we have learned—he asks God to bless him and his friends in their perilous indulgence. After serving out liberally the "hot stuff from the jug," Bob exclaims, "A merry Christmas to us all, my dears. God bless us!"

Were it necessary, we could quote columns in illustration of the truth we have before stated, that drinking, *free* drinking, even to intoxication, with all its terrible consequences, was not reckoned by Mr. Dickens among the follies or wrongs of the age which he felt called upon to rebuke or to aid in reforming. On the contrary, blows aimed by the good men of his time at the drink system he skillfully parried, and their efforts to effect a reform he held up to undeserved ridicule. However excellent the influence of his writings otherwise, on this *one* subject he was wrong, terribly wrong; wrong in opinion, in feeling, and in practice, and the influence of his writings, however excellent in relation to other matters, tends directly to popularize and perpetuate the drinking customs of society, nowhere more prevalent or destructive than as they existed directly under the eye of the writer.

But what is the explanation of all this? How could one with such wonderful, aye, almost microscopic power of observation, fail to *see* the drink system in its proper light? The gin-palaces of London and drink-shops generally are not among the indifferent things of this earth, and likely to escape observation from their very insignificance. They are powers in the earth for good or for evil. Was there any difficulty in determining which? Did fashion or custom so cloak the evil that *he* could not see the facts and the truths beneath or behind them? They never, elsewhere, concealed a truth or a wrong from *him*. In relation to other matters, his eagle eye looked through such flimsy coverings, as the sun looks in at an open window when no cloud or curtain intervenes. Was there nothing in the drink system, with its legitimate, everywhere present, and manifold miseries, to interest him? He was not certainly the "Doctor Jeddler" of his own pages, to whom, before reformation came, the world and all its affairs seemed but a ridiculous farce, fit only to provoke a laugh or point a jest. He felt for and eloquently pleaded the cause of all who were wronged and crushed, except the millions who suffer from the terrible oppression and wrong of the drink-traffic and the drinking customs. For these he had no plea, no word of encouragement or hope, and no word of denunciation for the villainous system by which they are crushed. The divine word gives us the key with which to find the truth here.

"Wine is a mocker" (a deceiver). The idea is that of being cheated, deluded, as the reader will see by reading the verse through: "And whosoever is deceived *thereby*, is not wise."

Dickens, though a man of wonderful powers, was not proof against the deluding influence of wine. Isaiah tells us that "the priest and the prophets" of his time "erred through wine." He said, "They err in vision, they stumble in judgment." Men, even *our* priests and prophets, have not become angels since the time of Isaiah, and wine is wine still, and as potent to deceive as ever. Dickens was, in this matter, no worse nor better than other great and good men of our age, who ignore this great question; and who, by example and precept, sustain the most wicked and destructive system that now curses the earth. More than one-fourth of the clergy of England, and some of the same class in this country, lend their influence to the weight that is crushing the hearts and hopes of thousands, corrupting the public morals, and opposing itself *squarely and defiantly* to every good influence and institution. Our Senators and Congressmen, more than half of them, drink. Learned judges, lawyers, and doctors drink. They know that tens of thousands of their countrymen go down annually to drunkards' graves; and they know, too, that by the utterance of truth, and the practice of self-denial, they could personally greatly lessen the evil, but they choose to drink. They smack their moist lips over their liquors, bow to each other over the table, drink and laugh, and seem utterly regardless of the influence they are exerting. Submit to the consideration of these gentlemen any other agency producing a thousandth part the mischief and misery of the drink system, and you will instantly learn that they are neither stupid nor heartless; but in reference to *this* matter, they are living illustrations of the truth of God's word: they are deceived, deluded, and many of them by the same influence doomed and damned. The infatuation of men, even good men, in reference to the use of intoxicating liquors, is really amazing. We could point to learned Professors of Colleges or schools of Divinity who have pleaded for wine, and continued to drink it, while it was ruining their sons and desolating their homes. We reckon it among the most disagreeable of all our duties as the conductor of a reformatory journal to speak thus of the errors, follies, and faults of our great men, our men of genius and learning, for whom, otherwise, we feel a respect amounting often to absolute reverence; but to treat with leniency their manifest and mischievous errors would be neither scriptural, kind, nor just. It would be practicing cruelty to the millions who are misled by their example, and whose hard lot in life is rendered more hard by their evil influence. It should ever be remembered, that neither genius, learning, nor exalted position can sanctify a wrong or neutralize the influence of error; but, on the contrary, give added power to both. Falsehood and profanity did not change their characters when practiced by the eloquent apostle Peter, nor was adultery rendered a virtue or respectable by the example of a David.

The Logic of Facts.

In the earlier stages of the temperance enterprise, those who labored to advance it had little to do with theories and philosophical speculations. Their attention was chiefly occupied with a multitude of most deplorable *facts*, which every thoughtful, honest observer traced at once to the use of alcoholic liquors as their immediate procuring cause. There was no mistaking the paternity of the mischief. The relationship was too intimate and obvious. Thousands of good men, all over the land, desirous of lessening the evils to which their attention had been called, and the cause of which they now clearly perceived, resolved at once to try the effect of abstinence, anticipating, many of them at least, some present evil in the contemplated change in their habits, but willing to suffer, if need be, if by so doing they could mitigate the manifold evils of intemperance. These friends were happily disappointed. As the result of their abstinence from alcoholic liquors, they became physically and mentally more vigorous, and could endure protracted labor and extremes of heat and cold better than before the change in their habits. In short, they discovered that a measure of self-denial which they had practiced for conscience sake, and from a benevolent desire to do good to others, had promoted their own health and happiness in an eminent degree. These results of abstinence from the use of liquors by those who had previously used them for years in all their varieties and forms, under all circumstances, and we might almost write, in all quantities, *have been uniform*, according to the declaration of those who were best qualified to judge, they having personally tested the matter. Their united testimony comes up to us as the sound of many waters—as with the voice of an earthquake. All the biblical quotations and interpretations of our few wine-drinking clergymen, and all the wire-drawn theories of our whisky-drinking doctors, cannot alter these facts. There they stand in the aggregate, like Bunker Hill Monument, massive and grand, a memorial of the past and a beacon for the future.

Now, any theory of the action of alcoholic liquors on the bodies of men and their various organs and tissues, which is utterly inconsistent with this aggregation of facts, MUST BE FALSE. A man might as well undertake to prove to us by some curious process of reasoning that fire will not burn us, or that food is not needful to the comfort and sustenance of our bodies. The contact of a heated iron with our fingers, or a fast of twenty-four hours, will prove too strong for all such theories.

What we must Teach.

Thousands violated the laws of their physical being before the commencement of the temperance reform by swallowing alcoholic liquors; but they did it in ignorance of the law and its requirements; and we have no more reason for questioning their Christian character in consequence than we should the conscientiousness or Christian character of men who, through ignorance and errors of diet or improper exposures, bring upon themselves dyspepsia or an inflammation of the lungs. No moral guilt is incurred by the violation of the laws of one's physical being while he remains in ignorance of the law; unless, indeed, he has shut his eyes against the light, or neglected to improve the means of acquiring knowledge which God has placed within his reach. He does not escape the physical penalty, however. The body is injured, and, through its mysterious connection with the mind, the intellect suffers. Nor does the injury stop here. The affections, appetites, and passions of the man are influenced materially by the state of the body; and in swallowing alcoholic liquors all these are perverted or inflamed according to the measure of the physical injury.

Thus it will be seen that, when the mind of the Christian man is enlightened on the subject, he can no more put alcoholic liquors in his stomach and keep a conscience void of offence than he could swallow daily a moderate dose of any other poison, expose himself needlessly by breathing a tainted atmosphere, or take burning coals in his hand. All the discussion as to whether it be a sin *per se* to drink a glass of alcoholic wine, is a waste of breath.

The answer to two simple questions will settle the matter. Is alcohol a poison at war with vitality? If so, does Mr. A—— B—— know that fact? If he is acquainted with that fact, he compromises his character as a Christian man, if he meddles with it; unless, indeed, it be prescribed to him by some medical adviser as a medicinal agent in some abnormal condition of the system.

Our work proper, as temperance reformers, is to convince all men that alcohol, the active principle even in pure wines and liquors, is an enemy to life; that its influence interferes injuriously with the functions of the stomach, the brain—in short, all the important organs of the body; and that its mischievous influence will extend by the operation of fixed laws to the mind, the social affections, and the moral sensibilities of the consumer. We must not stop here, but must call the attention of the people to the warfare which intoxicating liquors wage, through their mischievous influence on the human brain, upon agriculture, the manufacturing interest, commerce, education, civil government, and religion; and we must strongly and sternly appeal to the consciences of all who have been enlightened on the subject, and demand their active coöperation in the work of removing the scourge. In all our efforts we must bear in mind constantly that the law primarily violated by the use of intoxicating liquors is a physical law. This we must constantly teach, and as constantly urge, that the first and manifest duty of men concerning it is to practice abstinence—personal, rigid abstinence—for the same reason, primarily, that we should abstain from the use of arsenic, corrosive sublimate, opium, chloroform, or prussic acid. In the light of those truths, it will not be difficult for any man of ordinary understanding to perceive the true relation of temperance, or the doctrine and practice of abstinence from intoxicating liquors, to Christianity, the church, the ministry, religious revivals, or any other interest of society or class of men.

Foundations and Connections.

Is it right or safe to use alcoholic liquors as a drink? Innate consciousness will not help us here. To enable us to answer that question, we must have learned, either from experience, observation, or study, the effects of such drinking upon the physical constitution of man; for if any law be violated by such drinking, it is primarily a law pertaining to life and health, and a knowledge of those laws is not, with men, intuitive, but acquired. Now, here is just where the difficulty lies, in reference to this great and beneficent work of reform.

The knowledge acquired by a long habit of drinking, comes, alas! too late in a vast majority of cases; for the nervous system has, by the previous use of the drug, been diseased, and will often clamor, while life lasts, for the *present* relief afforded by the destroying agent. We therefore wish to induce our young men to abstain from all use of intoxicating elements; but we do not wish them to learn the folly and danger of such use by personal experience. But how else are they to learn the saving, restraining truth? Will you point them to the cases of A, B, or C, who have become drunkards and are ruined? They will point you to D, E, or F, who have drank for many years, and are still esteemed gentlemen, perhaps Christians. Talk until you are hoarse, of the extreme poverty, vice, crime, and moral degradation of men through drink, and they will answer, they are taught to answer by thousands of Christian gentlemen, some professors of colleges, and a few of our reverend clergy, that all *that* is justly chargeable to excess in the use of the drink; and, as each young man deems himself capable of avoiding excess, your argument does not reach him, and he continues to follow the teachings of those who by example and precept, declare to him that he may drink in moderation, at the demand of fashion or inclination, without sin or special danger. Now here is a work to be done which fierce denunciation of drunkenness and the liquor traffic, nor startling word-pictures of accomplished ruins, nor appeals to conscience, or self-respect, or fear, or all together, can perform; for here are minds as yet unconvinced of the danger and the wrong of drinking alcoholic liquors, *if excess be avoided*, and they intend to avoid excess.

The truths of science, the ascertained relations of alcoholic liquors to the physical organizations of men, must now come to the front and fight our battle for us, or victory can not be ours. The moment these relations are fairly comprehended and appreciated, your way is clear for effective appeals to the judgment—to Christian principle, if parties possess it, to native benevolence, to educated conscience, to interest, affection, and fear. But while there is wanting in those we address a knowledge of fundamental truths, your other measures and grounds of appeal are as ineffective, with logical minds, with thinking, educated men, as would be an assault on Fortress Monroe with cavalry or infantry, before heavy shot and shell had made breaches in its walls. Every thing in its place and season. Iron-work, paint, varnish, and cushions are essential to a fine carriage; but before these, there must be wheels, thills, and a body: cube root and equations, by all means; but before these, subtraction and multiplication. Buttons? yes, certainly, but a coat first.

But we shall be told, perhaps, that the verdict of science is not sufficiently settled on this question to afford us a reliable basis. Then we have none which will answer our purpose. If it be not proved conclusively that alcohol is at war with the principle of vitality in man, we are all afloat, and can only argue the question of drink or no drink as one of policy, or of Christian expediency, which few but conscientious Christians will be governed by; and this side of the millennium we can have no hope of reaching controlling majorities.

Starvation, and Consequent Feebleness.

Until the temperance men of our country to whom God has given large wealth and extensive influence shall show their respect for the cause by assigning to it its proper place among the great benevolent enterprises of the age, and sustaining it, not only by their example, their words, their prayers, and their votes, but also by their charities, in the same manner and to an equal extent to which they sustain other enterprises not a whit more needful or worthy, the cause will languish. As it is, they give to other enterprises in round numbers and to temperance in fractions. So strange is this infatuation that we have known scores who, for a quarter of a century, declared publicly, again and again, their devotion to the cause and their belief that its triumph would secure untold blessings to the country and the world, and then crown all by bequeathing to the missionary society ten thousand, to some college another ten thousand, to the Bible society five thousand, to the tract society five thousand perhaps, and so on, and to the treasury of the temperance cause *not one cent*.

When will this great enterprise, while it is thus, be able to command, to an adequate extent, the educated talent of the country to present its claims to the people? The liberality of a few good and wise men, here and there, constitute noble exceptions to the rule, and bring out, by contrast, in bolder relief the mistaken and killing parsimony of the masses even of our Christian rich men. Had the earnest and devoted but mistaken friends of this cause, who have wealth in abundance, treated it for the last fifteen years *with the same liberality they have other enterprises*, the efficiency of the National, and of every State organization, would have been increased ten-fold.

Fellow-laborer, if God has given you wealth, you will some time think of making your will. If you shall therein give of your property to aid other enterprises and nothing to the temperance cause, let us respectfully suggest that you tell why in an explanatory note. If nothing more suitable shall occur to you, you may copy the following words, and fold them up with that important instrument, your will:

"In this, my last will and testament, I have made

bequests of my property to all the enterprises of the age which I considered worthy of special support. As, when I have passed away, some may wonder that I gave nothing to the temperance cause, which they heard me so often extol while living, I hereby inform them, that I meant simply to pay the cause a pleasant compliment, which cost nothing, but considered it utterly unworthy of any more substantial support."

Slightly Intoxicated.

"The New Haven *Palladium* tells a horrible story of brutality to a wife, to the following effect: Alexander McCrady went with his wife from Plymouth to Waterbury, to pass Christmas. On the way home they quarreled, and McCrady, who was slightly intoxicated, seized his wife and threw her out of the wagon, breaking both bones of her leg below the knee. He then told her she must walk the rest of the way; but the poor woman being unable to rise, he got out, and fell to beating and kicking her. He finally threw her into the wagon, and on arriving home, threw her into the yard, where she lay nearly insensible, while with a knife he cut off every particle of her clothing. He then tied a rope around her and drew her under a shed, where he left her with a parting kick—stabled and fed his horse, and went to bed. We live in a Christian land!"

The Christianity of the land will not prevent the repetition of such brutal conduct while men continue to drink intoxicating liquors. Comparatively few drink that they may be brutal. Occasionally an individual *wishes* to commit an act from which his better nature revolts, and he drinks with the purpose to silence the admonitions of conscience, blunt his moral sensibilities, and enable him to do, without compunction or shrinking, a deed of blood. Thus did Strang, at Albany, many years since, when he would murder Whipple; and such cases are by no means rare. Most crimes are, however, committed when men have reached, *unintentionally*, the stage of madness and bewilderment.

Gentlemen who drink for a spree, as they call it, to feel jolly, for the fun and frolic of the thing, or for the narcotic effect of the third stage, to drown care, or lessen a keen sense of obligation to themselves, their families, their creditors, their country, or their maker, God, do not study the subject as they ought, before trying so perilous an experiment. Will they allow us hereby to instruct them that, in a thorough spree or a drunk regular, there are three stages?

The first is a stage of excitement, wherein the party is generally disposed to mirth. He laughs, sings, shouts, and is boisterous. The last stage of the regular drunk is marked by a disposition to coma, or sleepiness, mental stupor, generally with an indisposition to move, almost a total loss, for the time being, of the mental and moral faculties, and such imperfect use of his muscles that he reels and staggers, and perhaps falls, if he attempts to walk. It is in neither the first nor the third stage that crime is committed, or such brutal deeds are done as that above described; but in the second stage, wherein the mirth is ended, and the stage of stupor is not yet reached. *Just there* is an intermediate stage wherein all the mental and moral faculties are in a state of confusion, not as yet *paralyzed* or *suspended*, as in the stage of narcotism, but confused, a stage of insanity or mental bewilderment, during which the kindest-hearted man of your acquaintance may kill his wife, child, parent, or most intimate and best beloved friend.

It is in that second stage of drunkenness that nine-tenths of our murders are committed. Reynolds was evidently in that stage when he killed Townsend, Chambers when he shot Voorhies, and in that stage the brutal deed above described was done. Read the above sad story, dear reader, in the light of the foregoing comments, and see what was the condition of McCrady when he committed that terrible crime; a crime, in the production of which every supporter of the drinking system and liquor traffic was a party.

Temperance and the Doctors.

"In what state of mind did the man die?" asked a gentleman of a Christian brother who, the day previous, had spent some time with a dying friend.

"I cannot tell you anything about his state of mind, whether cheered by Christian hopes or otherwise," said the friend; "for he was for the last twenty-four hours of his life completely intoxicated by the large quantity of liquor given him, with a view to support him in his sinking condition; and," added the gentleman, who was a faithful and devoted Christian, and often in the chambers of the sick to speak words of comfort and Christian counsel to the suffering, "I cannot, *these days*, get any comfort or do any good by visiting the sick and the dying, for a large portion of them die drunk. So much brandy is given them that the feeble brain reels under its influence, and they have no realizing sense of their condition."

That was no fancy sketch. Few patients, under the care of the majority of our physicians, are permitted to die from the effects of incurable disease alone. The powerful anæsthetic, alcohol, is permitted to have a hand in the extinction of vitality.

It is not, of course, given for that purpose; but here, as elsewhere, the "mocker" does work he was not commissioned to do. Too many of our physicians disbelieve, as yet, the grand truth, stated by Dr. T. K. Chambers, of England. He says, "To recapitulate, we think that the evidence, so far as it has yet gone, *shows the action of alcohol upon life to be consistent and uniform in all its phases, and to be always exhibited as an arrest of vitality.*"

The distinguised chemist, Professor Silliman the elder, once remarked to me, while conversing on the subject of the temperance reform, in which he was deeply interested, that, whatever the doctors might say, "Alcohol was closely related in its chemical composition and influence to chloroform and ether." The French class the three articles together under the general term of anæsthetics. Who would think of administering chloroform or ether to a sinking patient *as a restorative?*

Anæsthetics are valuable when we have an important surgical operation to perform; and why? Because they paralyze the nervous system. They kill, for the time being, one of the functions of living human beings, namely, the power to feel; but they do something more, it seems. Dr. Hamilton, medical inspector of the United States Army, while admitting the great value of those articles in surgical cases, in lessening suffering, says, "Anæsthetics (alcohol is one of them) produce certain effects upon the system which tend *to prevent union by the first intention,* (the immediate healing of wounds without the formation of pus,) and consequently they must be regarded as, indirectly, promoting suppuration, secondary hemorrhage, erysipelas, and hospital gangrene." But why do they do all this? The only answer is to be found in the words of Dr. Chambers, as quoted above. They " arrest vitality." Yet our doctors prescribe it to the feeble and sinking with the view to *promote* vitality.

Although contradicted by facts all around us, a majority of physicians still hold to the notion, and inculcate it by their remarks in the sick-room and elsewhere, that alcohol possesses the power to support a feeble patient, not by its present or momentary effect as a stimulant or irritant, but for days and even weeks. Hence its prescription in fevers of low type, and hence too its prescription for nursing mothers, a prescription of which any physician ought to be ashamed. But nursing a strong and vigorous child, it is often said, makes a heavy draught on the mother. Granted; and therefore you should look well to her nutrition. If a hearty breakfast does not give her needful support to the dinner hour, beat an egg thoroughly, add to it half a pint of new milk, with sugar and a little spice to give it a pleasant flavor, and let that be taken at ten o'clock, and a similar draught at four P. M. in addition to the ordinary three meals, being careful that all the food taken shall be rich in the elements of nutrition, and easy of digestion. Fresh pork, smoked meats, sausages, and crude vegetables, as cabbage, beets, etc., should be avoided. If the digestion be faulty, search diligently for the cause of trouble. It may be too much care about her infant or older children, if she have them; about domestic affairs which go wrong through some one's neglect, possibly that of her husband in not providing competent help.

It may be that she is suffering (thousands are) from continual anxiety lest want should be at her door, while her husband is wickedly wasting his earnings in dissipation, in the continued use of intoxicating liquors, or burning up a small income in cigars at ten cents each. It may be a continual worry of mind induced by the presence of an unfeeling, coarse, crabbed nurse, who is unfit to nurse aught save a feminine bear, and even at that her bad temper would be infectious, and spoil the disposition of otherwise respectable cubs. We have seen some such nurses during our professional life. It may be that the food of the mother is not well prepared; the meats are tough, the bread heavy, the toast burned, and the butter rancid. Who would not have indigestion under such circumstances? We repeat, *find out the cause* of the indigestion, and remove it, rather than cover up the trouble for the time being by drugging the nerves of the stomach with ale or whisky. If a local stimulant be needed, which will rarely happen if the foregoing directions be attended to, half a teaspoonful of Brown's essence of ginger* is far better than a glass of ale, though nursing mothers who have been accustomed to use ale will probably insist that the ale is best, for reasons which I will not specify. A good lady some time since asked me if I thought it likely that the drinking of ale or milk-punch by a nursing mother would affect the child. "Of course, madam," I replied. "But why did you ask the question?" This was her answer: "Why, all the while my daughter followed the prescription of her doctor and drank milk-punch, we could scarcely keep the little one awake, even while dressing it. It slept nearly all the time, day and night."

"Yes, madam," I replied, "and it was precisely the same sleep that the poor drunkard enjoys, when we find him stretched by the fence or on the sidewalk." Will such an influence, brought to bear for weeks on the delicate brain of an infant, have any effect upon its future life? Reader, ponder that question.

The Longevity of our Temperance Fathers.

"With *long life* will I satisfy him, and show him my salvation."
Psalm xci.

In Chapter XIII, on page 188, I have spoken of the longevity of our early temperance reformers as quite remarkable.

At the time that chapter was written, I could not justify my statement by facts as extensively as I desired. I am now able to give a pretty full catalogue of names, familiar as household words to men who have but a tolerable knowledge of the history of the temperance enterprise. Against the names of such as have gone to their reward, I have placed the age to which they severally attained, so far as I am now able. Brethren who can aid me in filling the blanks, will confer a favor by doing so, that I may perfect the list for future editions of this work, should they be called for. In my catalogue are the names of some who still live and who have lost none of their zeal for the advancement of a cause they early espoused. Can any class, profession, association, trade, or calling, in this country, show a record of its prominent men or leaders which for average length of life will compare with the following? If so, let it be produced:

THE LONGEVITY OF OUR TEMPERANCE FATHERS.

Justin Edwards,	66
Rev. Nathaniel Hewitt,	77
Lyman Beecher, D. D.,	88
Rev. Calvin Chapin,	80
Daniel Frost, Esq.,	77
Rev. John Marsh,	80
Jonathan Kittredge, Esq.,	71
John Tappan,	84
Rev. William Colyer.	
L. M. Sargent,	81
Reuben Diamond Mussey,	86
Prest. Nott,	93
Prest. Heman Humphrey,	83
E. C. Delavan,	79
Gerrit Smith—still living,	75
William Goodell—still living,	79
Judge Daggett, Conn.,	87
Chancellor Walworth,	78
Rev. John Pierpont,	81
Rev. Dr. Wayland,	69
Christian Keener, Baltimore, Md.	
Nathaniel Emmons, D. D.,	95
Rev. Dr. Beeman,	86
William Lloyd Garrison—still living,	67
Joshua Leavitt—still living,	77
Hon. Lewis Cass,	84
Aristarchus Champion,	88
Gen. Riley—still living.	
Rev. Thomas P. Hunt—still living,	75
Gen. John H. Cocke, Virginia.	
Pres. Hitchcock,	71
Rev. Dr. Patten, New Haven,	73
Rev. Thomas Williams, R. I., still living,	84
Hermon Camp, N. Y., still living,	88
Judge Foote, N. Y., still living.	
Arthur Tappan,	79
Billey Grey.	
Rev. Jacob Ide—still living,	82

Form of Organization for Local Temperance Societies.

PREAMBLE.

Whereas, The formation of societies pledged to abstinence from the use of intoxicating liquors has, with the blessing of God, largely contributed to lessen in our Country the amount of intemperance and its attendant evils, and as we desire to perpetuate and render effective in this community, every instrumentality which may guard the present and the rising generation from the guilt and woes of drunkenness, it has seemed good to us, citizens of   to associate ourselves together for the purpose suggested, and for our guide and government we adopt the following

CONSTITUTION.

Article I. This Society shall be known as the   Temperance Alliance or Union.

Art. II. The Officers of this Association shall consist of a President, Vice President, Secretary, Treasurer, and   Councillors; who together, shall constitute the Executive Board of this Association; and these officers shall possess the powers, and perform the duties usually attached to the offices they hold, and shall severally discharge their official functions until their successors shall have been duly appointed.

Art. III. The regular meetings of this Association shall be holden on the   of every month, and the annual election of officers shall take place on the   of

Art. IV. Within the period of one week after the annual election, the retiring officers shall deliver to their successors in office, all books, records, moneys, and property of every description belonging to the Society.

Art. V. The members of this Association pledge to each other, and to the world, that they will abstain from the use, as a beverage, of all intoxicating liquors, that they will not manufacture or traffic in them to be thus used; that they will discountenance such manufacture, traffic, and use by others, and that they will make direct and persevering efforts to extend the principles and blessings of temperance, and to recover the intemperate to habits of sobriety.

Art. VI. A further condition of membership in this Society shall be the payment to its treasurer, at each regular meeting, by each member, of such sum as he or she may set against his or her name at the time of signing this constitution.

Art. VII. It shall be the duty of each *adult* member of this Association to report to its Secretary, or other of its Councillors, any known violation of its pledges; and such officer shall immediately, without exposing to the public the name of the offender, cause him or her to be visited by some member of the Association, and kindly and earnestly exhorted to a confession of the fault, and a renewal of his or her obligations to the Society. For a refusal to comply with the terms suggested, and a persistent violation of its pledge on the part of the offending member during the period of

his or her name shall be stricken from the records of this Association; but in no case shall the name of an individual be expunged from our records until persevering efforts shall have been made for his or her recovery.

Art. VIII. This Constitution may be altered or amended, at any regular meeting of the Society, by a vote of two-thirds of the members present, previous notice having been given of the proposed alteration at some regular meeting of the Society.

A strict compliance with the provisions of the sixth article can alone render the association influential, or save it from disgrace and ultimate disorganization. Funds *must* be had, and can a more reasonable and equitable method be conceived for the pecuniary support of the Society, than the one adopted? Suppose a society formed under this constitution with two hundred members. Each *monthly* meeting would put into its treasury a specific and considerable sum. Now your officers have something to work with. We must either *tax ourselves* to break down the liquor system, or be taxed roundly to repair the mischiefs—support the paupers and punish the crimes it will cause.

The regular meeting, whether monthly or semi-monthly, should be of an *educational* and high character, so as to command the respect of all. The demand which will thus be created for instructors or lecturers, will be met, when it shall be understood that our societies are *able* and *willing* to pay for instruction as well as associations of a purely religious or literary character. The exercises at some of the regular meetings should consist of short speeches of ten or fifteen minutes each from members, either bringing out local facts and commenting on them, or discussing some important phase of the question which they may have been recently investigating. It may be objected, that, to organize on this plan and sustain such organizations, involves systematic labor. True, and no association can exist and thrive without it; and if the professed friends of temperance are not willing to labor and make some pecuniary sacrifices to achieve a success, they do not deserve success, and will have no cause to complain if their families, friends, and all worldly interests shall be forever taxed and tortured by the curse of drunkenness and its concomitants.

CONCLUSION.

Reader, if you have carefully studied the preceding pages and believe the facts stated, you now know just as well what should be done to check the evil of intemperance which may be prevailing in your community, as you know how to warm your dwelling, cool a heated surface, or check the growth of weeds in your garden. The moral and Christian men of your vicinity (I hope there are many such) have it in their power to institute measures, which, if steadily supported, will assuredly lessen among your people the consumption of intoxicating liquors and the manifold evils which ever attend their use. These measures are simple, safe, and in no wise conflict with the nicest sense of honor, of Christian obligation, or loyalty to one's country. They honor the laws of God, for they enjoin obedience to them. They are auxiliary to the Christian church, for they inculcate self-denial for one's own good and the good of others. No *other* system of measures known to us has ever checked to any considerable extent this terrible evil in any age or part of the world. You see men all around you hurrying to ruin through the use of alcoholic poisons. You know from observation that in the case of such you have nothing to hope for until their resolves to live a better life, formed many times and broken as often, shall take the form of a specific solemn pledge to abstain entirely hereafter from the use of strong drinks, and until that pledge be *recorded* in the presence of their fellow-citizens, so that they shall feel themselves committed to the right side in this great conflict, a point of immense importance. You certainly know that men who attempt to break the strong cords of artificial appetite and habit need social, moral, and often physical helps, which they are not likely to find except in a society organized especially to afford them. Churches do not undertake the business of general education. That work is assigned to schools, academies, and colleges. Banks do not often engage in the business of insurance, or insurance companies in building railroads, or railroad companies in spinning cotton. *Special* organizations are needed to accomplish important and special results.

Train up the young in Sabbath Schools, and without temperance societies to guard them as they advance in years, against the influence of social drinking, thousands who at twelve sing the sweet Sabbath School hymns will at twenty join in the ribald songs of the bar-room or the social drinking party.

There are just as many ways to prevent it as there are to prevent the spread of small pox. One. No more. Neither in His Word or His Providence has God ever revealed more than one certain preventive of drunkenness—that is the pledge and practice of total abstinence from all intoxicating liquors.

Neither Noah or Lot where pledged to abstinence or practiced it. They both sinned and suffered through drink.

The Nazarites and Rechabites were pledged and practiced abstinence, and they were safe. The Corinthian Christians were not pledged to abstinence, nor did they practice it. Some of them fell into sin through drink.

The church in this country for the first quarter of the present century was not pledged to nor did it practice abstinence. And it was almost decimated in its male membership by this scourge and curse of the earth. The church now is safe from this destroyer so far as it is pledged to and practices abstinence—not a step farther. That the practice of abstinence will not generally prevail where men are not pledged to it all history shows. That there will be no *general* system of *pledging* without the existence of special organizations to promote that end, reader, you know. The matter may therefore be summed up thus: Without organizations, having a membership pledged to abstinence, no considerable check can be put to the terrible evil of intemperance. With the use of those means, blessed of God in all ages, we can check it. Do not these facts settle the question of personal duty? What remains now but for you and such of your fellow-citizens as you can induce to join with you, to set up a standard in your community at once against the common enemy? Lamentations over the evil, however sincere, or half-hearted resolutions to do *something in some way*, at some future time, will avail naught. Prayers to God for help will avail naught, *un-*

accompanied by efforts of your own of the right kind in the right direction and persevered in. We may be quite sure that God will work no miracle to relieve us from the ravages of a dreadful scourge, which we have the *power* but not the *will* to arrest. To secure the blessings of temperance to your community will tax your *resolution*, your *time*, your *purse*, and your *patience*. Do you anticipate the possession of any great blessing in this life at a less price?

If you adopt the measures suggested, resolutely, promptly, and persevere in their employment, you will not labor in vain. You *will* secure a personal blessing, you will bless your family, (if you have one,) the community around you, the Christian church, our beloved country, and through its influence elevated and purified, you will bless the world. If these incentives are insufficient to induce right action *now*, you may ere long find *others* in the general demoralization and ruin which intemperance will create around you, in which you, or some of those dear to you, shall in some way *certainly be involved*. In the preparation of the preceding pages I have, with a solemn sense of my obligations to truth, to God, and my country, sought to do my duty. Reader, will you set about doing yours?

www.ingramcontent.com/pod-product-compliance
Lightning Source LLC
Chambersburg PA
CBHW030546300426
44111CB00009B/880